THE UNIVERSAL FLAME

H. P. BLAVATSKY

THE UNIVERSAL FLAME

Commemorating the Centenary of The Theosophical Society

Editor

L. H. LESLIE-SMITH

The Spark hangs from the Flame by the finest thread of Fohat.
—*The Secret Doctrine.*

As from a blazing fire, of one same nature, sparks fly forth by the thousand, even so . . . do creatures manifold come forth from That beyond decay and thither go again.—*Mundaka Upanishad*, II, i, 1.

1975

THE THEOSOPHICAL PUBLISHING HOUSE

ADYAR, MADRAS 600020, INDIA

68, Great Russell Street, London WCIB 3BU, England

Post Box 270, Wheaton, Illinois 60187, U.S.A.

ISBN   0-8356-7506-8

PRINTED IN INDIA

At the Vasanta Press, The Theosophical Society,
Adyar, Madras 600020

Foreword

The Universal Flame is being published to mark the centenary of The Theosophical Society. The Society was founded in New York in 1875 and later moved its Headquarters to Adyar, now a suburb of Madras in Southern India, but at that time eight miles from the centre of the city. Adyar has remained the spiritual and administrative centre of the Society's work since the original founders took up their residence here in 1882; and it is therefore a real happiness to present from International Headquarters this collection of essays to a world in which a growing interest in the search for Truth about Man, the Universe and God is becoming everyday more apparent.

The articles, contributed by members of the Theosophical Movement in a number of countries, deal with basic principles of the Wisdom Religion, which may be considered the most ancient and universal philosophy known to man. The book seeks to present in terms that are easily comprehensible the fundamental nature of the deep and stimulating ideas of this philosophy, known throughout the modern world as Theosophy—Wisdom of, and about, God.

No comprehensive details of doctrine are given here; the authors point rather to the manner in which the reader in our modern and unpredictable world may relate this way of looking at life to the numberless problems that affect every individual, group and country today. The Society is much indebted to Mr. L. H. Leslie-Smith for accepting and carrying out with devoted care the onerous task of editing this volume.

Theosophy is universal in its true nature and encourages its students to examine a philosophy that is perennial and verities that are eternal. The Wisdom that we seek to realize is ancient indeed, since all the greatest teachers of mankind have been concerned to make it available, in part at least. But, being an expression of life, it remains ever fresh and new to those who know how to free themselves from the prison house of the mind—good servant, but poor master—which can be a stumbling block to him who sets out on the road to self-discovery. For the Wisdom is even more of the heart than of the mind, and wise is the man who has found the correct balance between these two.

As H. P. Blavatsky, one of the chief founders of The Theosophical Society, has stated, the archaic doctrine, comprising the Wisdom Religion, is the oldest philosophy in the world and is the inheritance of all nations. This commemorative book is sent out in the hope that men and women of all nations may be led to a closer consideration and knowledge of that eternal doctrine which is inherently their own.

JOHN B. S. COATS,
International President,
The Theosophical Society.

ADYAR, MADRAS, 1975

Key to Abbreviations

H.P.B.	H. P. Blavatsky
S.D.	*The Secret Doctrine* by H. P. Blavatsky
Key	*The Key to Theosophy* by H. P. Blavatsky
Isis	*Isis Unveiled* by H. P. Blavatsky
B.C.W.	*H. P. Blavatsky Collected Writings* by Boris de Zirkoff
M.L.	*The Mahatma Letters to A. P. Sinnett*
T.P.H.	Theosophical Publishing House, Adyar, Madras; London; and Wheaton, Ill., U.S.A.
	(from whom Theosophical books can be obtained)

Contents

		PAGE
Foreword	. . . . .	v
Key to abbreviations	. . .	vii
Introduction	. . . .	1
Enduring Wisdom for a Changing World	. .	7
Universal Law	. . . .	20
Progress to Fulfilment	. . .	32
Human Phases of Consciousness	. .	43
The Panorama of Human Existence	. .	58
Comparative Religion	. . .	72
Philosophy East and West	. .	84
Broadest and Most Catholic System	. .	96
The Wisdom in the Christian Tradition	. .	113
The Concept of God	. . .	123
A Messenger and a Message	. . .	130
The Mahatmas or Adepts	. . .	139
Towards a Scientific Metaphysic	. .	149
Relation of Consciousness to Thought	. .	161
Mystical Quest for Reality	. . .	171
One's Own Path to the Way of All	. .	183
Yoga: The Science of Without and Within	. .	190
Interplay of Individual and Group	. .	200
Personal Problems in a Troubled World	.	215
Towards Understanding Ourselves	.	226
For All Time	. . . . .	234
Source of the Immemorial Wisdom	. .	236

Appendices

Excerpts from Inaugural Addresses of the six Presidents	.	249
The Theosophical Society	. . .	253
Freedom of Thought	. . .	255
Our Contributors	. . . .	257

H. S. OLCOTT IN 1875

INTRODUCTION

In the latter part of 1875 a group of people in New York who were interested in pursuing and promoting research into occultism decided to form a society to further that aim. The name chosen as seeming best to express their purpose was The Theosophical Society, Theosophy implying divine wisdom; and its objects were to " collect and diffuse a knowledge of the laws governing the universe." Notable among the founders were Mme. H. P. Blavatsky, a Russian woman of high birth with remarkable spiritual and psychic gifts; Col. H. S. Olcott, a distinguished agriculturist who had served in the American Civil War; and W. Q. Judge, a New York lawyer. Olcott was elected Chairman and Judge was appointed Secretary.

During the next few years the objects and rules were several times redrafted. For instance, in 1879, after the two chief founders (Blavatsky and Olcott) had transferred the headquarters of the Society to India, a meeting of its General Council was held in the palace of the Maharajah of Vizianagram at Benares. Changes in the rules gave the title " The Theosophical Society or Universal Brotherhood " and the first rule: " The Theosophical Society is formed upon the basis of a Universal Brotherhood of Humanity." The final revision of the objects in 1896 gave the three objects as we have them today:

1. To form a nucleus of the Universal Brotherhood of Humanity, without distinction of race, creed, sex, caste or colour.

2. To encourage the study of Comparative Religion, Philosophy and Science.
3. To investigate unexplained laws of Nature and the powers latent in man.

Like many another idealistic organization, alas, the Theosophical Society has not been without its stormy periods by reason of personal differences, in spite of the first object. Some were resolved internally, but others proved too difficult and led to secessions from the Society, the last serious one being nearly fifty years ago. There are thus today several theosophical bodies within the Theosophical Movement, all having the same roots and tracing their doctrines to the period before the death in 1891 of H. P. Blavatsky—"H. P. B." as she was always known to those who studied her works and teaching. Happily we can record that most branches of the movement are now on friendly and cooperative terms. The splits belong to history and it would seem best to leave them there, with no attempt to apportion blame.

The Theosophical Society has no dogmas. The one requisite for membership is acceptance of its first object, regarding universal brotherhood. It is stated that for Theosophists the " bond of union is not the profession of a common belief, but a common search and aspiration for Truth," echoing the aim stated at the founding meeting a hundred years ago. Nevertheless, certain doctrines are presented for consideration, and for acceptance if found reasonable and not contrary to known facts. One may recall the advice given by the Buddha some 500 years B.C., not to accept anything because of hearsay, because handed down from antiquity, because it is said in some book regarded as sacred, because of the authority of any teacher, but only when it is corroborated by one's own reason and consciousness.

What then is Theosophy and whence comes it?

Col. Olcott and Mme. Blavatsky declared that they were inspired and instructed to start the Society by personages variously called Adepts, Mahatmas, Masters of the Wisdom, who were said to have achieved perfection at the human level and to be members of a spiritual hierarchy existing to guide mankind and to further its evolution, so far as men and women will allow themselves to be helped. These two people dedicated their lives to the infant Society with utter self-sacrifice and in the face of incredible difficulties, hardship, opposition and abuse. H. P. B. stated that she was taught by certain Mahatmas the principles of an esoteric philosophy that was nothing new but was contained in scriptures of the great religions hidden under glyph and symbol. Every religion was said to be a partial expression of this philosophy. The new factor was that some of this immemorial Wisdom, which had been kept secret except for such initiated persons as were given the key to its understanding, was now to be given out publicly in the hope that mankind was ready for it.

In carrying out this task H. P. B. strongly challenged the rigid orthodoxy of both science and religion, for which she was bitterly attacked. The challenge has since been repeated by scientists and theologians themselves, as well as by thinkers in other walks of life. The whole climate of world thought has changed during this century and many theosophical statements that were scoffed at a hundred years ago are now accepted as fact or as acceptable hypotheses.

Some Fundamentals

The basic postulates of the Perennial Philosophy or Ancient Wisdom presented in Theosophy may be summarized:

1. One Life pervades the universe and keeps it being.

2. The phenomenal universe is the manifestation of an eternal, boundless and Immutable Principle beyond the range of human understanding.

3. Spirit (or consciousness) and matter are the two polar aspects of the ultimate Reality. These two with the interplay between them comprise a trinity from which proceed innumerable universes, which come and go in an endless cycle of manifestation and dissolution, all being expressions of that Reality.

4. Every solar system is an orderly scheme governed by laws of nature that reflect transcendental intelligence. " Deity is Law," said H. P. B. The visible planets of the solar system are its densest parts; it also contains invisible worlds of exceedingly tenuous matter interpenetrating the physical. The entire system is the scene of a great scheme of evolution.

5. The spirit of man (often called the soul) is in essence identical with the one supreme Spirit, " that Unity (as Emerson put it), that Oversoul, within which every man's particular being is contained and made one with all other ".[1] The gradual unfolding of this latent divinity takes place by means of a process of reincarnation, in accordance with the Cyclic Law, seen everywhere in Nature, of periods of activity alternating with periods of rest and assimilation.

6. " Whatsoever a man soweth, that shall he also reap." This is the Law of Karma, under which men weave their own destiny through the ages. This is the great hope for humanity, for man can indeed become the master of his future fate by what he does in the present.

The articles that follow deal with some aspects of these hypotheses, as the various writers see them. Obviously the whole ground cannot, even sketchily, be covered, and there may be considerable omissions. This is in no sense a text-book of Theosophy. The aim has been to present certain

[1] *Essays*: " The Oversoul ".

broad principles of what has been called the Wisdom Religion, and a general outline rather than detailed exposition of any part. There is inevitably, and with advantage, some overlapping, as authors approach the subject from different angles. Theosophical doctrines, some of which are now supported by modern thinkers in scientific, philosophical, psychological and other fields, are put forward for consideration and not as dogma to be unthinkingly accepted.

" All is Life "

The keynote of these postulates will be seen to be wholeness. The one Life sustains all, the " inanimate " as well as the " living ". " Esoteric philosophy teaches that everything lives and is conscious ",[1] in varying degrees. " All is Life, and every atom of even mineral dust is a life, though beyond our comprehension and perception." [2] The poet Alexander Pope saw it as " one stupendous whole " that

> Lives thro' all life, extends thro' all extent,
> Spreads undivided, operates unspent.

There is an interrelationship of all that exists, all linked together. As the countless cells of our bodies are so many lives within a greater life, so all parts of nature comprise a multitude of lives within total Life. The vast range of nature is thus considered a whole, lesser unities within bigger ones, wheels within wheels; a wholeness of each atom in a cell, of the cell in the organism; the wholeness of individual man, of the earth, the solar system and so forth, beyond imagining, a continuous unseen network.

Life seeks ever to express itself. It would seem then that the universe and man and the long processes of evolution

[1] H. P. Blavatsky, *The Secret Doctrine*, I, 47, 1st ed., I, 120, 6-vol. ed., T. P. H.
[2] *Ibid.* I, 248; I, 293.

are manifestations of total Life. The evolution of forms that it is the province of science to investigate may thus appear to be a means, a method, of the progressive unveiling of the potentialities of Life itself—and the evolution of that Life takes us beyond the scope of physical science into metaphysical and philosophical regions. Theosophy envisages a vast scheme of the evolution of Life, which reveals itself stage by stage through mineral, vegetable, animal and human kingdoms, and beyond, in ever greater complexity and richness.

As the doctrine of the one Life gives wholeness to the universe, so does the doctrine of the identity of the spirit of man and of the universal Spirit show the essential unity of the human race. It also gives the key to the wholeness or integration of every man—a spiritual being disclosing himself progressively through psychic and physical mechanisms.

Wholeness is the clue to the understanding of man and the universe. Those who have deeply pondered these ideas and found therein some measure of illumination realize, with the mystics of all time, their intimate relationship with their fellows and with all nature, of whose entire process man is a part and not something separate. Here is a true foundation for morality, free from dogma. Here is the basis for a new way of life that can integrate men and women individually, can integrate them as individuals in groups, and further integrate those groups in the wholeness of mankind. It is the ancient way of holiness or wholeness, in line with nature and evolution; and it can bring inward peace and tranquillity regardless of all externals.

ENDURING WISDOM FOR A CHANGING WORLD

The One remains, the many change
and pass—SHELLEY.

JOY MILLS

TWENTIETH century thought has been shaped by two
fundamental movements. One, based on discoveries in
physics, has propelled man into space for the exploration
of the solar system; the other, born of research in biology
and psychology, has carried man inwards towards the exploration of life and consciousness. For every question asked
concerning the nature of universal processes there is a question
about the quality of life, the boundaries of the human mind,
the ethical and moral implications of man's knowledge.
Each probe inwards in the examination of consciousness has
been matched by probes into outer space. The names of
the giants of the age reflect this dual movement: Einstein and
Freud, Planck and Jung. Pierre Teilhard de Chardin
represents that singular individual who, versed in the disciplines of science and religion, combines in his researches
the dual movement of the age.

Knowledge, however, whether of the inner recesses of the
mind or of the outer structure of the universe, does not arise
in a vacuum. Every thinker who advances the frontiers of
knowledge in any field is related to the social milieu of his
day; his work proceeds not only from his own research and
contemplation but also from the collective spirit of his time.
Each man who contributes to the house of knowledge builds

on foundations laid by his predecessors. The shape of the house reflects the needs of the tenants as well as the general trend of the day. The analogy may be apt indeed for, in view of the polar movement of knowledge in this century, it may not be without significance that modern architecture also shows a duality: many structures are sprawling, open, space-releasing, drawing occupants outwards towards broader horizons; other buildings are space-confining, closed, window-less, as though to turn the occupants away from the vision of the sky to contemplation of the immediate interior concern.

Some men need confining walls; others must have open doors. Some seek without for the clues to life's meaning. Others turn within to mine the depths of individual being for purpose and significance. Ultimately, both directions serve the same goal, for what we fear to face is not total destruction, but total meaninglessness. Meaning, however, is derived less from the knowledge gained from the dual movement of scientific investigation than from the base out of which that movement proceeds. Only if the universe, including man, is rooted in meaningfulness can purpose inhere in all the processes of the universe. In an age when man has split the atom and deciphered the genetic code in his search for the secrets of matter and of life, he will surely come to see, as some thinkers do already, the underlying intention which infuses the system with purpose and order.

Today's philosopher, seeking support for a holistic view of man and the universe, has an easier time of it than his predecessor did a hundred years ago; whether he buttresses his idealism with the physical sciences or with psychological insights, he will find the thicket of scientific materialism considerably thinned and the fog of religious orthodoxy largely dissipated. Whatever resistance remains to the concept of an ordered and orderly universe in which man is rooted, not as an alien object but as a participant in the same conscious life process, arises from failure to perceive the dramatic advances in human thought which the last century —and particularly the last fifty years—has witnessed.

If human experience and scientific discovery are to be significantly related, then certain universal principles must be postulated that are both basic and comprehensive. The revival of interest in direct, personal encounters with the interior realms of consciousness, whether they are attempted by hallucinogenic drugs, meditation or yoga, or the forced awakening of psychic faculties, has proceeded apace with interest in and research on the external conditions which support conscious life, including studies ranging from an analysis of moon rocks to an examination of the ocean floor, from experiments in atomic fission and fusion to experiments in genetic restructuring and physiological reorganization. There is urgent necessity for a metaphysical system that will combine the data of personal and non-personal research and at the same time give direction to man's endeavours. In an age of unparalleled advances in human knowledge, the need is for a wisdom that will liberate the human spirit before we destroy the human race.

Wisdom Tradition

Embedded in the cultural stream of every civilization, underlying every religious system, emerging periodically through myth and legend, is a wisdom tradition comprising fundamental and universal truths whose simplicity permits innumerable ramifications, interpretations, permutations, transformations. Restated in the ninteenth century under the name Theosophy, the wisdom tradition has always been verifiable by experience and by scientific validation. As one of its principal exponents wrote in the last century: "Theosophy is no new candidate for the world's attention, but only the restatement of principles which have been recognized from the very infancy of mankind."[1] An examination of those principles reveals their timelessness and their timely relevance to our present condition.

"Eternal truth needs a human language," wrote Carl Jung. Language reflects the growth of human consciousness, and only as consciousness becomes aware of universals can language convey the quality of living truth. We can speak only what we know, and what we know must be expressed both in language and in life. For this reason, generations of seers and sages representing all cultural heritages, all religious traditions, have borne witness as *knowers* to the wisdom of the ages, which is also the ageless wisdom. The language of their knowing begins not with the separate syllables of facts, but with the complete sentences of immortal ideas.

Consequently, as H. P. Blavatsky pointed out in presenting anew the primary concepts which comprise the theosophical philosophy:

> The Secret Doctrine is the accumulated Wisdom of the Ages. . . an uninterrupted record, covering thousands of generations of Seers, whose respective experiences were made to test and verify the traditions, passed on orally by one early race to another, of the teachings of higher and exalted Beings, who watched over the childhood of Humanity.

When asked how wise men preserved the knowledge of universals, Mme. Blavatsky continued:

> . . . by checking, testing, and verifying, in every department of Nature, the traditions of old, by the independent visions of

[1] *M.L.*, pp. 34-35, T. P. H.

great Adepts; that is to say, men who have developed and perfected their physical, mental, psychic, and spiritual organizations, to the utmost possible degree. No vision of one Adept was accepted till it was checked and confirmed by the visions—so obtained as to stand as independent evidence —of other Adepts, and by centuries of experience.[1]

The Hermetic chain of Greek mystical tradition, the Guru-parampara of the Hindu, the Apostolic Succession of the Christian, the Bodhisattva ladder of the Buddhist, all refer to the existence of a living tradition transmitted and communicated from teacher to disciple, teacher following teacher, in a never-ending chain the links of which are living men, " just men made perfect," " Masters of Wisdom and Compassion ". The importance of the tradition lies less in who these teachers were or are than in what is transmitted—a wisdom that unifies all knowledge and gives purpose and direction to man's efforts to understand himself and the world in which he moves.

The undying tradition, the timeless wisdom, now termed Theosophy, is far more than a collection of doctrines or an assemblage of facts. It is an evolving living whole, as alive as the universe which is its visible expression. Whether stated in religious or philosophical terms, or demonstrated by science, the Wisdom has its final validation in that most intimate experience of knowing which is the essence of mysticism. Unfolding in a natural sequence of ideas which may be examined, tested, and corroborated, the Wisdom itself cannot be limited or defined. Its comprehension, therefore, can only be partial and approximate, depending on the mode of consciousness prevalent at a particular time. In exploring the metaphysical principles underlying the theosophical tradition

---

[1] *S.D.*, I, 172, 1st ed.; I, 316, 6-vol. ed., T. P. H.

one may find the way that leads towards the Wisdom. Such exploration will inevitably show the relevance of the ideas to the contemporary human situation.

One Essential Life

Chief among the basic principles of the theosophical system is that of a universal Reality, in which all is grounded —one living, non-material, creative reality from which everything in the universe emerges in an evolutionary unfolding. The one essential life permeates all nature; all creatures are its reflections. Reality *is*, no matter what happens in the universal force field of infinite potentiality. All that is transient obeys the laws of the universal, impartible one Reality. Consequently, the self-existent One never *does* anything, but nothing can happen except in accordance with its inherent nature, for the self-existent essence of all makes possible all existences.

> It is called ' Substance-Principle,' for it becomes ' Substance ' on the plane of the manifested Universe . . . while it remains a ' Principle ' in the beginningless and endless, abstract, visible and invisible SPACE. . . It is latent in every atom in the Universe, and is the Universe itself.[1]

In and of itself that fundamental Reality is timeless being or "be-ness"; it is raw awareness, consciousness without conditioning and therefore " unconscious " since there is nothing of which to become conscious; its essential nature is harmonic, permitting the beauty and bliss of order to arise in natural sequence. The existential Christian theologian, Paul Tillich, has written of " essential being " as contrasted with " existential being," referring thereby to the full potentiality of the infinite " ground of being " or God which is only partly expressed at any time in the world of actuality, but which must be present

[1] *S.D.*, I, 272; I, 316.

for existence to emerge. Although orthodox Christianity
has usually tended to personalize, if not anthropomorphize,
the concept of an immutable root-principle or essence, eastern
religions have generally viewed reality as an impersonal,
universal life pervading all nature. The cross-fertilization of
religious thought—by increased interest in the west both in
comparative religion and in the practices of various Buddhist
schools; and in the east by a reawakening to the depth and
meaning of Asian religious traditions—has helped to liberalize
views everywhere and to point to one divine source, a unitary
root cause. The essential brotherhood of all men is the necessary corollary of such a concept. The unity of all life further
implies a web of interrelationships among all living things;
if man is to survive, he must learn to live in accordance with
nature's law of unity, accepting his responsibility for any
damage to that intricate web of life.

The second premise of theosophical metaphysics arises
naturally from the first and states that the universe and all
phenomenal forms are periodical manifestations of that
primary Reality, the universal Substance-Principle. Matter
is an emanation of Reality, periodically manifested or precipi-
tated. Matter is, in this sense, a precipitation of energy,
never divorced from its source but appearing externally as
the transient and periodic manifestation of the one Reality;
the universe of be-ness projects the universe of process. That
projection is in accord with the inherent rhythm of
consciousness.

Everywhere there is the pulsebeat of Reality, sometimes
quickened to self-awareness as in man, sometimes slowed
down to nearly immeasurable cycles as in the geologic ages.
As an American scientist has said: " The pulsebeat of planet
Earth has not yet been counted. But a pulse is there. . .

a rhythmic throbbing in the magnetic shell enclosing the planet arises from the solar wind. . . Within the magnetic sheath, Earth's atmosphere expands and contracts ".[1] It is well recognized that the rise and fall of the oceans cannot be measured exactly because the terrestrial crust, on which we who would measure that ebb and flow are riding, also undulates in answer to the tidal pull of the moon. Other studies concern the bio-rhythmic cycles of the human being. Throughout nature, the law of periodicity may be observed.

Worlds and Atoms

This second postulate requires an inherent dynamism within the primal Reality, recognized by its effects. Hence, universes come and go as periodical manifestations of an unchanging non-material Reality. The phenomenal world, then, is an emanation, an unfolding of that which has been infolded during a previous cycle. According to H. P. Blavatsky,

> The Secret Doctrine teaches the progressive development of everything, worlds as well as atoms; and this stupendous development has neither conceivable beginning nor imaginable end.[2]

The universal field, the " One Homogeneous Divine Substance-Principle," is non-operational. The activation within that field of what is called *Fohat*,* the inherent dynamism of the system, produces transient universes, which are characterized by constant change. Therefore all process happens sequentially; time becomes a measurement for evolution. Within the primal Reality, the abiding factor is duration; as that Reality manifests itself, duration is reflected in

[1] John Lear, " The Pulse of Earth," *Saturday Review*, Feb. 1, 1969, p. 49.

[2] *S.D.*, I, 43; I, 115.

* A Tibetan term referring to the active potency in nature; the universal propelling vital force whose manifestations include electricity, light, heat, etc.

sequence, which is time. That which was infolded in simultaneity is now unfolded sequentially. For some philosophers this concept has led to the view that since everything is transient, it is therefore illusory, meaning non-existent. A logical extension of such a view has been nihilism, a philosophy directly contradictory to Theosophy, for it fails to recognize the essential meaning of what is transient and temporal as a reflection of underlying reality. While the " One Radical Cause " alone is characterized by immutability, " the Universe is real enough to the conscious beings in it." [1]

> There can be no manifestation of consciousness, semi-consciousness, or even ' unconscious purposiveness,' except through a vehicle of Matter. But inasmuch as the phenomena of *our* plane are the creations of the perceiving Ego*—the modifications of its own subjectivity—all the ' states of matter representing the aggregate of perceived objects ' can have but a relative and purely phenomenal existence. . . From the standpoint of the highest metaphysics, the whole Universe . . . is an Illusion. . . But the illusion of him who is in himself an illusion differs on every plane of consciousness; and we have no more right to dogmatize about the possible nature of the perceptive faculties of an Ego. . . than we have to identify our perceptions with, or make them a standard for, those of an ant, in *its* mode of consciousness. [2]

The concept that the phenomenal world reflects the realm of the Real, Plato's world of the archetype or the noumenon, may be illustrated by the electromagnetic field of modern physics. The effects of this field are best exhibited in a simple experiment with iron filings placed on a surface under which a magnet is brought into operation. Electrons in a

[1] *S.D.*, I, 274; I, 317.

* The word Ego is used in theosophical writings for the reincarnating Individuality; not, as in modern psychology, for the evanescent personality.

[2] *S.D.*, I, 329; II, 42-43.

magnetic field take up patterns according to the lines of force of the field. The field itself is changeless, non-material, existing everywhere in space whether or not particles are present to be influenced by it. The changeability and temporality of anything that operates within the field give rise to the concept of the illusory nature of " things " as objects; in this sense, one can never see a thing as it is, but always as it was for, even in the time interval that elapses in the process of " seeing ", what was perceived has undergone change.

Consciousness Universal

A further basic premise of the theosophical philosophy is a radical departure from generally accepted scientific thought at present. It propounds that " Everything in the Universe, throughout all its kingdoms, is CONSCIOUS: *i.e.*, endowed with a consciousness of its own kind and on its own plane of perception." [1] The work of Teilhard de Chardin has gone far to demonstrate that consciousness is inherent in matter from the beginning, and there is also experimental evidence of a rudimentary consciousness in minerals and plants. Some evolutionists suggest that the distinction between matter and consciousness is fading with further evidence that the root of consciousness may be locked up in matter itself. Poets and mystics through the ages have conveyed an intuitive feeling that life courses through all things, flower, rock, animal, star.

If, then, the fundamental Reality, non-partible and non-material, a seamless web, is through and through conscious, that consciousness must inhere in all that emerges as pheno-menal. All is embedded in the Real, revealing itself in the

[1] *S.D.*, I, 274; I, 317.

sequences of time according to cyclic law. Evolution is marked by the growth of consciousness; forms come and go, change, alter and improve by trial and error, expressing in orderly progression the limitless potential of the background reality, which is universal Consciousness. " The whole order of nature evinces a progressive march towards a *higher life*." [1] Some biologists, among them Dr. Edmund W. Sinnott, see a goal-seeking mechanism present even in protoplasm. Teilhard de Chardin, Julian Huxley and others suggest that side by side with greater complexity of form there is enrichment of consciousness, so that " purposiveness " is characteristic of the entire evolutionary process.

Purpose gives rise to design, pattern, order; it emerges from within. This basic principle recognized by the life sciences, both biology and psychology, is fundamental to the esoteric philosophy: " The Universe is worked and *guided*, from within *outwards*." [2] Physics finds that what appears to our senses as stable solid is a wild dance of electric forces, governed by electromagnetic and gravitational fields. Biology suggests an inner guiding principle, " self-representation ". And in some schools of psychology " self-actualization " accounts for an inner guiding principle of unfoldment unique to each individual and governing psychological growth, including potentials for creativity, love, intelligence, etc.

Nowhere does nature provide a more dramatic example of these primary principles than in the metamorphosis of some animal forms. A caterpillar, at a certain stage in its growth, when a mechanism in the brain triggers a new impetus, winds itself in its cocoon, isolates itself from its former environment and uses its own resources for an amazing transformation.

[1] *S.D.*, I, 277; I, 320.
[2] *S.D.*, I, 274; I, 317.

2

The larval organs disappear; what was once a crawling, earthbound creature, is now reduced to an amorphous emulsion having no discernible structure. By some process of reorganization, directed by a mysterious dynamism, this formless emulsion transforms itself into a creature of wings and beauty, adapted to a different environment and for a different mode of life. Yet the final pattern is present from the beginning in the cell of the simplest organism.

These, then, are the metaphysical principles underlying the theosophical tradition. They find their ultimate expression, their magnificent summation, in man—man as the localization of all that is present everywhere in the universe, man who, as the Pseudo-Dionysius put it, "must not only learn the truth; he must suffer it." For the theosophical vision presents man as part of the whole flow of evolution, though far from mature in an evolutionary sense. Recognizing one universal Reality, man must come to know himself as part of the seamless web of life, in which whatever happens anywhere in the universe affects all living things from star to atom. Aware of the dual principles of rhythm and harmonious but ever-changing design, he must learn to move in accordance with universal law. In man, consciousness is self-consciousness; through choice, he learns the price that must be paid for every advance in knowledge until, self-committed, in full self-consciousness, he works to further the entire process of which he is a part, forgetting the claims and desires of the transient self in a purpose more in tune with universal purpose.

Whatever evidence may be marshalled by science, whatever witness may be given by religion or philosophy, the validity of the immortal principles of the wisdom tradition that is Theosophy must be found in their practical value in the lives of men. In the fiery furnace of life's experience we have to learn to transmute universal principles into the gold of wisdom. Einstein sought to distil from the principles of physics a unified field theory which would account for all known phenomena; Jung looked to the *unus mundus*, the unitary world, as the ground towards which the psyche of man ever gravitates. As the twentieth century moves into its final decades, as a cycle of 100 years since the founding of the Theosophical Society closes upon itself, modern man is desperate for a unified vision that will relate all parts of knowledge into a meaningful whole. In his absorption with fragments of information gleaned from such diverse activities as moon landings and the dissection of cadavers, man suffers from cosmic nearsightedness. Theosophy offers no panacea for the complex problems of our times; only man can solve the difficulties brought about by his own blindness. But the ideas and principles presented by that ageless wisdom which today is called Theosophy may give him the means, the corrective lenses, to restore his vision.

———

Theosophy is that ocean of knowledge which spreads from shore to shore of the evolution of sentient beings; unfathomable in its deepest parts, it gives the greatest minds their fullest scope; yet, shallow enough at its shores, it will not overwhelm the understanding of a child. It is wisdom about God for those who believe that he is all things and in all, and wisdom about nature for the man wh accepts the statement found in the Christian *Bible* that God cannot be measured or discovered.—W. Q. JUDGE.

UNIVERSAL LAW

Deity is Law, and vice-versa—
H. P. BLAVATSKY.

GEOFFREY A. FARTHING

A STUDENT of spiritual matters is at once confronted with the problem of finding a firm base for his studies. He soon discovers a field of speculation and general ignorance except among a few unusual people, as, for example, the mystics, who have had some transcendental experience. All accounts of such experience have much in common, regardless of the language used in describing them; and this adds strength to the testimony.

Theosophical teaching and method of approach differ from those in most religious studies. First, the doctrine is said to be based on knowledge: the accumulated wisdom of the ages, established by generations of seers using spiritual faculties still only latent in most men, and continually verified. Secondly, the student is advised to proceed carefully and critically, basing all progress on what he already knows and what he comes gradually to know as indisputable fact. This knowledge can come only through one's own being, one's subjective faculty; for example, of the kind " I think, therefore I am ". From here the inquirer can proceed to ask what other faculties we have, what is their nature, are they common to others, what degree of control have we over them, what are " we " essentially; and how do " we " relate to others and to our surroundings?

There is an occult maxim " as above, so below ", and a rule of analogy which says that the things and events of the physical world reflect and express the inner spiritual or subjective worlds. With these guidelines we may consider the theosophical teaching of universal Law.

The physical world has been found to be governed by law. It is this that makes possible the findings of science. Every discovery, whether in the depths of space or in the atom, confirms an orderly universe that obeys, or is the embodiment of, law. By reason of the maxim and the analogy quoted above, Theosophy extends this principle to the psychic (mental-emotional) and spiritual aspects of the universe, which are beyond the limits of the field to which science has restricted itself. Originally, however, science meant knowledge; knowledge of all kinds, and from whatever source, was within its sphere. If there are laws regulating the universe, then they must apply to its entire range and cannot be limited to the merely phenomenal aspects; and those laws must constitute a body of truth. Here is the basis for the theosophical student's search for truth.

Francis Bacon wrote: " I have taken all knowledge to be my province ".[1] The advancement of learning and its ever-increasing mass of detail have long since rendered a repetition of that claim impossible, and the need to specialize has still further limited the scope of any one person. In order to examine the vast and increasing range of human activities and interests, it has been necessary to divide them artificially into subjects. Thus we have history, geography, biology, chemistry, economics, physics, philosophy, religion, sociology and the rest; and these are split into ever smaller sections, any one of which takes the best part of a lifetime to master.

[1] Letter to Lord Burleigh, 1592.

Yet these all impinge on one another, and all together constitute a whole. In fact, no one aspect of life can properly
be understood except in the context of total Life. Similarly,
we can regard the many laws of nature as aspects of one
inclusive universal Law. But for the purpose of the present
study we may distinguish five facets. Some elements of these
are self-evident, easily related to our ordinary lives; others
are for us at present only theories.

Aspects of the One

First, causation. This presupposes that all manifestation
must have a beginning, a period of existence, and an end,
and that something must have caused the beginning.

Causation as used here does not imply a primeval creation
by which a universe, or anything in it, was caused to come
into being *ex nihilo*—out of nothing—which is a philosophic
absurdity. Origins are taken to mean changes of state, either
of what already exists as matter and form, or of and by
a postulated eternal substance-principle. This principle is
thought of as homogeneous and characterless in itself, equated
with space, and becoming differentiated periodically to form
the basis of matter as we know it. These periods are of almost
inconceivable duration. At the end of each period, all is
said to revert to the original condition of " non-being ".
The root substance, however, continues endlessly, becoming
alternatively " fertile " and " infertile ", in a cyclic pattern,
under the influence of " spirit ", the source of all dynamism.

During a period of activity the eternal substance-principle
is activated by the spirit, and the interaction shows as energy.
The substance-principle and the energy-principle are, however,
never really separate. The two are aspects of the everlasting
One, the fount and origin of all. The primordial power, the

One, for ever sleeps and wakes according to cyclic law, which paradoxically is the power itself.

In any phase of manifestation the one basic substance—energy, from which the matter of forms is ultimately derived—undergoes a transformation: there is a putting together in a different way of something pre-existent. This is the process commonly referred to as creation. Dissolution, inevitable in due season, follows creation. For instance, in the building and growth of our bodies, pre-existent matter in some form —gas (air), liquid (water or milk) and solid (food)—are selected from what is breathed, drunk or eaten, and assimilated in a marvellously ordered way. A new body is born, grows and is sustained. Then in due time the body dies. This is natural process, nature's way, even with universes.

Such causation, postulating the one spirit-substance, may not be apparent; but scientific thinking seems to sense the need for an essential basic plasma underlying the energy-matter of research.

Linked with causation is a second aspect of the Law—progression through time. The great cycles, the cycles within cycles and the tiny cycles within these never return completely to their starting point. They progress like spirals along the axis of time.

Coupled with this also is the premise of the universe as a unity and an entity, with all that is contained in it comprising a total process maintained by an exhaustless potency which we know as power, force, energy. The universal potency and the law under which it operates are aspects of the one Source of all being.

The idea of fundamental Unity, the One, the All, may be acceptable as necessary for comprehending the total natural process and its laws, though it may not be possible to find proof to satisfy a sceptic. However, scientists now talk of a web of invisible links that relates each particle in the universe to every other. This parallels a statement in *The Mahatma Letters to A. P. Sinnett* [1] that "nature has linked all parts of her empire by subtle threads of magnetic sympathy".

A third aspect of the Law has to be understood against a background of universal and perpetual motion. Before the beginning of any *thing*, a universe included, there must be movement. So absolute abstract motion would seem a necessary hypothesis, symbolizing the continual possibility of recurring genesis. All things come and go according to a rhythm. Abstract motion incessantly pulsates; but there are periods of activity followed by periods of rest—of unimaginable length for a universe, but short indeed in the ephemeral life of a butterfly, and brief beyond thought in terms of rates of vibration in atomic physics. Whether one regards light as a wave motion or as particles, the idea of something extremely small persisting in a certain state for a very short time underlies both theories. Electro-magnetic radiation, of which light is an aspect, underlies the whole manifest universe. We come to know that even matter is, so to say, consolidated vibratory energy. The basis of all is motion.

This alternating cyclic aspect of the Law already referred to, is seen throughout nature: in the seasons, the tides, waking and sleeping, in-breathing and out-breathing, the heart beat and the blood pulsing through our bodies, in the rarefactions and compressions of the air that constitute sound. It shows itself also in the great rhythm of life and death, of existence and " non-existence ". Theosophy affirms that there is Being even behind non-existence, a subjective state as opposed to an objective one. At death and after we do not cease to be; we

[1] p. 267, 1st ed; 263, 3rd ed., T. P. H.

cease to have existence only in the physical and then in the psychic world. Alternating activity and rest apply also to the inner levels of being, where time and space as we know them are different, or perhaps do not exist. The doctrine of reincarnation would seem to be a necessary corollary of the cyclic law.

Balance of Nature

A fourth aspect of Law shows itself in the harmonious inter-relationship of all that comprises the universe. We see order and balance in a vast dynamic process where nothing is static for an instant. There is apparent stability in the rocks that withstand the seemingly endless assault of sea and weather; yet even these do not endure for ever. Land masses remain long enough for untold generations of living things to come and go and fulfil their natural functions; perhaps for millions of years, but still not for ever.

In nature there is a total balanced economy. This is illustrated in the sustenance provided for all her creatures. In the long term, supply meets demand, until maybe a species is due to disappear from the stage of existence. Then another branch of life burgeons forth, and the great cyclic process of coming and going continues. But a total equilibrium is always maintained—an overall and marvellous harmony. We may see what we call waste in thousands of seeds being produced for every one that is needed to ensure the continuance of the species or line it represents; but the apparent chaos of waste is merely the disintegration of form that is part of the process of preserving essential balance.

There may indeed be chaos in human affairs, for man is the one free agent in the universe; and he can, and does, disturb nature's laws, at any rate for a time. It is said that man suffers only from two causes: ignorance and inertia or laziness. The former will produce inharmonious action, the latter no action, and therefore no experience, and it is only by experience that we learn and develop.

This leads to a fifth facet of universal Law, which ensures that whatsoever a man sows that shall he also reap. Actions are always followed by compensatory reactions, and if events are regarded in isolation this is the law of cause and effect. But one cannot isolate events. Every effect becomes in its turn a cause, and the chain is endless. Thus the present is the effect of causes stretching back into an infinite past. Likewise all that exists now, and all that is occurring to it, will be the cause of our tomorrows and their happenings. This aspect of the one Law has been called the law of continuity. Harmony is constantly restored by action being followed always by compensating reaction.

Karma and Reincarnation

In this great process, man, possessing self-consciousness as well as memory and intelligence, has some power to make a choice, to act as he wishes, and to upset the balance of nature both outwardly and in himself. Nevertheless, under the law of adjustment or balance, the result of any cause for which he is responsible will be returned in some way, sooner or later, to him. In eastern terms this is karma, in the common application. But derivatively karma simply means action, and is the vast process of continuous cause and effect constituting the total process of nature during the period of living activity, according to which the fruits of previous periods of existence become the seeds for the next. In another sense, this aspect of Law underlies the predictability of scientific experiments, precisely similar causes producing precisely similar results. The law is inexorable:

> It knows not wrath nor pardon; utter true
> Its measures mete, its faultless balance weighs;
> Times are as nought, tomorrow it will judge,
> Or after many days.[1]

When ignorantly or wilfully, man acts contrary to natural
law or against the inmost law of his own nature, suffering
inevitably follows, whether to the individual or to a group.
But his pain is an educative factor, so that he slowly learns
from experience to act differently. Every moment we are
changing the present and determining the future. We weave
our own destiny, and therein lies the great hope for humanity.
Hence karma has been called " An immutable law of absolute
Love, Justice and Mercy." [2]

> The Karma—all that total of a soul
> Which is the things it did, the thoughts it had,
> The " Self" it wove—with woof of viewless time
> Crossed on the warp invisible of acts.[3]

Karma is " an unfailing redresser of human injustice; a
stern adjuster of wrongs; a retributive law which punishes
and rewards with equal impartiality. It is no respecter of
persons, and it can neither be propitiated nor turned aside
by prayer " [4]. In fact, it precisely lets " the punishment fit
the crime ", and likewise the reward suit the merit.

The unity of all that exists ensures that the law works at
levels other than the physical, which is why H. P. Blavatsky
put forward the proposition that karma is

> ... the *Ultimate Law* of the Universe, the source, origin and
> fount of all other laws which exist throughout Nature. Karma

---

[1] Sir Edwin Arnold, *The Light of Asia*, VIII.

[2] *Key*, p. 201, T. P. H.

[3] *Light of Asia*, VI.

[4] *Key*, p. 198.

is the unerring law which adjusts effect to cause, on the physical, mental and spiritual planes of being. As no cause remains without its due effect from greatest to least, from a cosmic disturbance down to the movement of your hand, and as like produces like, Karma is that unseen and unknown law *which adjusts wisely, intelligently and equitably* each effect to its cause, tracing the latter back to its producer. Though itself *unknowable*, its action is perceivable.[1]

Also Karma is the law of readjustment which ever tends to restore equilibrium in the physical and broken harmony in the moral world.[2]

And in *The Secret Doctrine* H. P. B. states:

The law of Karma is inextricably interwoven with that of Reincarnation... It is only this doctrine that can explain the mysterious problem of Good and Evil and reconcile man to the terrible and *apparent* injustice of life... Karma creates nothing, nor does it design. It is man who plans and creates causes, and Karmic Law adjusts the effects.[3]

Inherent Intelligence

Theosophy also postulates that the total process of nature and the stupendous operations of the Law are manifestations of inherent intelligence in everything. This intelligence is a derivative of consciousness. Universal consciousness and universal intelligence are regarded as fundamentals, necessary for an understanding of cosmos. They constitute the essential nature of life operating at all levels. They also comprise, in some measure and in some manner, the essential nature of every manifested thing; whether manifesting sentiently or not, everything responds to stimulus. In man this response is

[1] *Key*, p. 201.
[2] *Ibid.*, p. 205.
[3] *S.D.*, II, 303 and 305, 1st ed; III, 304 and 306, 6-vol. ed.

highly developed. Development from a rudimentary state to the complex and sophisticated condition in living creatures illustrates the process of unfoldment of the potentialities of life, and shows the progress through time of the workings of universal Law. The actors, the actions and the acts of this stupendous play all constitute manifested Deity, yet Deity transcends every manifestation and ever remains in its absolute, unconditioned and unqualified peace, enduring, unchanging and boundless.

Such are some of the aspects of the great Law. In total, it is indescribable. In particular, we see its applications everywhere and in every circumstance of life. If we consider deeply our own being, circumstances, acts, we find we are the result of its operations. Within the broad bounds imposed by nature, our circumstances are as we and our fellows have made them. Mankind is entirely responsible for its lot, and within the whole human family each group carves out its particular niche by what it says and does and is. If acquisitive, selfish and aggressive, it tends to be isolated and feared. If cooperative, helpful, peaceful and making for happiness, it is welcomed. The modern cry is for man to take charge of his own destiny. Unconsciously, he has always been responsible for it. But if we are consciously to shape the future, the rationale of the process and the method may be found in karma; remembering that " Karma is the force that impels to Reincarnation ".[1]

We can, however, progress only by effort. Effort means action, and action means change. In our action we affect not only ourselves but our surroundings. What we create reacts on us; our surroundings affect us psychically as well as physically.

[1] *Key*, p. 211.

In the long reaches of time and in successive lives, and with
the law of periodicity applying to ourselves, we grow in wisdom,
understanding and effectiveness. Our understanding becomes
the understanding of nature, our wisdom that of right action.
And understanding and wisdom expand in time beyond the
bounds of physical existence. We become more aware of,
interested in, and capable in our inner activities and powers,
which reflect something of the invisible forces and energies
of nature behind the appearance and obvious effects of manifested existence. Gradually, in psychological and spiritual
terms, we develop our own inner powers and learn the laws
of these inner realms.

The One, the All, it must be emphasized, is in the theosophical view not an entity within cosmos. It is cosmos itself.
" All existence is one thing ". Consciousness is that by which
we become aware. Animals as well as men are possessed
of this faculty. It would seem that whereas the content of
consciousness—that of which we are aware at any given
moment—is different for each one of us, awareness itself is
the same in everyone. Consciousness has a common quality,
which argues a universal origin: absolute consciousness. Again,
consciousness in varying degrees is a quality of life, ranging from
mere response to environment to alert and wide perception in
man through his senses. This shared characteristic of life
surely indicates a common life, the One, at the source of
everything.

The working of the Law, particularly in restoring and
maintaining balance and harmony, strongly suggests the intelligence we have postulated. But whence is derived intelligence that can order the working of a universe down to its
smallest details? The question justifies the hypothesis that
a universal Intelligence operates in and through all things,

coeval with the one Life. Universal order and finely regulated interdependence and harmonious relationship bear witness to it. But the intelligence postulated is not that of a super entity, an idealized projection of ourselves, but universal Intelligence as an aspect of one universal Mind.

Granted a universal Intelligence, it is hard to see how, without an overruling entity through whom it can work, it could be effective. We may get some light on this from the saying " Unity manifests in diversity ". Intelligence becomes operative through vast hierarchies of intelligences ensouling all substance and form, both in the world we know by our senses and in the unseen world with its various levels of being and beings. Universal Law as the one Law, one universal Mind and one common Intelligence are all of the One and the All.

A Theosophist is one who gives you a theory of the works of God, which has not a revelation but an inspiration of his own for basis.

A man once abandoning the old pathway of routine and entering on the solitary pathway of independent thought— Godward—he is a Theosophist, an original thinker, a seeker after the Eternal Truth, with an inspiration of his own to solve the Eternal problems.—THOMAS VAUGHAN (1622-66)

PROGRESS TO FULFILMENT

Some call it evolution and others
call it God—W. H. Carruth.

Madeleine Leslie-Smith

The idea of evolution is relatively new in the western world,
dating only from about the middle of last century. But it has
always been part of the secret archaic Wisdom of the east, as
N. Sri Ram has pointed out:

> It is a fallacy to think that in ancient times no one knew
> anything about the extraordinary phenomenon we call
> Evolution and its enormous significance. The archaic
> teaching on the subject is explained in *The Secret Doctrine* by
> H. P. Blavatsky, but is also indicated in the form of certain
> basic truths in the *Gita* and other now less well-known books
> from which she quotes.[1]

So H. P. Blavatsky brought to the somewhat crude and
incomplete views of western thinkers ideas of the Ancient
Wisdom and its teaching about evolution. All the religions
of the world are based upon these teachings, although in
many instances they are distorted either by literal and
dogmatic interpretations or by only partial statement of the
basic teaching; or they are overlaid with ritual, ceremonial or
codes of priestcraft.

Modern Theosophy, the most recent expression of the
Wisdom, is concerned with these fundamental concepts of
which each religion is an incomplete version, and it encourages

[1] *The Nature of Our Seeking*, p. 111, T. P. H.

each individual to discover for himself as much of the truth as his mental faculties and spiritual capacities enable him to perceive.

Theosophy, however, sees evolution as something deeper than the gradual adaptation and growth of forms to suit outward circumstances. It is not merely the development of physical form. It is a continual process at three different levels of being. At the highest level, called monadic, it is more an unfoldment than a growth. Here consciousness is one and undivided; its latent power is released into potency as evolution at the lower levels progresses. Our understanding of this level is helpfully symbolized by the unity of the ocean in which is an infinity of individual drops of water. This is the ocean of eternity where One and many are united.

The second level of progressive expansion is that of mind, where each man, as a separate unit of the One, is evolving his intellectual and intuitional powers. The centre of each man's being is a spark of the divine Unity, or Monad, and this centre is often referred to as the monad of that individual. This explains the seeming paradox of the Monad being at the same time One and indivisible and also the core of each separate unit of life. For every living unit (including that of so-called inanimate objects) has its spiritual heart or monad, enshrouded in matter and awaiting the opportunity of releasing its potentiality during successive ages.

The third area of evolution is that with which we are most familiar: physical form. Here is evolved through countless generations a form more suited to the environment and more expressive of the life within. Thus the modification of the form is achieved by the dual pressure of the life-force within and the circumscribing physical world without.

3

According to the ancient teaching, then, evolution is the means by which the Spirit—the One—expresses itself in matter as the many. The several strands in the rope of evolution are bound each to each, and each supports and gives strength to the whole.

Expansion of Consciousness

The unfolding of spirit can be seen as the gradual expansion of consciousness throughout the whole of the manifested universe, both that aspect of it which we can perceive with our physical senses and that infinitely larger portion which is hidden from our ordinary human faculties. The One can be apprehended as the driving force within and behind all the kingdoms of nature, from the simplest mineral forms to the level of human beings—and beyond. The dynamic power of the indwelling Spirit directs the evolution of the form; and the outer circumstances are the means by which that Spirit impels the form to acquire greater responsiveness and sensitivity to express the indwelling life.

Evolution implies movement, progression. In the *Stanzas of Dzyan*, given in *The Secret Doctrine*, movement, or breath, is said, together with space, to be the ultimate source of all that exists—the one constant: " ceaseless eternal breath, which knows itself not ".[1]   H. P. B. elaborates it:

> . . . eternal ceaseless Motion . . . called in esoteric parlance the " Great Breath ", which is the perpetual motion of the universe, in the sense of limitless ever-present SPACE.[2]

This outbreathing and inbreathing, or motion, is a symbol of the formation and withdrawal of all that exists in the

[1] Stanzas, II. 2.
[2] *S.D.*, I. 2, 1st ed., I. 70, 6-vol. ed.

phenomenal worlds from atom to universe. It implies that each unit of existence (external, objective being), based on the eternal spiritual " be-ness ", follows a path of change and progress, of gradually increasing complexity, and then gradual withdrawal again to the spiritual, formless condition symbolized by the ceaseless breath.

We can individually focus our attention on the outer world of increasing complexity or on the inner world of subjective being or spirituality. As children our attention is obviously turned mainly towards the exciting phenomenal world. And yet children, especially, seem to have a subconscious awareness of an inner world which is often hidden from their elders, whose habits of thought and concern with external problems tend to blunt their perception of that interior world. As we go through life the focus of our attention alternates between the outward processes of evolution and the inner realization of the source of these processes, according to our age and temperament. This is also true of the human race as a whole. There is the evolutionary drive at the physical level to greater complexity and wider objective knowledge, and at the same time the inward urge of the spiritual sphere for ever fuller expression. This then is the dynamic message of Theosophy: that evolution at the physical level is an outward expression of a spiritual drive or movement whose source is within and beyond the reach of human thinking. In other words, evolution is spiritually based. It is also a continuous process:

> The Secret Doctrine teaches the progressive development of everything, worlds as well as atoms; and this stupendous development has neither conceivable beginning nor imaginable end.[1]

[1] *S.D.*, I. 43; I. 115.

Man stands now, according to occult tradition, at roughly the mid-point of his cycle of evolution. It is understandable therefore that most of the race is still immersed in considerations of material and physical import. But, having achieved a firm basis in an objective world, the way ahead for mankind is to transfer attention to the realms of spirit— to turn from the knowledge of the world without to an understanding of the world within.

The outward movement from what H. P. Blavatsky calls " be-ness ' to the various states of being, begins at a level of consciousness which is entirely beyond the reach of man's thinking processes. *The Secret Doctrine* speaks of it only in metaphor and allegory. We can but try to follow the metaphor, accepting what seems reasonable to us, and frequently reminding ourselves that words also are but symbols of the facts they represent, and that the whole presentation in word and symbol is like a two-dimensional plan of a three-dimensional structure. In this way we shall leave room for our own expanding awareness to fill out progressively an incomplete skeleton draft.

The beginning of the outbreathing of the universe is described as " Number proceeding from No-number ". That is, the eternal pulsation of be-ness (no-number) energizes a portion of that be-ness to become One (number) and from that One proceed the many (i.e. numbers).

The One in action becomes threefold. It has three aspects, it " acts " in three ways. These three modes are described in different terms in religious teachings: Self, Not-self and the relation between them; Father, Son and Holy Ghost; Brahma, Vishnu, Shiva; or, the terms most frequently used in Theosophy, Will, Wisdom and Active Intelligence. These modes are the basis of the teaching about a trinity in all religions.

From Trinity to Septenary

Will can be understood to be the power, the drive behind all manifested things, the enthusiasm to create, to achieve. Love-Wisdom is that aspect which draws together and unites those units which are in accord and holds apart those that are inimical to each other. (This power can be seen even in the chemical reactions of the mineral kingdom.) Intelligence is an aspect latent in all that exists, as the guiding principle, long before it becomes self-conscious knowing in the human being. These three, inherent in every object, every activity in the universe, form the ocean, so to speak, the spiritual basis and ensouling energy, of the entire objective universe. This objectivity is not limited to what is objective to our own restricted senses, but extends also to that much wider sphere of awareness to which our expanding faculties will attain in the further course of evolution. From this basic trinity, the " Seven Builders " are evolved. A septenate naturally arises from a triad because, through their interrelations, the three components can group themselves in seven ways and no more. These are the modes of being which, in their combinations and permutations, make the diversity of all living beings.

Much of the Ancient Wisdom is based on numbers. We may accept them and their relation as fact, or as allegory to help us to understand in some measure the mystery of the formation of a universe, a world or an atom. The idea of the seven builders, or intelligences, emananted from the One, who evolve the material universe, is as old as thinking man : compare the seven Rishis, the seven orders of Angels, the seven Spirits before the Throne, and so on. The pattern of sevens lies behind all the information given in the old teachings, the entire objective world being a complex of these seven basic influences.

The process of evolution appears to be a gradual limitation

and separation of the One into units whose work is to become increasingly aware of self and not-self. This is the evolution of consciousness, taking place within the limitation of form. As we have seen, it is the ensouling consciousness that causes the modification or evolution of the form to suit its growing awareness and need for Self-expression and self-awareness. At last, after unimaginable ages of evolution, the human form as we know it on this planet is evolved as the vehicle through which human intelligence can be expressed. Then man, having learned of self and not-self, by his gradually extended concern for the outer forms, starts to resolve a paradox. Eventually he comes to realize that self and not-self, thou and I, are in truth One.

The septenary scheme of our solar system takes place on four planes of consciousness, successively " descending " to levels of awareness of thought, of feeling, of subtle physical (" etheric ") matter, and finally to the level of ordinary physical matter (solid, liquid and gaseous), and then " re-ascending " to the " higher " planes. Of the seven areas of development our earth is the fourth and the densest; and it alone " is within our plane or means of perception ".[1] The scheme is often pictured as seven globes arranged like beads on a string, with two globes on each of the subtler levels and the earth only at the dense mid-point, the whole group being termed a chain. But as they represent states of consciousness they should not be thought of as necessarily spatially separated, but perhaps interpenetrating each other, like water and sand in a jar. Activity is focused on each successively, and on each of the seven consciousness develops awareness at different levels. These correspond to the mineral, plant, animal and human kingdoms, preceded

[1] *S.D.*, I. 152; I, 207.

by three others at a sub-mineral stage, of which science as yet knows nothing, but which are referred to in ancient writings. The teaching is that the ensouling consciousness passes to vivify forms at a higher level when it has achieved its goal of perfection at a lower one.

The Present Stage

In the process of reaching its present stature humanity as a whole is said to have passed through earlier modes of consciousness (mineral, plant, animal) elsewhere than in the scheme of evolution to which our earth belongs. We started our human experience in the first highly subtle area, or globe, of this chain, progressed to the second and so on, until we had completed a first series of activity and experience in each of the seven areas. This sequence is said to have been repeated three times (three rounds) and we are now passing the mid-point in our progress through the fourth cycle.

During the present active cycle on our planet there have been successive types of human beings, developing their faculties in different cyclic phases of growth, referred to in *The Secret Doctrine* as the seven root races, of which five have so far appeared. These do not correspond to modern ethnic groups, but to the unfolding of potentiality at different levels and the development of corresponding sensory organs at the physical level. Although physical types may show genealogical descent, all present-day humanity has available in common the kinds of consciousness developed by earlier races. All normal human beings have five senses with which to observe the outer world. The basic brain equipment, for instance, of an uneducated tribesman from a tropical rain forest is identical with that of a highly learned philosopher or scientist. It is not the outward appearance of the physical body that indicates an evolved individual but his ability to use his physical apparatus and express his ideas through it.

Traditionally, man at the beginning of his human training possessed the faculty of hearing—the power to sense vibrations from without. Adam and Eve " heard " God in the Garden of Eden.[1] Then sequentially were developed the senses of touch, sight, taste and smell.

It is interesting to note that the first three senses—hearing, touch and sight—enable man to be aware of the world without and to understand his place in it. The senses of taste and smell then enable him to refine and sensitize both his own personality and the environment in which he lives. If we accept the postulate that perfected man will have seven senses, then it is probable that we are already beginning to evolve in our fifth root race a new form of perception, possibly some form of intuition which will be part of the normal equipment of future races.

The present fifth race type is descended from the preceding ones and has not as yet reached the goal set for it, but, looking to the future, we can assume that a sixth race type will eventually appear. The evolution of a new race type now can scarcely follow the pattern of the birth of earlier races. For them a group of men could be isolated from the rest of mankind by natural barriers such as mountains or seas and develop required characteristics without extraneous influences. Obviously that is not possible. It seems likely that our future progress will be not so much a matter of physical type but of mental and psychic affinity, so that from the best of all the races a new and more responsive type will be born.

[1] *The Bible*, Genesis III, 8.

The workings of karma must be considered here. The reincarnating Ego * will have for his parents those who can provide him with the conditions he needs for continuing his evolution. Those with already highly developed abilities will be born into conditions where those abilities can be used and further developed. One who is still at an early stage of human evolution will choose a simpler environment where the demands made on him will not be beyond his powers of response.

Thus we see that each race type has acquired for mankind a new dimension of awareness, and each has therefore had its special contribution to make to the evolution of humanity. This applies to the individual as well as to the group. Each has its individual physical ancestry and also the accumulated experience of past incarnations to draw on. Each can bring its unique quality to the group and the world. Some will emphasize the philosophical aspect, some the intellectual, some the artistic; all aspects are necessary for the wholeness, the health, of mankind.

What is the special contribution that present-day humanity can make? What will be the new area of awareness which will make this contribution possible? We are said to stand just beyond the mid-point of the evolutionary cycle in our associated group of centres of activity—our chain. We have gained a wide knowledge of the material world and great skill in handling our environment. To an almost obsessive degree we are conscious of ourselves as separate individuals in an objective world. Our outward journey to the complex confines of the many is nearing its completion. Now mankind must begin to turn its face homewards, to realize itself as a unity, sparks within the divine Flame.

* See footnote p. 15.

Men must assume conscious and deliberate control not only of their own progress and environment, but also ultimate responsibility for the guiding and evolution of life on the whole planet and at all levels. Until now we have been guided and watched over by intelligent beings who completed their human experience on other chains than that to which we belong. These express themselves through the forces of nature and are themselves the expressions of the trinity of Will, Wisdom and Intelligence of which the whole universe is an aspect. Gradually man must take over the work which has hitherto been undertaken by his elders on the ladder of evolution.

What then should be our special contribution to the whole? Since an extension of awareness seems to be the way of progress it is to be expected that some new faculty will be developed. It is possible that this new awareness might be in the nature of a spiritual insight which would enable man to perceive with immediate certainty true spiritual values and their application to the world in which he lives. In fact, on his return journey man may rediscover that perception symbolized by hearing, as Adam and Eve heard the voice of God in the Garden of Eden. With this perception of That which stands within or behind the substance of the universe, man will be able to take up conscious cooperation with the One Will in evolution.

HUMAN PHASES OF CONSCIOUSNESS

V. Wallace Slater

> What a piece of work is man! How noble
> in reason! how infinite in faculty! . . . in
> apprehension how like a god!—HAMLET.

WHAT is man, who has been called the crown of nature on this planet, the creature whom Julian Huxley said was evolution become conscious of itself?

Yet unless one is a scientist, with the constant urge to gain more knowledge, why should one bother about how man is constituted? The overriding reason is that on our views depends our attitude to life—and death—and our attitudes govern how we behave, our conduct and our whole way of living.

The theosophical view is that man is not just the physical body that is born, lives, dies and disintegrates, nor is the brain the whole thinking principle. Furthermore, although man is limited by his individuality, this limitation does not apply to the experience of his essential nature. There appears to be a quality in human consciousness that expands individual man to embrace the whole human species. In Theosophy this is expressed by the term life-wave, meaning that abstract essence, life, that embraces the whole of the human kingdom, and every other kingdom of Nature.

At the material level the individual is limited in consciousness to his physical body. His senses of smell, sight and hearing extend that consciousness beyond the limits of the body. Thought extends it still farther. Thus the individual may be seen to embrace, not only the whole human species, but the whole of nature. The theosophical notion is that man as individual is a microcosm containing within himself the general principles of the whole universe, the macrocosm.

Evolution from the lower kingdoms has proceeded in a manner to develop the individual animal as a separate personality in the human kingdom. It is the emphasis on the individual at the mental level that enables man to understand his part in the whole scheme of human evolution—not just his physical anatomy, but the emotional, mental and altruistic aspects of his consciousness.

But first it is necessary to establish the general idea that man is a principle that embraces both the individual and mankind. By analogy it is as if humanity, the life-wave now ensouling the present human kingdom, were the radiating light of the sun and that each individual is a sunbeam. The sun in this analogy represents the divine Paradigm, the archetypal model or pattern for the creation of all forms. Each ray creates a projection of the divine Paradigm in the manifested world. It is thus that we may form a picture of man the individual as the microcosm, reproducing within himself all the characteristics of archetypal man as the macrocosm.

Expressed in the language of western religion, man was created in the image of God. He is in truth an incarnation of God. " Ye are gods; and all of you are children of the Most High ".[1] " Ye are the temple of the living God " [2].

[1] *Bible,* Psalm LXXXII, 6.
[2] *Ibid.,* II Cor. VI, 16.

Theosophical literature describes man and mankind as that being in whom highest spirit and lowest matter are joined together by Intelligence.

Body, Soul and Spirit

With that introduction to the nature of man in general, we may now proceed to the constitution of individual man in particular. Duality is the inherent idea in the human mind, whether one believes in the existence of one part of the duality after the death of the body or not. The first elementary conclusion of man about himself is that he appears to be such a duality of matter and spirit, a physical body and a spiritual or non-material " soul ". At this stage we will call this " soul " the I-making principle.

The physical evolution of man proceeds by heredity from two physical bodies to the physical body of their offspring. But the offspring has an identity separate from the parents, not only in the material body but in that abstract experience called consciousness. Different schools of thought identify consciousness with different aspects of experience: the mind, intelligence, feeling, the will, the ego, the essential nature of life, and so on. Psychologists have presented the view that there is a peak experience of consciousness that is aware of itself as an entity " which is different from the humdrum levels of earth-based, instinctive life ". Dr. L. J. Bendit calls the dual existence instinctive man and essential man.[1]

Materialists may argue that the essential man is so dependent on instinctive man that on the death of the body both fade into nothingness. Yet most men have always accepted the idea that essential man or soul or Ego * (the I-making

---

[1] L. J. & P. D. Bendit, *The Transforming Mind*, p. 22, T. P. H. 1970.

* See footnote p. 15.

principle) continues to exist or to BE after the death of the physical body.

Philosophers and sages throughout the ages have expanded the dual aspect of man by separating the non-physical into two entities, thus making man threefold: body, soul and spirit, to use St. Paul's terms.

The theosophical view supports this idea that man is triune: spirit (*nous*), soul (*psyche*) and body (*soma*). The body is the material form; the soul is the psychic nature; spirit is the transcendent Self or spiritual Ego existing at a level of being outside or beyond the world of material and psychic experience. In this context the body and soul are called the personality because it is assumed that the higher consciousness or spiritual Ego gains its experience in consciousness of outer things through a *persona* or mask. Thus we have a duality in which the lower entity embraces both material and psychic levels of existence and the higher entity stands apart, above or within according to one's line of thought about spiritual matters.

The experience of self, the personal identity, is centred in wherever consciousness is located at a given point in time. During waking consciousness this is clearly in the body, but there is a feeling that one is also living as from an inner psychic world, that there is a vague sensitive non-material entity that is aware of bodily reactions and responds by its ability to decide what the body shall do. This we call the *psyche*. When the body is quiescent, only half-awake, the inner feeling becomes more real. It is as if consciousness moves out of the physical world into a psychic realm.

The withdrawal of consciousness from the physical senses to the psychic level awakens some still deeper feeling of an

" I-ness ", a sense of Self-hood which bears the same relation to the psychic as that does to the body. This we call the spiritual Self or Ego.

Sevenfold man

Waking consciousness is a blend of sensation, feeling (including the emotions) and thinking. If to this we add the physical body then the personality is fourfold.

The theosophical view is that man is a sevenfold being; seven aspects make up the constitution of man. These may be considered in different ways according to how one tries to visualize their existence:

(a) *As bodies.* Here one begins with the dense physical body and pictures a series of subtler bodies co-existing with the physical, the spiritual being the most subtle. Some schools of thought regard these higher bodies as replicas of the physical having extension in space; spiritualists claim to be able to contact them after death.

(b) *As sheaths, vehicles or vestures.* These terms are based on the idea that the spiritual Self of man descends into matter, taking on more and more dense material as it descends. At each stage spirit accepts an additional limitation, a veil over pure spiritual consciousness.

(c) *As fields of force.* This expression is an attempt to link up with modern scientific thought. The idea is that the physical body has a field of force around and within itself just as a magnet has a magnetic field extending beyond the bar of metal. The mental body or sheath then becomes rather less formal in shape. One has a picture of higher aspects of consciousness operating in a more diffuse sense, rather as a cloud or aura around the physical, but in realms that become more and more subtle.

(d) *As principles.* This is the philosophical approach, using the term principle as an element or original essence of the universe. Principles are subjective rather than objective. It is assumed that the lower aspects of consciousness, physical, emotional and mental, may require forms for their expression, but beyond that there are fields of consciousness that are outside our powers of visualization; they are formless. For example, consciousness is experienced in many different ways and in different forms, but it is an abstract principle; it is not the forms as such.

The objection to the more formal terms for the constituents of human consciousness is that they imply clear-cut divisions. Our various realms of conscious activity are inextricably interwoven. It is possibly as inaccurate to say that man is sevenfold as to speak of the spectrum as consisting of seven colours. So one should think of consciousness ranging from highest spirit to lowest matter by imperceptible gradations.

However, scientists have always found it useful to analyse a subject into its constituent parts. The following classifications of the constituent parts of man's total being are therefore presented in the spirit of what has been said above. Psychologists use different ways of considering the fields of consciousness from so-called waking consciousness to the universal unconscious. Similarly Theosophy presents the constitution of man in different ways.

There are two main types of septenary to be found in theosophical literature. They are given below—one as principles, the other as bodies. The former is based on the qualities of each " constituent " as part of a whole, the latter on the form of each " constituent " as if they were separate entities.

I The Seven Principles

Spirit, divine will   ⎫
Wisdom, pure reason   ⎬ Upper triad
Mind, creative intelligence ⎭

Animal desires   ⎫
Sensitivity   ⎬ Lower quaternary
Vitality or life   ⎪
Physicality   ⎭

II The Seven Bodies

Spirit   ⎫
Intuition   ⎬ Ego
Causal body (higher mental)   ⎭

Lower mental body   ⎫
Desire (emotional) body   ⎬ Personality
Etheric double   ⎪
Dense physical body   ⎭

In **II** spirit and intuition are not really bodies but centres of higher consciousness. The causal body is the vehicle for spirit and intuition to have access to the outer world during incarnation in a physical body. It is also the repository of experience between incarnations, assuming one accepts the idea of reincarnation.

Comparing **I** and **II**, the principles of the lower mental and desire bodies are grouped together as animal desires; the etheric double is represented by sensitivity; and the dense physical body is represented by physicality, a word implying the properties of material things: inertia, resistance, etc. This gives us six principles, but vitality is added, thus making

4

seven. Vitality is not given in II, because it is not a separate
body or centre, but a life principle.

These two examples, I principles and II bodies, illustrate
what was said earlier that clear-cut divisions should be avoided;
one must be prepared to hold broad views and to accept
different arrangements according to one's method of approach.

Personality

A detailed personal examination of the constitution of
man naturally begins with the physical, the body studied by
anatomists and physiologists. Even at this level we have
systems within systems: the skeleton and muscular structure;
the heart, arteries and veins with the circulation of the blood;
the nervous system, voluntary and sympathetic; the diges-
tion and excretory system; the glandular system with hormone
control of bodily functions; and other auxiliary systems.

Materialists may claim that man is only this complex of
chemical structures and reactions, and that intelligence and
all other characteristics of man are but the end-products
of the physical evolutionary process. The theosophical view
is that the body is held together as a living organism by non-
physical forces. The primary force is vitality, that something
which makes a living thing live. It is associated in animal
bodies with breathing. Indian psychologists call it *prana*.
The idea is not generally accepted by biologists, but there
are a few who are prepared to admit that there are phenomena
associated with living organisms that cannot be explained by
purely materialistic means.

The etheric double is the field of force around the physical
body. Clairvoyants say that a body of ethereal substance
permeates the physical body and extends beyond the surface
of the skin about six millimetres. They refer also to an aura

extending several centimetres. The term double is used because it is not a separate vehicle of consciousness any more than the electric field around an electric conductor is a separate force.

The etheric double appears to be the vehicle for that force we have called vitality, life or *prana*. This explains why in table I we have two principles vitality and sensitivity for the one body, the etheric double. The characteristic of the etheric is sensitivity; vitality (*prana*) is a life principle which is associated with all levels of consciousness and therefore in table II it is not a body but the life principle of all the bodies. In normal activity it is specially associated with etheric and dense physical. It is possible to experience the flow of *prana* and the extension of physical consciousness into the etheric double by the practice of deep breathing and meditation, but that is outside the scope of this chapter.

The next principle to be considered is that which has been called animal desires; this is associated with two bodies, desire (sometimes called emotional or astral) and lower mental. Desire (feeling and emotion) and thought are so closely related in consciousness that it is not easy to separate them. Hence they have been taken as one principle in table I.

The term animal desires is meant to imply that this principle is associated with the animal part of man and the material world rather than with the spiritual. It is, as it were, a veil between the higher Self, associated with spirit, and the outside world. It is the *psyche* of threefold man, the bridge between spirit and matter, and it is assumed to have a limited lifetime.

Consideration of the evolution of man indicates how the animal-desire principle activated two vehicles. We may now find it difficult to feel pure emotion, but primitive man behaved more as animal-man and his psychic sensibility was

more clearly identified with sensation, feeling and desire.
We see this reproduced in the early life of a child. Gradually
the nervous organization develops with the awakening mind
that begins to exercise control over the desire nature, to be
selective in what the child wants. So one comes to the realization that there is a body of desire and an emotive-mind.
These are given a variety of names in theosophical literature:
emotional body, astral body, body of feeling; and lower
mental body, lower mind, vehicle for concrete thought.

The most commonly used expressions are emotional body
and lower mental body. The latter is associated with that
element of the mind which is directed downwards to the feelings
and emotions. The emotional body is associated with desire and
instinct, and seeks experience in physical behaviour. We shall
see that these two bodies are so blended as to behave as one.

Thus table II for the personality might be given in terms
of behaviour thus:

Feeling ——————— Thinking

Vitality (etheric)

Activity (physical)

The whole personality of physical and psychic (body and
soul) is regarded as one's lower self and transitory. It is the
Ego or higher self that lives throughout reincarnations. The
body dies and so eventually does the "soul". A new incarnation takes place by the descent of the Ego into new vehicles of
consciousness at the lower levels of thinking, feeling and acting.

Ego

So we come to a consideration of the nature of that higher
Self. This higher consciousness of man is taken to be that
part of our nature which operates with abstract ideas, broad

views and a clear understanding. The mind of man is dual: the lower mind is concerned with concrete thought and linked with emotion and feeling; the higher mind is concerned with abstract ideas and linked with a principle that has been called the intuition, but is probably better described as enlightenment, inspiration, illumination, understanding, insight.

If we wish to have clear-cut divisions, then the higher Self, the Ego, is a triad: mind, enlightenment and spirit. These are arbitrary expressions for levels of consciousness.

Mind is the thinking principle. Enlightenment is characterized by wisdom and pure divine love, intuition, harmony and illumination. The two linked together constitute the higher Self or spirit of man, the illumined mind. It exists after the death of all the lower vehicles and therefore is called the reincarnating Ego.

At a still higher level is the pure Self, the highest principle of man. In table I we called it divine will to distinguish this will from the capricious will of a fractious child or the obstinacy of a fanatic. With the enlightened mind we have an upper triad corresponding with the lower triad of feeling, thinking, vitality.

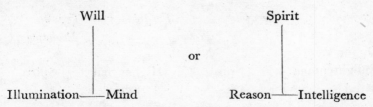

At this level it is well to drop the idea of bodies and keep to principles, as a more abstract expression.

The principle of divine will is both universal and individual. Thus man, through this, his highest principle, is rooted in the universal Self or Spirit of the universe and yet he also has an individual existence in his own higher Self. It is this principle that gives the illumined mind an identity as a spiritual consciousness, manifesting as understanding, judgment, discrimination.

Symbolical classifications

Some further examples of the sevenfold classification of the phases of consciousness will now be given. These must not be taken too rigidly but as symbolical of relationships. For example charts I and II indicate that there are two mental phases, or two minds, one higher and the other lower. But there is only one mind at the central point of consciousness. When that mind functions in conjunction with desire we call it lower mind. When it is "enlightened" we call it higher mind.

The constitution of man is complex and the "parts" are not clearly separate entities but blend one into the other. Even that statement must not be taken too literally, for some aspects can be regarded as separate under certain circumstances.

III

Sevenfold	Threefold	Twofold	Type of Evolution
Divine Will ⎫ Enlightenment ⎬	Spirit	Higher Self	Spirit
Mind ⎭		(Ego)	
Lower Mind ⎫ Desire ⎬	Soul (psychic nature)	Lower Self (personality)	Intelligence
Etheric ⎫ (vitality) ⎬ Physical ⎭	Body		Physical Form

Chart III indicates the idea that in man there are three parallel schemes of evolution: spirit, intelligence and physical. The central feature is the mind that bridges spirit and soul, Ego and personality and may be intellectual or psychic. Here the mind is taken to be a guiding Intelligence that preceded the creation of all forms. It is man's middle principle energized by divine Intelligence assumed to be primal.

IV

FORM		1		LIFE
		2		
		3		
Spirit	4			
(divine will)	5	1		
	6	2		
	7	3		
			4	Enlightenment
		1	5	
(H.M.)		2	6	
		3	7	
Mind	4			
	5	1		
(L.M.)		6	2	
		7	3	
			4	Emotion
		1	5	
(etheric)		2	6	
		3	7	
Physical	4			
	5			
(dense physical)	6			
	7			

Another way of looking at the principles is based on the idea that there is throughout creation a duality of life and form, for example that emotion or desire is the life of the lower mind. Chart IV illustrates this, and shows that the life principles overlap the forms. It is assumed here that each principle has seven sub-principles of graded subtlety, 7 being the most dense. This is, of course, a symbolical representation to give an idea of relationships: horizontally between life and form; vertically between life and life, and form and form (higher and lower).

One may use the chart to invoke an experience of the transmutation of emotion into the harmony of enlightenment; of physical into intellectual thought and thence to divine will.

Taking this idea of life and form, *The Secret Doctrine* postulates a general life principle of *prana* and a general form principle called the auric envelope, since all forms require a surrounding envelope or skin.

Monad

The highest principle of man as an individual is his will. In the charts it has been called divine will or spirit. As already indicated, this principle is twofold: universal and individual. The universal aspect is called in theosophical literature the Monad, a name given to highest Spirit. In this sense the Monad is above or beyond the sevenfold man, bearing a similar relation to the Ego as the Ego does to the personality. The individual monad is taken to be that spark of divinity within each one of us. There is however only one Monad for the human hierarchy. This Monad operating through divine will gives individuality to the human spirit. For Monad we should probably have said monadic essence, the rays of which become the individual monads of man.

Most of the problems of the modern world, both those of corporate man (nations) and individual man, arise because people are everywhere caught up in a materialism that confuses and identifies the real human being with the personality through which he tries to express himself in physical life. Unfortunately the religions have failed in their task of presenting man as essentially a spiritual being, conviction of which changes one's whole moral outlook, one's attitudes, one's way of life. Hence the importance of the ideas we have here tried to outline.

Behold the truth before you: a clean life, an open mind, a pure heart, an eager intellect, an unveiled spiritual perception, a brotherliness for all, a readiness to give and receive advice and instruction, a courageous endurance of personal injustice, a brave declaration of principles, a valiant defence of those who are unjustly attacked and a constant eye to the ideal of human progression and perfection which the sacred science depicts—these are the golden stairs up the steps of which the learner may climb to the Temple of Divine Wisdom.
—H. P. BLAVATSKY.

THE PANORAMA OF HUMAN EXISTENCE

The Pilgrim of Eternity—SHELLEY.

HELEN V. ZAHARA

WHO am I? Where did I come from? Why am I here and where am I going? These searching questions have haunted the thoughts of men in all times, and neither science nor religion has been able fully to explain them.

In the west for many centuries the predominant belief has been that man experiences but one life on earth. In the view of orthodox religion he is a special creation of God and the state of his after-life depends on his earthly actions. But evolutionary theories developed by materialistic science last century have caused wide rejection of these concepts. Man became regarded simply as a biological product of the evolutionary process, and death the end of the individual. Neither point of view allows for the theory of pre-existence or explains the inequalities of human conditions.

In eastern thought, with its doctrines of reincarnation and karma, can be found some of the otherwise missing pieces in the puzzle of man's existence. These concepts give meaning to the evolutionary process and remove the conflict between science and religion. A spiritual dimension is added to the theory of evolution, without denying the physical evidence, and both life and death are seen from a much wider viewpoint.

To re-awaken the ideas in the west was part of the task undertaken by H. P. Blavatsky and her spiritual teachers through the Theosophical Movement a hundred years ago. This effort has had a profound effect on western thought.

To grasp fully the magnitude of human existence may be beyond our power, but an immense and extraordinary vista is opened up when we take into account the theory of reincarnation. This is especially so if we view it within the context of a universal cycle that embraces all manifestation. Perhaps nowhere is it put in greater perspective than in the three fundamental propositions of the esoteric philosophy which appear in the Proem of H. P. Blavatsky's *magnum opus*, *The Secret Doctrine*, published in 1888. Here, within the space of a few paragraphs, are far-reaching concepts which supply the links so vitally needed to fill out man's view of himself and of the world.

Before coming to the propositions, the Proem introduces a principle which is basic to the whole esoteric system; There is ONE LIFE, eternal, invisible, yet omnipresent without beginning or end. . . .[1] This is repeated in different words in the first fundamental proposition which speaks of "An Omnipresent, Eternal, Boundless and Immutable PRINCIPLE"[2] The one Life is the one self-existing Reality, the Absolute.

The second fundamental proposition of *The Secret Doctrine* refers to the cyclic nature of "numberless Universes incessantly manifesting and disappearing" within the boundless plane of one eternal universe, and "the absolute universality of that law of periodicity, of flux and reflux, ebb and flow, which physical science has observed and recorded in all departments of nature".[3]

---

[1] *S.D.*, I. 2, 1st ed.; 1, 70, 6-vol. ed.
[2] *S.D.*, I, 14; I, 79.
[3] *S.D.*, I, 16-17; I, 82.

These two postulates should be kept in mind when considering the third proposition, which relates to man and is of the utmost importance when pondering the theme of life and death. Having been introduced to the concepts of one boundless existence and the law of periodicity, we find the same principles govern man. As it is put:

> The fundamental identity of all Souls with the Universal Over-Soul, the latter being itself an aspect of the Unknown Root; and the obligatory pilgrimage of every Soul—a spark of the former—through the cycle of Incarnation, or Necessity, in accordance with Cyclic and Karmic Law.[1]

Evolutionary Pilgrimage

In those few succinct statements we are presented with the awesome, all-embracing picture of the universe. There is one Life, that one Life is in man, and man in his inmost essence is identified with the universal Over-Soul, an aspect of the unknown Root. However, in accordance with cyclic action, man is embarked on a long evolutionary pilgrimage governed by karmic law.

Karmic law is the universal principle of causation, which operates at every level of manifestation, and applies to universes as well as to all beings. Every action produces its reaction or result, and so we observe the law working as a succession of interrelated causes and effects. Karma is also described as the principle of harmony, because it tends to restore balance and equilibrium, and therefore it is also a law of justice and righteousness.

When a universe appears as a result of cyclic motion, there occurs what is poetically described as the outbreathing of the Great Breath—a compulsion from within the ocean of Being.

[1] *S.D.*, I, 16-17; I, 82.

Sparks from the pure essence of the over-Soul (to use the imagery of *The Secret Doctrine*) issue forth and must thereafter pass through every elemental form of the phenomenal world, in the first stage through natural impulse as part of the outgoing process.

As the life wave moves from the highest or subtlest levels of spirit to the lowest or densest fields of matter, consciousness is imprisoned in dense forms, and then gradually through the evolutionary process begins to free itself, moving from mineral, through vegetable and animal kingdoms, to the human kingdom. The process is complex, and involves many cycles, immense aeons of time, and the interaction of multitudinous beings and forces of nature, visible and invisible.

When life enters the human kingdom individuality arises, self-consciousness develops, and choice becomes possible. Then man becomes subject to karma in a new way; his efforts are "self-induced and self-devised" as his consciousness ascends thorugh all degrees of intelligence. This brings us to the very difficult subject of destiny and free will. The pilgrimage for every soul is said to be obligatory (that is our destiny, we might say), it is part of the universal karma. But now we learn that, having acquired individuality, we are responsible for our own evolution. The factor of free will has entered, and this is subject, of course, to the law of karma. Says *The Secret Doctrine*:

> The pivotal doctrine of the Esoteric Philosophy admits no privileges or special gifts in man, save those won by his own Ego * [Self] through personal effort and merit through a long series of metempsychoses and reincarnations. [1]

From this larger perspective, the struggles, the pains and the joys of life appear less futile. It seems that the abrasive

* See footnote p. 15.
[1] *S.D.*, I, 17; I, 83.

effect of such experience is necessary for our evolution through many lives. Just as minerals, plants, and animals survive by adapting to their environment, so man learns and grows through experiences in many cultures, lands and ethnic groups, in male and female bodies, in different periods of history, building qualities and capacities, unfolding latent powers of body, emotion, mind and spirit, moving to that state expressed in the *Bible*, as the " the stature of the perfect man ".

In referring to the universality of the law of periodicity, H. P. Blavatsky gave as examples: day and night, life and death, sleeping and waking. In recent years there has been extensive research into cycles and rhythms, and it has been found that rhythmic fluctuation characterizes the phenomena of at least 36 separate disciplines. Astronomy, physics, oceanology, bacteriology, mammalogy, climatology, terrestrial magnestism, physiology, botany, history, sociology and economics are examples. Edward R. Dewey, President of the Foundation for the Study of Cycles (affiliated with the University of Pittsburgh) states: " The number of phenomena in which cyclic behaviour has been observed is so great as to suggest that behaviour of this sort is a fundamental characteristic of nature ".[1] Apart from the mighty cycles of nature, observed in the pulse of the earth, in solar rhythms, tides, seasons, and in other ways, there are numerous rhythms that affect man himself. These include time sense, biological clocks, natural rhythms in the nervous system, heart rate, pulse wave, respiratory rate, sexual cycles, the pattern of emotions, the energy cycle, war and peace, crime, and other aspects of human behaviour.[2]

[1] Paper issued May 3, 1965.

[2] See *Biological Rhythm Research* by A. Sollberger, Elsevier Pub. Coy., 1965; and *Cycles in Your Life*, by Darrell Huff, W. W. Norton & Co., New York, 1964.

Wheels Within Wheels

So it is well established that within nature there are large and small cycles, and these are amazingly interrelated. It is, therefore, not difficult to expand this concept and to grasp the idea of a rhythmic process of activity and rest, or flux and reflux, of descent and ascent, of movement from within outward and return, of outbreathing and inbreathing. This governs the whole of manifestation, from universes to atoms, and includes man. Each cycle is complete in itself, and at the same time is part of a larger cycle. For example, each cell in man's body has its own life and yet is part of the physical organism experiencing its cycle. Thus all the cycles of nature are linked together in an endless chain of causation, which has no conceivable beginning or end.

Inner changes are also involved in the evolutionary process. With each outward and inward movement there is (figuratively speaking) an upward movement, which means growth and unfoldment.

It is now being recognized by science that man is using only a very small fraction of his potential. Sensory capacities, the brain, and other faculties have enormous possibilities; but, from the theosophical standpoint, even these represent only a portion of man's powers which remain to be awakened. Man is seen as a reflection of the macrocosm, and has latent within him the powers of the whole universe of which he is part. To develop these is the purpose of his evolution, and the meaning behind the process of reincarnation.

Most people do not have any memory of having lived before because with each new birth the individual functions with a new brain mechanism. At the same time it is not unusual to have the feeling of having met friends or relatives before, of recognizing places as if having been there in some earlier time. Also in the learning process there might be a sense of already knowing a particular subject. These experiences could represent intimations from the past. There are also qualities, capacities and characters with which we are born, which are only partly explained by heredity, and which could be carried over from previous experience.

Child genius also provides possible evidence of reincarnation. Mozart, who began to compose at four, is considered a classical example. He was born into a musical family and therefore heredity and environment were important factors, but there seemed to be an innate capacity which gave that added quality or genius. There are cases where heredity does not provide the explanation, as with Isaac Newton. Genealogists who have traced his background have not been able to discover whence his mathematical genius arose.

We can find many recent examples of youthful prodigies. Mabelle Thompson, in the U. S. A., at the age of four could solve trigonometry problems and read advanced textbooks on mathematics and astronomy. Senaka Senanayake of Ceylon painted brilliantly at seven and produced art reminiscent of Manet, Monet, Van Gough, Sisley, Picasso and of the abstractionists. A boy in Korea, Kim Ung Yong, read, wrote and spoke Korean, Chinese, German and English at the age of two and a half. Jeffrey Hurrt, a Negro naturalist, was accepted by the American Museum of Natural History in New York to do research there at the age of eight. Tony Rolle of New York was described at eight as " the Mozart of the 20th century ", with an understanding of tonal colour and phrasing rare in one so young.

People display different levels of enlightenment and spirituality; some have little intelligence, others have highly developed minds. Some are criminals, others are saints. These suggest different stages of unfoldment on the evolutionary path.

Although most people do not have direct memory of having lived before, there are exceptions, and there is an impressive body of testimony from people who have had such experience, occurring to themselves or to someone close to them. It seems that children who die young may sometimes reincarnate quickly and bring some memories through.

Survival Evidence

Dr. Ian Stevenson, Emeritus Professor of Neurology and Psychiatry, University of Virginia, U. S. A., published in 1960 an essay entitled " The Evidence for Survival from Claimed Memories of Former Incarnations ".[1] He stated that he had studied several hundred accounts of claimed memories of former lives, as well as cases of those who have had apparent memories of places and have described some events of which the person had no previous knowledge.

Six years later he produced a bigger work, *Twenty Cases Suggestive of Reincarnation.*[2] He travelled to various countries to study evidence at first hand—sometimes alone, sometimes with colleagues—interviewing the claimants and their families, friends and neighbours, checking records and verifying statements. He had reports of nearly 600 cases, of which he and his colleagues had personally investigated about a third.

None of this evidence, nor all of it together, can amount to proof, but it can suggest probability. Moreover, reincarnation is an ancient belief which forms part of the religious outlook of probably more than half the people of the world,

[1] *Journal*, American Society for Psychical Research, April and July 1960.
[2] American Society for Psychical Research, New York, 1966.

including in particular Hindus and Buddhists. They associate with it also the law of karma, cause and effect, as governing the conditions into which they are born.

In the west also, many thinkers have found the concept of rebirth to be valid, among them Plato, Pythagoras, Schopenhauer, Schweitzer, Benjamin Franklin, Walt Whitman and Thomas Edison.

The *Bible* has passages in both Old and New Testaments implying that an acceptance of reincarnation existed at the beginning of the Christian era. It is also referred to in the writings of the early Church Fathers, including those of Origen. But the rejection by the Council of Constantinople in A.D. 553 of pre-existence and, by implication, reincarnation, had a far-reaching effect on the thinking of millions of people in the centuries that followed.

What is it that continues after death? The student of Theosophy would say the Self, for whom the body has been but a tool. The materialistic view is that consciousness is a product of brain cells and therefore disappears at death. Yet, apart from evidence of after-death communication, there comes ample testimony, from those who practice yoga and meditation, of the possibility of realizing oneself as a centre of consciousness working through, but separate from, the physical body, emotions, and even the mind itself.

There is some scientific evidence pointing to mind and brain being separate. Sir John Eccles, an eminent Australian neuro-physiologist, has described experiences of patients undergoing brain surgery, who are conscious, so that the result of the surgery can be assessed. When the brain is exposed, electrical stimulation of the motor area administered by the surgeon causes the patient's arm or leg to move, even though the patient has not willed to move it.

Dr. H. Tudor Edmunds, writing on mind and brain separation, refers to brain waves recorded on the electroencephalograph (EEG) during hypnosis. The mind of a subject is deluded by the suggestion of the hypnotist that the eyes are shut when they are actually open. He acts as if he is blind while the brain records on the EEG that the eyes are open and seeing. This indicates that the mind is acting independently.[1]

There is also the testimony of many people who have had out of the body experiences, travelling away from their bodies during sleep, and subsequently verifying what they had seen.

Death and After

Clairvoyants record that, while the centre of consciousness seems to be in the brain, there is a magnetic centre of life in the heart, and as death draws near this moves from the heart to the brain. We find references to a magnetic thread which links the soul to the body and brings it back after sleep and other forms of unconsciousness. But this breaks at death, and then it is not possible for the soul to re-enter and occupy the body. This magnetic thread is likened to the silver cord in Ecclesiastes, in the *Bible*, where there is the reference to death, " Or ever the silver cord be loosed".

From the occult point of view the transition is said to be peaceful for the individual, even though his body may appear to be suffering. This is confirmed by a two-year survey of deathbed observations by nurses and physicians conducted by Dr. Karlis Osis, research director of the Parapsychology Foundation. They found that with seriously ill people withdrawal is frequently aided by visions and experiences which help them pass over peacefully. Visions or hallucinations of

[1] *Theosophical Journal*, London, March/April, 1972.

religious images or of beautiful scenes were experienced in 884 cases. Visions of persons occurred in 1,370 cases; in most instances these represented persons who had already died, usually relatives. Where non-relatives appeared in the visions, they were generally living persons. These experiences tend to support the idea found in theosophical literature that persons passing over in death are aided in the transition.

According to occult teaching, at the point of death, as the Ego (the Self) is about to begin withdrawal from the physical body, the individual reviews his life; " As in a dream, the events of a long life, to their minutest detail, are marshalled in the greatest order in a few seconds in our vision."[1] People who have reached the point of death and have been revived confirm such experience.

The original statements in the Theosophical Society regarding the after death process were given in Letters of the Mahatmas to A. P. Sinnett, which were later published. These state that with disintegration of the physical body there also occurs the disintegration of its subtle counterpart called the etheric double (which may, however, last long enough to appear as a wraith) and the life principle, called *prana*. For the Self there follows a period of unconsciousness which may last for moments, weeks, or years. During this time there occurs a period of separation between the higher and lower principles (spiritual and astral). The quintessence of all nobler affections, aspirations and the most spiritualized portions of the mind are drawn into the spiritual Self in a blissful state of consciousness called devachan. What remains is a shell of the old personal self, which may gradually develop a kind of hazy consciousness of its own, until it also eventually disintegrates. It is this shell that may be contacted by mediums

---

[1] *M.L.*, 20 c., p. 128, 1st ed.; 124, 3rd ed.

in seances; but—according to the Letters this is not the real Self (except perhaps in the case of premature death). True communication can be attained only by a person who is *en rapport* with the one who has died and can raise his consciousness up to the higher spiritual level of devachan.

One must, however, note that a different description of the after death process appears in some works by theosophical writers. One such exponent was C. W. Leadbeater, a notable clairvoyant, who recorded what he saw of after death conditions. According to him, the average individual finds himself, after death, in the " astral plane ", where life continues with similar (though subtler) conditions and interests as in physical life. It is, therefore, possible for a person still living on earth to communicate with an individual after death, either through a medium (which is not recommended for various reasons), or in thought, or during sleep. A person with clairvoyant vision can observe and even sometimes communicate with one who has passed over. Gradually after a period, there is a dropping of the astral " body ", the instrument of feeling, and then of that of thought, called the mental body. Then comes a further withdrawal of the individual into his higher Self in the heavenly devachan.

This would seem to be at variance with the original teaching. It is well to remember, however, that greater knowledge has often shown apparently impossible theories to be but different, and incomplete, aspects of the same fact.

Though the veil over after-death conditions is but slightly raised, one can think of it as a process of unrobing, peeling off a heavy overcoat, then removing dress or suit, then undergarments, until the Self remains in its pure state. There follows a blissful time of gestation, an assimilation of the fruits of the meritorious actions of the past life, and eventual rebirth in another body. In the new personality there appear tendencies and qualities carried over from the past in accordance with karmic conditions that the individual has himself created, and which he needs for further experience and unfoldment.

The periods between incarnations are said to range from a short time to many centuries. The average is supposed to be one hundred times the length of life here, but this may vary, depending on the evolutionary level of the individual and other factors. This means there must be billions of beings out of incarnation at any one time. Even though the population may rapidly increase, the number out of incarnation would seem to be many times the total in incarnation. Since the cyclic law must apply throughout the universe, it is reasonable to suppose that flow will be followed by ebb, as a result of natural or other causes, perhaps by the action of man himself. The present is only a chapter in the vast panorama, and the movement of the evolutionary process will continue through long aeons.

If we can envisage something of this stupendous scheme, our view of death is radically changed; it is seen as a stepping-stone along the way and not something to be feared. Furthermore, if we accept the theories of reincarnation and karma, we shall realize that we ourselves have brought the world to its present sad impasse, and it is for us to determine the future course of civilization.

The dimensions of human evolution and potentiality are immeasurably widened when we view them in the light of such part of the metaphysical system of the ancient esoteric philosophy as is presented in our day in Theosophy.

While no one fully comprehends the cosmic process, it is possible, in moments of introspection and contemplation, to become aware of our immortal nature and the one Life that binds us all together. A recognition of the one Life and its periodic manifestation, with reincarnation as an inevitable corollary in accordance with karmic law, provides a basis on which to build those deeper values and meanings that humanity desperately needs.

———

Sometime ago I came across a book called *Theosophy of the Upanishads*, written some decades before The Theosophical Society came into existence, which shows that Theosophy is a certain wisdom, not just a name by which a group of people are divided from the rest of humanity. The name Theosophy was chosen, I believe, in order to identify it with a Wisdom which existed in the past, not only at one particular time, but at different periods, and to indicate its profoundly philosophical and transcendent character. That which is spiritual is ageless; it is only the forms that can be dated. When we use the word Theosophy, we refer to a universal Wisdom which has been studied in all ages, exists in the present, and operates in nature all the time.—N. SRI RAM (*The Theosophist*, Dec. 1955).

COMPARATIVE RELIGION

Man is by his constitution a religious
animal—EDMUND BURKE.

E. JAMES BURTON

SIR J. G. FRAZER in *The Golden Bough*, and many other scholars
later, noted (by painstaking recording of events and practices)
recurrent attitudes towards life the world over, as communities
emerge from hunting to pastoral and agricultural economies,
and in the process are placed in new and revealing life patterns.
Religion, a total attitude of man to life, has been defined by
Howerth (supported by Warde Fowler) as " effective desire
to be in right relationship with the power manifesting itself
in the universe." [1] Unity of purpose underlies variant
approaches and diverse practices. Religion can be studied
in these comparative aspects; relating, with admittedly differing and partial perceptions, to a universal formative impulse.

When great cultures developed, each tended to evolve its
religious system further in the light of environmental pressures,
particular civilization, and resulting insights. Experience
and opportunities encouraged specific emphasis in creative
relationship. What we call Hinduism is comprehensive
in scope, majestic with traditions of the ages; Buddhism was
born within its realm of influence. Confucianism and Taoism,
remarkable systems, emanate from the teaching of two Masters

[1] See for this reference and various others, E. G. Kellett, *A Short History of
Religions*, ch. 1, Penguin.

of Wisdom, for there are those who draw into manifestation, state coherently, and then transmit, deeper apprehensions of mankind. But acceptance of such seemingly complete life models did not remove the will to learn from others, as Lao Tse learnt from Indian thought. Buddhist missionaries spread their ideas through the far east, but could respect and absorb existing insights from peoples whom they met. There was constant cross fertilization, for living religion is organic, not static and dogmatic. Judaism, for example, learnt its angelology from Zoroastrian and Iranian sources. In ancient Egypt we see how a rich environment—archetypal realities of fertilizing Nile water and unconquered solar radiance—fostered an awareness which came to be shared by other Mediterranean nations.

The ancient peoples were conscious that their gods were common to differing cultures; no one civilization or people had an exclusive or unique claim to truth. When by conquest or travel they entered another land, they frankly recognized that their new neighbours shared, in their religion, certain basic aspects of life and reality which they themselves approached in their own particular cults. Thus the Romans identified their Juno with the Greek Hera, their Mars with the Greek Ares, their Venus with Aphrodite.

This identification often enriched some cult or approach; a fresh area of life was apprehended and refined. Later, when the Romans were ruling in Britain, Celtic deities were thus identified with Roman gods, with worship of the creative powers of being. In other words, they realized that there was a common heritage upon which men entered, a world of being which all humanity shared, however simply, and sometimes crudely, less developed peoples might represent this in their personalized concepts of deity.

This is not to say that new apprehension, awareness and sensitivity did not sweep through the religious practice of the classical world, as elswhere on the planet. Such, for example, was the vivifying and civilizing influence of the cult of Dionysos, god of creativity, of fertility in all its aspects, god of dramatic art and saviour figure, divine life within all things, however much the teaching was debased by the less sensitive. Such too was the survival at Eleusis, during the waves of Greek conquest, of mystic death and life enactment, the rising of Persephone. These two aspects were retained side by side, equally valid in the Greek culture. Later came parallel devotion to Isis, a quest for a spiritual beauty and asceticism that attributed all life to her, as chronicled by Apuleius in the closing chapters of *The Golden Ass* when redeemed from ass-hood to humanity.

The Early Church

So, too, in the early Christian church there was fusion of Greek thought with Judaistic religious insight, a vivid flame of aspiration and controlled perception. In the gnostic thinkers the process continued, seeking validity in religion, expressed for instance by Iamblicus in *On the Mysteries of the Egyptians, Chaldeans and Assyrians*; or in his *Life of Pythagoras;* and indeed by the Neo-Platonic writers in general. Of such ideas the Cambridge Platonist Thomas Taylor said in 1821:

> Thus all beings proceed from, and are comprehended in, the first being; all intellects from the one first intellect; all souls from the one first soul; all natures blossom from one first nature; and all bodies proceed from the vital and luminous body of the world.
>
> And lastly, all these great monads are comprehended in the first one, from which they and all their depending series

are unfolded into light.   Hence this first one is truly the unity
of unities, the monad of monads, the principle of principles,
the god of gods, one and all things, yet one prior to all.   No
objections of any weight, no arguments but such as are
sophistical, can be urged against this most sublime theory. . .
It can only be treated with contempt in degraded, barren
and barbarous ages.[1]

Although in the early church this common heritage of
religion was accepted and indeed utilized, invigorated by
experience of the Christ life, the barren and barbarous ages
in the west lost this sense of a shared wisdom and life. Add to
this the fact that the mediaeval church, faced with barbarian
opposition, protected its practices with a hard, dogmatic
and authoritarian facade.   As a corrective to this narrowed
outlook, some significant movements towards comparative
religion were bound in due time to appear.

In the first part of the nineteenth century scholars began
to explore the treasures of eastern thought or, as the brothers
Grimm, to show that Sanskrit and English came from the
same parent language stock; and artists began also to acknowledge the validity of exotic and remote cultures and master-
pieces. . These activities presented a challenge to the church.
Just as scholars and artists had to broaden, or rather deepen,
their experience and knowledge of the unity of the human
quest, so now western religion had to accept the undoubted
resemblances between other faiths and current Christianity.
No longer was it possible to accept such explanations as early
missionaries in the New World gave: that striking analogies
between catholic practice and experience and those of native
civilizations were the work of devils.   Yet for nearly a century

[1] Thomas Tayler, *Introduction to Iamblicus* or *The Mysteries of the Egyptians,
Chaldeans* & *Assyrians*, Stuart and Watkins.

the church strove violently to point out the differences, since all other religions were presumed false. If a point of resemblance could be found within Christianity, then Christianity would also be false. About the same time the church was also engaged in a critical struggle with scientists, who exploited any resemblance as showing that Christian thought was erroneous. Indeed, all religious thought, as they understood the term, was a delusion, all religious systems alike condemned. Even well into the present century some Christian scholars sought to deny any affinity or common experience between their own faith and other religious ideas. Moreover, in this latter half of the century many theologians still argued from a position of a special revelation in the Christian faith.

Across all this, with clear perception, came the words and utterances of H. P. Blavatsky. Instead of resemblances proving equal falsity, she said that they indicated truth, a basic truth in the experience and situation of humanity, which emerged in the various religious systems as circumstances, necessity and natural genius demanded. The way to unity was not by minimizing the difference and particular insights of religions, but by the pursuit of each religion to its source and end, the eternal and unchanging nature of all things, the Wisdom from old, valid also for all the future.

At this point it may be useful to examine the word religion, which has two very different meanings. In itself and in its fuller sense it signifies the relationship between the life that is in each one of us and the total Life in all, through all, sustaining all. It is the active unity between the individual consciousness and the whole life process—that which unites, binds, the one to the many and the whole. It retains us within creative being, gives us *dharma*, teleological function, a significance within the bewildering, varied and shimmering ever-changing *māya*, enabling us to find our "Way" through all the changing scenes of life, glory and beauty, sadness and struggle, all of which bring something of ultimate fulness, height and depth, of Being.

And every man has his religion. At the lowest material level, perhaps, just the pursuit of extra money, which he thinks will bring him "life" and happiness and fulfilment. Even the life-weary dehumanized "hollow men" of T. S. Eliot have a religion, even though it is a death wish, a negation, a refusal of the reality.

This significance, of universal import, dating from classical times when to speak of a particular *religion* was deprecated, must be distinguished from the connotation of the word religion as applied to a *specific* faith. The usage arises when a great number of people in a land or culture share similar beliefs, have equal insight and apprehensions, led by some great teacher or inspired by a common spiritual experience. We talk then, rightly, of their religion. This common outlook and experience is called a particular religion: Christian, Buddhist, and so on. This is a limited meaning of the word, or rather it leads to a secondary meaning. Thus the question "Are you religious?" would still mean to most people today: "Do you go to church, or to your temple?" and so on. But all men are religious however imperfectly, and those who never go near a place of worship may well have a tremendous creative relationship with life which springs from a high religious impulse, even if it is not channelled into a particular religion.

Only One Religion

Thus the term comparative religion establishes again the ancient consciousness that basically there is only one religion, one search for significance and relationship with the whole environmental process of life.

In her preface to *The Secret Doctrine* Madame Blavatsky wrote:

> This book is not the Secret Doctrine in its entirety, but a select number of fragments of its fundamental tenets. It is perhaps desirable to state unequivocally that the teachings, however fragmentary and incomplete, contained in these volumes belong neither to the Hindu, the Zoroastrian, the Chaldean, nor the Egyptian religion, neither to Buddhism, Islam, Judaism nor Christianity exclusively. The Secret Doctrine is the essence of all these. Sprung from it in their origins, the various religious schemes are now made to merge back into their original element.

Aware that her work has " many shortcomings ", she said:

> All that she claims is that its logical coherence and consistency entitle this new Genesis to rank at any rate on a level with the "working hypotheses " so freely accepted by modern science. . . .
>
> The aim of this work may be briefly stated: to show that Nature is not " a fortuitous concurrence of atoms " and to assign to man his rightful place in the scheme of the Universe; to rescue from degradation the archaic truths which are the basis of all religions; and to uncover, to some extent, the fundamental unity from which they spring.[1]

The Secret Doctrine inaugurated an awareness within the materialist west of a fundamental basic unity, apprehension of Reality, which underlies all man's attempts to establish living relationships with the " one primeval universal Wisdom", the teachings of which were, for example, " at least partially known to several of the Fathers of the Church ".[2]

[1] *S.D.*, T. P. H.
[2] *S.D.*, Introductory.

H. P. Blavatsky stressed the influence of Neo-Platonism and its place in the unifying perception of inter-religious relationship and basic identity, just as Taylor did before her. But her vision and grasp developed deeper apprehension, bringing into western view eastern religious systems and esoteric knowledge in a startling and illuminating way.

One may see the implication and effect in the slightly later work *The Key To Theosophy*, which in its preface sums and " traces the broad outlines of the Wisdom Religion . . . meeting the various objections raised by the average western inquirer, and endeavouring to present unfamiliar concepts in a form as simple and in language as clear as possible ".[1] It is, moreover, valuable to note how effectively she dealt, earlier in *Isis Unveiled* and later in *The Key* with the then popular presentation of " salvation " and " vicarious atonement ", subjecting such teachings to a critical assessment that would today be favourably regarded by Christian thought. We are recalled to the fundamental principle, " Whatsoever a man soweth, that shall he also reap ".

Regarding perception of the essential, but imperfectly realized, Christian way, one may quote again: " Theosophy is the quintessence of duty. So is Christianity, when rightly understood and carried out . . . but then, were it not a lip-religion in practice, Theosophy would have little to do amidst Christians ".[2] The fundamental principle of religious relationship with life is clearly laid down: it must be a continuing activity. Theosophy inculcates action " instead of mere intention and talk ".[3] H. P. Blavatsky quotes Carlyle with approval: " The end of man is an action and not a thought,

[1] T.P.H.
[2] Key. p. 229.
[3] *Ibid.*, p. 230.

though it were the noblest ". Again in *practice* she sees the innate unity of the religions. Theosophy has a far higher standard than equal justice to all and love to every creature; it requires

> the giving to others more than to oneself—self-sacrifice. Such was the standard and abounding measure which marked so pre-eminently the greatest Teachers and Masters of Humanity, e.g., Gautama Buddha in history, and Jesus of Nazareth as in the Gospels. . . . In our opinion Father Damien, the young man of thirty who offered his whole life in sacrifice for the benefit and alleviation of the sufferings of the lepers at Molokai, and who went to live for eighteen years alone with them, finally to catch the loathsome disease and die, has not died in vain. . . . He was a true Theosophist and his memory will live for ever in our annals.[1]

Bursting the Fetters

Madame Blavatsky has much more to say on the practical activity that must characterize those who follow truly the vital and essential truths within each religious path, which stems from the one Life and the Wisdom Religion. All outer protestation and talk are meaningless; it is by their fruits that ye shall know them. Religion is an active and living relationship, emergent in manifest decision and event. One cannot over-estimate the importance of that principle of religion which, finding deep unity below credal statements, is a living way. Hence she affirmed that if the Theosophical Society was true to its mission, it " will gradually leaven and permeate the great mass of thinking and intelligent people with its large-minded and noble ideas of Religion, Duty and Philanthropy. Slowly but surely it will burst asunder the

[1] Key., pp. 237-38.

iron fetters of creeds and dogmas, of social and caste prejudices ".[1]

Thus was envisaged the whole scope of religion, creative relationship, active participation in and working with the total environment in all phases of being. Study of comparative religion leads to a perception of unity in all humanity seeking to achieve the way of fulfilment, expansion of conscious living within total Life.

What is the position today? Only those who are actively concerned with inter-religious studies can fully appreciate the new integration that has been achieved during the past decade. One example, among many, is the standard Christian work *Pauline Baptism and the Pagan Mysteries*, a massive study of " the problem of the Pauline doctrine of Baptism in the light of religio-historical parallels ".[2]

The author, Gunter Wagner, is associate professor at the Baptist Theological Seminary at Rushlikon-Zurich. After examining the text he compares relevant pagan rites in ancient Babylon, Egypt, Greece and Rome. There is a detailed and carefully documented account of Osiris, linked with the death and revivification of man, and associated mysteries, the resurrection of Tammuz and of Adonis, the Attic Mysteries, and so on. The select bibliography fills nineteen pages, with an average of thirty-five works on each page, all being relevant to comparative religion. Further, in every single area (e.g., that of Osiris) new knowledge gleaned in the past twenty years is overwhelming in import. The new approach is collaborative, giving a sense of unity in the continuing quest of mankind.

In the Roman Catholic church the results are even more striking. Scholarly studies emphasize an underlying unity

[1] Key, p. 305.
[2] Gunter Wagner, Oliver & Boyd, 1967.

6

of wisdom which animates religious activity, shared inevitably by all human beings who seek creative relationship with the cosmic Being.[1]

The same feeling of identity is evident in studies made by those concerned with other faiths. *The Tibetan Book of the Dead*, edited by W. Y. Evans-Wentz, parallel to his beautiful *Tibetan Book of the Great Enlightenment*, shows deep universalism. Agreement in depth with Pauline teaching, or the Vedanta, leads to a consideration of wall paintings in English churches. (That in Chaldon church, Surrey, for example, dating from about 1200 A.D., parallels a Tibetan painting of the " Judgement "). Such parallels must not be pressed but, in Evans-Wentz's words, these things suggest " that the thought forms and thought processes of orient and of occident are fundamentally much alike, and that despite differences of race and creed and of physical and social environment, the nations of mankind are, and have been since time immemorial, mentally and spiritually one ".[2]

Again, Nyanaponika Thera's *The Heart of Buddhist Meditation* [3] shows the deep unity of religious practice through meditation and disciplined mindfulness. Here indeed comparative study is superseded in meditation by shared apprehending. Such a book may be set beside Walter Hilton's *Cloud of Unknowing* or works of other contemplatives. One may also note the practical identity of the Tao with Christian religious structures.[4] Study of comparative religion leads to a synthesis in deeper awareness, with the possibility of a gradually unifying experience, lucid and harmonized.

[1] *The Vatican Declaration on the Relation of the Church to non-Christian Religions,* (Vatican II) 1966.

[2] p. 240, O. U. P.

[3] Rider, 1962.

[4] E. J. Burton, *Tao & The Christ Way*. (pamphlet)

There were many stages by which the study of comparative religion proceeded.[1] But what was the initiating impulse? What disturbed the isolation and contemptuous superiority of attitudes current in the mid-nineteenth century? History records the outward work, detailed research, however intuitively apprehended, associated with H. P. Blavatsky and those who followed her inspiring lead. Here was the *fons et origo*; and at that source of life, light and inner truth we may still be refreshed for the coming age.

[1] E. g., J. G. Frazer's monumental work, *The Golden Bough*, 1890-1915, valuable for content if not for conclusions; S. A. Cook, *The Study of Religions*, 1914; Punnard de la Bouyahe, *L'Étude comparée de religions*, 1922-25; and the more popular works, E. O. James, *Comparative Religion*, 1928; T. H. Robinson, *A Short Comparative History of Religion*, 1951, Duckworth; and A. C. Bouquet, *Comparative Religion*, Penguin.

We have no dogmas or creeds in the Theosophical Society, nor in its work; and thus it is that we have Hindu Theosophists, and Buddhist Theosophists, and Christian Theosophists, and Mohammedan Theosophists, and Jewish Theosophists, as well as other Theosophists who belong to no religion—except to Theosophy as the Religion of religions. Hence it is our bounden duty to cultivate in our hearts the spirit of brotherly love towards all, however they may differ from us in philosophical and religious or scientific opinions; but while we are thus absolutely free as members in our choice of religion and philosophy, we all hold to the prerequisite of a Theosophist, which is a belief in Universal Brotherhood and an adherence to the sublime ethics which Theosophy teaches.

—G. DE PURUCKER

PHILOSOPHY EAST AND WEST

*How Charming is divine
philosophy—*MILTON.

DAVID F. T. RODIER

AND

CHARLES S. J. WHITE

I

IN order to understand the relationship between Theosophy
and philosophy in the modern world we must first draw attention to the basic differences between the place of philosophy
in the modern world and philosophy in classical antiquity.
These are: (1) the different place of philosophy in the lives
of its students and (2) the different conception of the scope
of philosophy.

Throughout classical antiquity the philosopher served as
teacher, counsellor, and spiritual adviser to his pupils. The
study of philosophy was considered to be a " way of life "
making special demands on its students. Beginning students
were taught self-discipline and the cultivation of moral virtues
as well as the intellectual disciplines demanded by the study
of logic long before they were permitted to study the more
difficult questions of metaphysics. Thus, for example, Marcus
Aurelius, referring to his teachers of philosophy, records
that Rusticus taught him that his character required improve-
ment and discipline but that in improving it he should avoid

ostentatiously parading himself as a "man who practices much austerity or does benevolent acts in order to make a display."[1] While from Alexander the Platonist he learned "not frequently nor without necessity to say to anyone, or to write in a letter, that I have no leisure; nor continually to excuse the neglect of duties required by our relation to those with whom we live, by alleging urgent occupations."[2] In the same way, although most of the written treatises of Plotinus deal with technical philosophical questions and were written for advanced students, it is clear from Porphyry's *Life of Plotinus* that he considered moral discipline as a prerequisite to proper philosophic development, as is shown by his anger at Diophanes's defence of the idea that immoral behaviour on the part of aspiring students of philosophy is permissible.[3] Of course, both Marcus Aurelius and Plotinus are merely repeating the lesson of Socrates who insisted to Alcibiades that morality is a necessary prerequisite to intellectual development.[4]

The second way in which philosophy was a comprehensive discipline in classical antiquity was in terms of its scope. The first Greek philosophers of whose writings we have anything more than fragments are Plato and Aristotle. Both of them wrote extensively on questions of logic and the problems connected with the theory of knowledge as well as on ethics and on metaphysical questions such as the state of the soul after death, the existence of God and the ultimate nature of Reality. In fact Aristotle is known not only for the inclusive scope of his works but also for systematically arranging

---

[1] *Meditations*, I, 7.

[2] *Ibid*, I, 12.

[3] *Vita Plotini*, 15.

[4] Plato, *Symposium*, 215 ff.

a course of study for students which began with logic and then dealt with the physical world, man and his faculties, metaphysics, and ended with the systematic study of ethics, politics and art. This same comprehensive treatment of all areas of philosophy was also the goal of the philosophers of late classical antiquity. These writers, influenced as they were by Alexandrian Neoplatonism (" which was in essence Theosophy"[1]) present a system which unifies ethical demands and comprehensive subject matter. For most of them the goal of philosophy was to show man how all things came to be from the utterly transcendent, named (but not described) the One or the Good, and how man can return to this source by purifying himself morally and developing himself intellectually.[2]

A Merely Academic Discipline

In the modern period of western philosophy both the ethical demands and the comprehensive vision have been lost in the study of philosophy. The reasons for this loss are twofold. First there is the place of philosophy in our educational system and, secondly, there is the way in which philosophy is pursued. In the beginning of the seventeenth century a profound change occurred in western philosophy. This shift is so great that it is usual to date the beginning of modern philosophy with the publication of Francis Bacon's *Novum Organum* in 1620 and Descartes's *Discourse on Method* in 1637. For our purposes, what is significant about both works is the insistence that philosophy should no longer be the concern of specialists in the traditional literature but rather that the study of philosophy

---

[1] B. C. W. XI, 438.

[2] For a good survey of these writers see R. T. Wallis, *Neoplatonism*, New York, 1972.

was the concern of every well-educated person. While it was necessary at the time to bring philosophy out of the cloister and into the marketplace and to show the ordinary man that his beliefs about the ultimate and enduring questions were relevant to his day to day life, and while it was necessary to free philosophy from the restraints of religious requirements in order that it might meaningfully interpret the emerging new sciences, the unfortunate side effect of these changes was to eliminate the idea that the study of philosophy imposed any ethical demands on its students. For if philosophy can be studied by any educated man, then a special moral discipline does not seem to be required. It was also the renewed accessibility of philosophy to the ordinary man which, ironically, resulted in its renewed technicality and abstractness. Given that a little philosophy was the concern of any well educated person, it was inevitable that the study of philosophy became a regular part of the curriculum of higher learning. But this placing of philosophy in the normal college and university not only accelerated the elimination of any ethical requirement for its study—since the teachers no longer chose their students but taught equally anyone who enrolled—but the very fact of philosophy becoming an academic discipline meant that, more and more, only academicians would study it and that the result of their research would be primarily for each other and not for the ordinary man.

Throughout the nineteenth and twentieth centuries the status of philosophy has been that of a highly technical study, completely removed from daily life, making no especial moral and disciplinary demands of philosophers. And precisely this condition was attacked by those whom we in the second part of the twentieth century have come to regard as important philosophers. Kierkegaard mercilessly satirized those philosophers who could account for everything but the existential situation which forced man to philosophize. Karl Marx called for philosophers to stop merely interpreting the world and instead to try to change it. Nietzsche gave over the writing of formal philosophy for a more persuasive kind of writing which attempted to remake the reader.

In this context the rise of the Theosophical Society can be understood as a return to an older ideal of philosophy. In both its ethical demands and the breadth of its vision of the subject matter of philosophy, the Theosophical Movement returned to the prior western philosophic tradition for " Theosophy is . . . the universal code of science and the most transcendental ethics that was ever known." [1] From the very beginning the Society demanded of its members a positive commitment to human brotherhood and a willingness actively to work to advance the cause.

As Madame Blavatsky said, " The Society is a philanthropic and scientific body for the propagation of the idea of brotherhood on *practical* instead of *theoretical* lines " [2]; " . . . a true Theosophist must put in practice the loftiest moral ideal, must strive to realize his unity with the whole of humanity, and work ceaselessly for others." [3]

Training in Tolerance

The early history of the Theosophical Society is one long illustration of the need to accompany intellectual development with a practical commitment to the welfare of mankind, whether in the form of the Buddhist revival in Ceylon, schools for the outcastes in India, Indian Independence or Animal

[1] B. C. W. XI, 437.
[2] Key, p. 19.
[3] *Ibid.*, p. 25.

Welfare. Today this tradition of training in brotherhood and service meets the new member of the Society when he finds he must learn not merely to tolerate other points of view but positively to respect them. Not only does he have complete freedom in his own beliefs but he must, " within the limits of courtesy and consideration for others," fearlessly exercise and defend his and other's right of liberty of thought and of expression. This training in tolerance is not only a necessary prerequisite for an intellectual development which must dispassionately consider various conflicting positions and evaluate them without bias; but the tolerance of differing interpretations and schools of thought leads inevitably to a practical sense of universal brotherhood irrespective of race, creed, sex, caste, or colour.

But it was not only in the return to a vision of philosophy which makes practical demands on its students that the Theosophical Society represents a return to the older western philosophic tradition, but in the breadth of its vision of the subject matter of philosophy. Perhaps the most striking instance of this breadth can be seen by considering H. P. B.'s *Secret Doctrine* with its magnificent, sweeping treatment of both cosmogenesis and anthropogenesis. The basic questions of philosophy are here presented as concerned with the ultimate nature of reality, the laws of the physical universe, the history of the human race and the ethical demands of man's future evolution. There we see repeated the fundamental themes of late classical antiquity, the unfolding of the universe from the One and the way of return. These themes, although basic to the older traditions of western philosophy as represented by Plato, Aristotle and Plotinus and their great mediaeval successors such as Maimonides, Gabirol and Thomas Aquinas, have been largely ignored by contemporary philosophers, especially in the English speaking world where philosophy has come to be identified almost exclusively with problems in the theory of knowledge. It is to be hoped that students of Theosophy may seek to understand how contemporary research in the theory of knowledge and the developments of modern logic and verification theory help in the understanding of basic questions Theosophy raises, *e.g.*, the problem of the objectivity of clairvoyant investigation.

II

The Theosophical Society was the first religious organization in modern time to attempt a completely synthetic transformation of the religious history of mankind into an intelligible unity. Of course this could not be done without the introduction of a particular scheme and the advocacy of certain fundamental principles, a special doctrine that was elaborated in the main works of H. P. Blavatsky and added to or interpreted by other writers. We have already seen some of the connections through which modern Theosophy is related, notably in its ethical stance, to its spiritual and intellectual forbears in the earlier history of the West. We may now turn to consider the relationship of theosophical teaching to certain of the great eastern traditions.

Basic Themes

There is a published facsimile page in H. P. B.'s own handwriting of a section of *The Secret Doctrine* in which she sets forth the main elements of its teaching as follows:

> (*a*) An omnipresent, eternal and boundless Principle beyond the reach of words or thought—unthinkable and unspeakable.

(b)   The eternity of the Universe as a fixed abstraction, with periodical appearances and disappearances of objective manifestation; like a regular tidal ebb of flux and reflux; coeval with, as being in one sense identical with, the one Principle.

(c)   The unity all the Souls with the Over Soul or the unknown *Root* and the continuous transmigration of each ray of the one, infinite light, in accordance with cyclic and karmic law. . .[1]

It is with these basic themes in mind that H. P. B. develops the *Proem* to *The Secret Doctrine*, and they constitute, moreover, a fundamental thesis for which the complex elaboration of theosophical thought and experimentation seeks to give adequate conceptualization.

One might say that in the most general terms eastern thought is a vast meditation upon the possible relationship between man as he knows himself, particularly in the life of devotion and mysticism, and the larger cosmos to whose internal aspect he somehow hopes to relate. It is clear that the answers proposed for stating this relationship are extremely varied, but there are two positions that divide most of the issues between them. These are the theories of monism and dualism. It may be that man's driving need for a resolution of the paradox of his sensitive awareness of the reality around him, and yet for long periods of his history being nothing more than its responsive victim, leads inevitably toward such a twofold solution: either one can break through to a sense that the macrocosm continues the reality that man experiences in his internal states, or there is a submission to the Person whose reality is the other toward which man is drawn as a particle toward a magnet. Between these two extremes of

[1] I, facing p. 79, 6-vol. ed.

consummation there is the whole drama of self-transformation to unfold, either through arduous discipline or else in the instantaneous reorientation of one's experience of time and space.

In Indian literature we discover that in the Upanishads a clearer insight into the spiritual absolute (Brahman) began to take shape. This insight inspires many lines where the writers appeal to the absolute nature of their discovery. " Verily, this whole world is Brahman; Tranquil, let one worship It as that from which he came forth, as that into which he will be dissolved, as that in which he breathes "[1] and " Verily, what is called Brahman—that is the same as what the space within a person is. Verily, what the space within a person is— that is the same as what the space here within the heart is ";[2] and " This Self, verily, is a world of all created beings ".[3]

At about the same time as these more or less monist theories were beginning to be recorded in the Upanishads—to be used later by Shankara himself to undergird the Advaita Vedanta philosophy—a strong surge toward the dualist (or pluralist) position, respecting ultimate Reality, arises in the metaphysics of the Jaina and Samkhya philosophies, both of which stimulate important religious traditions in India. The Jainas discovered that there are two principles in the universe, the *Jiva* and the *Ajiva*, corresponding roughly to spirit and matter. The *Jivas* exist in infinite number and can come to emancipation through the efforts of spiritually minded men who are willing to undertake the arduous discipline that is requisite. Similarly, the exponents of Samkhya taught that matter, *Prakriti*, and Spirit, *Purusha*, are distinct, but that *Purusha* can be emancipated

[1] Chandogya, III, 14, 1.
[2] *Ibid.*, III, 12, 7.
[3] Brhadaranyaka, I, 4, 16.

from his involvement in *Prakriti* by a swift stroke of realization, after which he will be eternally free. At these early moments in Indian thought, the distinction between monism and dualism is more a matter of perspective than of metaphysical absolutes, for both *Jiva* and *Purusha* are thought of as universals. In later times, however, the influence of the yoga theory of Ishvara or Lord, as the supreme Spirit in the universe to whom the other spirits are subservient, and other decisively dualist philosophies, such as those expounded by Ramanuja and Madhva, inspire a multitudinous theistic tradition. The philosophical and religious interchanges between the monist and dualist positions continue down to the present day. In the teaching of the Theosophical Society, arising from H. P. B.'s basic schema in *The Secret Doctrine*, we see sometimes a hierarchical, sometimes an experiential alternation between the One and the Two or the many, but the prevailing thesis seems to be that all phenomenal reality must be understood against the background of a single fundamental unity.

Here we may turn to Buddhist thought to grasp another dimension of the perspective in *The Secret Doctrine* and other works in the theosophical literature. Buddhist speculative theory is the *alter* image of the Hindu in many respects. If one were to set the two systems side by side in diagrammatic fashion, one would discover that they chart the same metaphysical territory with amazing correspondence, but with underlying meaning that is very different. The principal distinction lies in the fact that the towering edifice of Buddhist thought rises on the foundation of the experience of a single man, Gautama Sakyamuni, who came, after his enlightenment, to be recognized as the Buddha. For him the whole religious and metaphysical enterprise is negated by the individual at the deepest level of awareness. *There* (which is really not a "there") is the fullness of Nirvana or Sunyata—non-being and emptiness. This metaphysical position does not allow for theistic dualism nor for the pregnant ontology of the Advaita theories. On the other hand, it is not only in Buddhist and Hindu mysticism that the guide books lead one to a brink beyond which the artifices of language and rational analysis cannot progress.

Occult Tradition

The occult tradition outlined in *The Secret Doctrine* profoundly illuminates the underlying relationship between Hindu preoccupations with Being and the " qualities " manifest in the phenomenal world, to which the numerous gods hold a symbolic key, and the Buddhist emphasis upon the transitoriness of all phenomena in response to which the Buddhas and all other heavenly beings are saviours in the midst of contingency but always pointing beyond themselves to the dark target. In this complex perspective one can see the relationship to other occult traditions as well, western and eastern:

> From the Unknown One, the Infinite TOTALITY, the manifested ONE of the periodical Manvantaric Deity emanates; and this is the Universal Mind, which, separated from its Fountain-Source, is the Demiurgos or the creative Logos of the Western Kabalists, and the four-faced Brahma of the Hindu religion. In its totality, viewed from the standpoint of manifested Divine Thought in the esoteric doctrine, it represents the Hosts of the higher creative Dhyan Chohans. Simultaneously with the evolution of the Universal Mind, the concealed Wisdom of Adi-Buddha—the One Supreme and eternal—manifests itself as Avalokiteshwara (or manifested Ishwara), which is the Osiris of the Egyptians, the Ahura-Mazda of the Zoroastrians, the Heavenly Man of the Hermetic philosopher, the Logos of the Platonists, and the Atman of the Vedantins. By the action of the manifested

Wisdom, or Mahat, represented by these innumerable centres of spiritual Energy in the Kosmos, the reflection of the Universal Mind, which is Cosmic Ideation, becomes objectively the Fohat of the Buddhist esoteric philosopher. Fohat, running along the seven principles of Akasha, acts upon the manifested substance or the One Element, as declared above, and by differentiating it into various centres of Energy, sets in motion the law of Cosmic Evolution, which, in obedience to the Ideation of the Universal Mind, brings into existence all the various states of being in the manifested Solar System.[1]

How many resonances vibrate from this remarkable passage! We catch a glimpse at last of the resolution of the apparent paradoxes of the Unknown One, the Infinite Totality and the Universal Mind for which the teachings of the several traditions herein discussed need no longer be thought of as at cross purposes.

[1] *S. D.*, I, 110, 1st ed.; I, 170, 6-vol. ed.

Science is the exploration of things with thought, and the finding of unity there. Religion is the exploration of life with feeling, and the finding of unity there. And philosophy is the exploration of the relations between life and things, and the finding first of harmony and then of unity there.

—ERNEST E. WOODS

BROADEST AND MOST CATHOLIC SYSTEM

> The fair-winged One who is but one,
> inspired poets, by their incantations,
> shape in many ways.—*Rigveda.*

J. MILLER

THE famous Rigvedic verse quoted above is perhaps the oldest expression extant in any of the world's scriptures of man's recognition of the one principle underlying and uniting all things, of a oneness to which men have always ascribed different forms and names. It has been variously translated and reduced to its bare meaning as: " truth is one, learned men call it by different names ".

The fundamental idea behind this assertion was voiced thus in the *Bhagavad Gita*:

> However men approach me, even so do I welcome them, for the path men take from every side is mine.[1]

In other words, each man chooses his own road to the ultimate realization of truth, each according to his need, development and temperament, and each one's method of search and endeavour is equal in the eyes of the Lord who meets each human being on his own ground. This is a universal message explicitly voiced in that " eternal religion ", the religion of India, later called Hinduism by those who failed to grasp its broad tolerance, inclusiveness and limitless appeal

[1] IV, 11.

to the simple-minded as to the lofty intellect, and who narrowed it down to a label referring only to a particular people living by a particular river.

The essential theosophic message is contained in these two verses; for Theosophy, the divine Wisdom (*theos sophia*) which lies at the foundation of all religions, is nothing other than the ancient, ageless wisdom expressed in a new form, given back to the western world in a modern language suitable to a different generation. It brings out the great truths which have been handed down in various ways throughout the ages of mankind's long history and explains some of the more abstruse philosophical conceptions. It is not a mixture or hotch-potch of oriental philosophies, as some superficial inquirers have mistakenly taken it to be, but the reformulating of their perennial meaning, with elucidations of hitherto unavailable texts. " Theosophy ", asks the inquirer, " then, is not as held by some, a newly devised scheme? " to which the answer is given: " Only ignorant people can thus refer to it. It is as old as the world, in its teachings and ethics, if not in name, as it is also the broadest and most catholic system among all ".[1]

It has been thought that Theosophy is more aligned to the oriental (Indian and far eastern) religious philosophies than to those of the west—though we should remember that Christianity originated, not in the west, but in the middle east, which also gave birth to Islam and Judaism. It is true that the original theosophic writings as extant in H. P. Blavatsky's works and the Mahatma Letters, revealed oriental doctrines and cast as much light as possible on these. This was deliberately done to break down the rigid western prejudice then prevalent regarding such eastern philosophies, to bring out their vital and intrinsic value and their depth and breadth

---

[1] *Key*, p. 11. T. P. H.

7

of insight, which alone could undermine the extreme materialism and bigotry of the age, and open men's minds to a deeper
and more tolerant outlook. It was thought that in expounding
eastern thought in a language that could be better grasped by
the west, a greater concern, born of deeper understanding,
might be fostered for our eastern brothers. This would help
to bring about a meeting of east and west on an equal basis
and a realization that the east too might have something
worth while to teach us. The first two objects of the Theosophical Society deal directly with these aims.

Later Theosophists who knew that Theosophy was the
very source of all religions standing beyond and above any
particular formulation of divine truth, turned to the investigation of other religions in the light of Theosophy. Here,
however, we shall concentrate on Theosophy in its relation
to the eastern philosophies.

Universe and Man

The great questions of Deity, of the origin of the world,
of man, of death and immortality, on which the oriental
religions have speculated and to which they have given
various answers, are set forth in early theosophic literature
(e.g. in the works of H. P. Blavatsky and A. P. Sinnett and
in the Mahatma Letters), and are discussed in the light of
eastern philosophies. Nowadays, when the gap between east
and west is much less than it was a hundred years ago, we
can more readily accept basic theosophic teachings such as
the conception of Deity as an impersonal absolute Principle
periodically emanating the cosmos which thus evolves out of
the ONE and eventually returns to IT, rather than as an
anthropomorphic arbiter of destiny creating the world *ab
nihilo*. We can more easily envisage one universal law of cause

and effect, action and reaction, the karma of Hindu philosophy, operating on all planes of manifestation—physical as well as emotional, mental and spiritual—constantly adjusting the effect to its cause and thus re-establishing harmony which contrary human action as constantly disturbs, a harmony which we find in the ancient Hindu scripture, the *Rigveda*, as " cosmic order " (*rita*), the very background on which the web of the universe is spun:

> The cosmic order is the base that bears the earth, by law the sons of the infinite stand secure.[1]
>
> Firmly seated are the foundations of cosmic order; in its shining beauty manifold are its aspects.[2]

The universal law of action and reaction leads us to its corollary, the doctrine of reincarnation, to many people so typically Indian, but no longer rejected *a priori* as too fantastic. It is more and more being accepted as a reasonable hypothesis explaining many a mystery of human existence and its apparent injustices. And it is now being realized that in one form or another reincarnation was known throughout the ancient world, and not merely in India. As you have sown, so are you reaping now; as you are now sowing so will you reap in the future; as you sow on the objective or subjective level, so will you reap on that particular level. Viewed in its wider implications, the doctrine of reincarnation is but an aspect of that law of eternal recurrence peculiar to the cosmos, the ebb and flow of all things, from the days and nights—the never failing dawns proceeding day after day to the appointed place,[3] waxing and waning and disappearing but to reappear again—to the seasons, the years, the stars and the " numberless

[1] X. 85. 1.
[2] IV. 23. 9.
[3] *Rigveda*, I, 123. 9.

universes, incessantly manifesting and disappearing " [1] upon the boundless plane of THAT which IS.

With the development of science—in particular geology, anthropology and archaeology—we can more readily contemplate the immense duration of the cycles of involution and evolution called the *days of Brahma* in Indian literature, during which the various kingdoms of nature came into existence one after another, and we may find that the *six days* of creation of Genesis may not be so different in their essential meaning —the duration of each day is not elucidated in Genesis.

These theosophic tenets are at one with Indian philosophy, but they are traced back by H.P. Blavatsky to the *Book of* DZYAN.

In writing her incomparable work, *The Secret Doctrine*, as basically a commentary to the Stanzas of Dzyan of which " extracts are given from the Chinese, Tibetan and Sanskrit translations of the original Senzar Commentaries and glosses on the Book of Dzyan ",[2] H. P. Blavatsky not only explained the Stanzas of Dzyan but also gave a key to the unravelling of the Vedas and indeed of every ancient cosmogony. In its vast sweep these volumes take into consideration all the religions, speculative philosophies and mythologies of the past and throw light upon the sacred books of the East—the *Vedas, Upanishads* and *Puranas* of India, the Buddhist scriptures, Chinese and Japanese religious thought, the Tibetan and Egyptian *Book of the Dead* (more appropriately called book of the great awakening) as well as those sacred books of the west from the *Popol Vux* of American Indians to the *Bible*, the *Siphrah Dzenioutha* of the Hebrews and the *Pistis Sophia* of the Gnostics. She claimed that the very " old book " from which she translated the stanzas which form the backbone of *The Secret Doctrine*

[1] *S. D.*, I. 16-17, 1st ed. I, 82, 6-vol. ed.
[2] *S. D.*, I. 22-23; I, 87.

is the original work from which the many volumes of
Kiu-ti were compiled. Not only the latter . . . but even the
Sepher Yetzireh . . . the *Shu-King*, China's primitive Bible, the
sacred volumes of the Egyptian Thoth-Hermes, the *Puranas*
in India, the Chaldean *Book of Numbers* and the *Pentateuch*
itself, are all derived from that one small parent volume.[1]

Vedas and Stanzas of Dzyan

It has not yet been possible to vindicate H. P. Blavatsky's
claim with respect to each and every one of these ancient texts,
especially since the original manuscript of the Stanzas of Dzyan
is still untraced by western scholars. But, assuming that
such a document does exist—and it would be stretching our
credibility too far to believe that the whole doctrine was created piecemeal by a single 19th-century woman—an examination of the *Rigveda* for example, in the light of H. P. Blavatsky's
commentaries and explanations, and a comparison of the
vedic texts with the Book of Dzyan, throws much light on
the Vedas and substantiates her statements.

The cosmogony of the *Book of Dzyan*, in its broad sweep
and fundamental ideas, is found in the Rigvedic speculative
hymns. Thus:

STANZAS:

> Darkness alone filled the boundless all, for Father, Mother
> and Son were once more one, and the son had not yet awakened
> for the new wheel and his pilgrimage thereon.[2]

> Alone, the one form of existence stretched boundless,
> infinite, causeless, in dreamless sleep; and life pulsated un-
> conscious in universal space, throughout that all Presence.[3]

[1] *S. D.*, I, xliii; I, 64.
[2] I. 5.
[3] I. 8.

RIGVEDA:

> The Unmanifest was not then or the manifest. Spatial depths or heaven beyond were not . . . . What ocean profound, unfathomable, pervaded?
>
> Darkness there was. At first hidden in darkness this all was undifferentiated depth.[1]

H. P. Blavatsky's method of elucidation was to go back to the ancient exegesists themselves and quote what they wrote on the subject, adding explanations in the light of esoteric philosophy. Thus, the puranic commentators explain the " one form of existence " by " cause " (*karana*) " but Esoteric Philosophy by the *ideal spirit of that cause*. In its secondary stage, it is the Svabhavat of the Buddhist philosopher, the Eternal Cause and Effect, omnipresent yet abstract, the self-existent plastic Essence and the Root of all things ".[2] Further on she explains that " Svabhavat, the ' plastic essence ' that fills the universe is the root of all things . . . Chinese mystics have made of it the synonym of ' Being '." [3]

STANZAS:

> There was neither silence nor sound; naught save ceaseless eternal breath, which knows itself not.[4]

RIGVEDA:

> . . . Undisturbed, self-moved, pulsated the One alone. And beyond that, other than that, was naught.[5]

" The ' Breath ' of the One Existence ", comments H. P. Blavatsky " is used in application only to the spiritual aspect of

[1] X. 129. 1-3..
[2] *S. D.*, I, 46; I. 118
[3] *S. D.*, I. 61; I. 130.
[4] II. 2.
[5] X. 129. 2.

cosmogony by Archaic Esotericism; otherwise it is replaced by its equivalent on the material plane—Motion ".[1]

Comparisons of this kind—and there are many[2]—may make us wonder whether there was not indeed, to use Max Müller's words as quoted in *The Secret Doctrine* " a primeval preternatural revelation granted to the fathers of the human races ",[3] as H. P. Blavatsky claimed, yet this was and is still being denied. " The Secret Doctrine " she maintained " was the universally diffused religion of the ancient and prehistoric world ".[4] " Whence . . . all this identity of ideas, if there were no primeval universal revelation ?"[5] she asks. " If we turn to the Chinese Cosmogony ", she goes on, " the most hazy of all, even there the same idea is found. *Tsi-tsai*, the Self-Existent is the Unknown Darkness, the root of the . . . Boundless Age . . . The ' great Extreme ' of Confucius gives the same idea."

In so far as man is concerned three fundamental teachings are succinctly expressed in the *Idyll of the White Lotus*:

1. The soul of man is immortal and its future is the future of a thing whose growth and splendour has no limit.

2. The principle which gives life dwells within us and without us, is undying and eternally beneficent, is not heard or seen or smelt, but is perceived by the man who desires perception.

3. Each man is his own absolute lawgiver, the dispenser of glory or gloom to himself; the decreer of his life, his reward, his punishment.[6]

---

[1] *S. D.*, I. 55; I. 125.
[2] cf., e.g. *S. D.*, I, 64; I. 133 with *Rigveda* X. 129. 3, X. 121. 1, X. 82. 5,
[3] I xxx; I. 53.
[4] *S. D.*, I xxxiv; I. 56.
[5] *S. D.*, I. 356; II. 71.
[6] By Mabel Collins, T. P. H.

To meditate on these three points is to enter into the core of every great religion. This is the theosophic method par excellence.

Deity and Humanity

We have here the idea of the divine indwelling spark in man, making him heir to immortality, this being the essence of all religious teaching. The divine spark, or that aspect of Deity within man, directly relates the latter to that aspect of the Deity without him, or macrocosmic God, the absolute Principle or transcendent One:

> Concealed in the heart of all beings is the Atman, the Spirit. . . . The man who surrenders his human will, leaves sorrows behind, and beholds the glory of the Atman by the grace of the Creator.[1]

> And when he is seen in his immanence and transcendence, then the ties that have bound the heart are unloosened, the doubts of the mind vanish and the law of Karma works no more.[2]

Transcendence and immanence, these two aspects of the One over which so many have quarrelled can be truly reconciled only in our own transcendental experience of that which the Upanishad summed up as: *tat twam asi*, That thou art. Thou art Brahman—not outwardly, but in our deepest depth, in our heart of heart. Compare this famous assertion with the third proposition of *The Secret Doctrine*:

> The fundamental identity of all souls with the Universal Oversoul, the latter being itself an aspect of the Unknown Root.[3]

---

[1] *Katha Upanishad*, II. 20.
[2] *Mundaka Upanishad*, II. 2 (Juan Mascaro's translation).
[3] I. 16-17; I. 82.

The too orthodox Buddhist may object to the idea of a permanent self in man. It should be remembered that the *atman* of the Upanishads, described in the *Idyll of the White Lotus* as a " thing whose splendour has no limit " and as " the principle which gives life ", is no human self but that divinity within man that links him to the cosmos and for which *nirvana* is but the natural state. The whole meaning of human evolution is thus apparent: to raise the human consciousness from the mundane, outward-turned level, to the inner God-attuned level, thereby making man the conscious link between matter and spirit, heaven and earth. This great goal was variously revealed in the past. In the *Rigveda* it found expression as Agni, the flame divine, " brow of the firmament, earth's centre " [1] " the wise . . . the holy, the friend ", the " vehicle of the transcendent " [2] " crouched in the cavern " whom " men filled with understanding find there when they have sung prayers formed within their heart ".[3] In similar manner, *fire*, in the Avesta, is man's great advocate: " Through thy fire, O Lord, we draw near to Thee and Thee alone! " [4] What is this *cave* where resides the flame divine? The *Chandogva Upanishad* states that

> He who knows this [space within the heart] attains eternal and all sufficient treasures.[5]

The idea of the *void*, of the *nothing* (to the senses and mind) which is everything, is well exemplified in Buddhist teachings and also subtly hinted at, in true Chinese manner, in the *Tao Te Ching*:

[1] I. 59. 2.
[2] I. 77. 3.
[3] I. 67. 2.
[4] *Yasna*, 36. 5.
[5] III. 12. 8.

Thirty spokes share one hub. Adapt the nothing therein to the purpose in hand, and you will have the use of the cart. Knead clay in order to make a vessel. Adapt the nothing therein to the purpose in hand, and you will have the use of the vessel. . . . Thus what we gain is something, yet it is by virtue of Nothing that this can be put to use.[1]

It is in man's heart of heart that man's oneness with the whole is known in reality and this oneness means that

He who is in the fire, and he who is here in the heart, and he who is yonder in the sun—he is one.[2]

The practical aspect of such realization is summed up for us in the Confucian text, *Chung Yung* or *Doctrine of the Mean*:

The way of Heaven is primal purity; the way of man is the realization of primal purity.

The means thereto were taught by the sage-ruler of China, Shun Ti, thus:

Man's mind goes easily astray; while the Essence of Tao is hidden aloft. Learn One-in-all and All-in-One and observe always constant mean.

The middle path, well known to Buddhism, is the safest.

To the last of the three truths given out in the *Idyll of the White Lotus* the Theist may object: if man is his own lawgiver, what of God? The " absolute lawgiver " is not man, the imperfect human being such as we know, but the *divinity* within the human, that which makes him one with the transcendent Principle and thus heir to immortal life, that divine centre from which he has to unwrap the many shrouds of heredity, upbringing, conditioning which he has allowed to wind around it. In its expression this third point is a Buddhist

[1] I. xi.
[2] *Maitri Upanishad*, VI. 17.

statement. When carefully considered it does not reject the theistic belief in a transcendent Absolute since the Deity within man is a spark of, and relates man to, that same Absolute: "thou art That". The Buddhist idea that the dewdrop slips into the shining ocean, or as we might say, the conception that the divine spark opens out or flashes forth to include the whole, shows where lies the point of agreement between these various ways of considering the one truth.

Birth and Death

The question of death is given special consideration in theosophic literature and much light is thrown upon the various hints scattered in the oriental religions.

In accordance with the law of cycles and eternal recurrence, birth and death are part of the vast cosmic process, in its ever renewal of all forms, in its everchanging panorama underlying the everlasting, unchanging Being. Theosophy emphasizes that the after-death life consists of states of consciousness into which we grow or to which we gravitate as a direct result of our past earthly life; heaven and hell are the effect of a cause created by ourselves when on earth:

> We create ourselves our devachan (heaven) and our avitchi (hell) while yet on earth and mostly during the latter days and even moments of our intellectual, sentient lives.[1]

This was taught as far back as vedic times where the defunct is described as mounting a one-poled vehicle which he "fashioned by means of mind during his life." [2]   In this mental chariot is placed " that which is to be handed over ", the harvest yield of life or essence stored up at the mental level.

[1] *M. L.* 127, 1st ed.; 124 3rd ed.
[2] *Rigveda*, X. 135. 3.

Since every "creation" implies a beginning and therefore an ending, neither of these states is permanent or eternal; they come into the main stream of our wider life and they pass away. "Nothing is permanent" teaches the Secret Doctrine [1] "except the one hidden absolute Existence which contains in itself the noumena of all realities." "All shall perish save his Face", echoes the Koran.

The dispersion of the various constituents of the human being that occurs after death as taught in the Mahatma Letters—"Dismemberments of principles . . . as a rule take place after the physical death of average humanity" [2]—is variously expressed in vedic verses and has given rise to much misunderstanding and misinterpretation in the scholarly world, indeed in the oriental religions themselves.

> By the first dying it goes apart dividing threefold; yonder goes it with one [part]; yonder goes it with another. Here with one it dwells.[3]
>
> Let the eye go to the sun, the spirit to the wind; go thou according to thy nature to heaven and earth. Or go to the waters.[4]

Whatever, in human beings, has an affinity to any of these, will gravitate thereto, while that which is unborn in man is kindled to awaken to its own real state:

> Do thou, Agni, kindle it with thy fervour, let thy flame and thy lustre kindle it . . . convey it to the world of the righteous.[5]

[1] S. D., I. 39; I. 113.
[2] p. 130; 126.
[3] Atharvaveda, XI. 8. 33.
[4] Rigveda, X. 16. 3.
[5] Ibid., X. 16. 4.

The Mahatma Letters clearly state that after the *first dying* (the physical death) there is what is called a *second dying* which occurs on the threshold of the soul's passing into that state of consciousness called heaven when all lower emotions are laid aside, just as the physical body had been cast away, and the essence of mind is carried off into " heaven ". This teaching may be compared with the Rigvedic verse:

> This one [light is] thine; yonder [is] one for thee too; with the third light unite thyself in mergence with thyself, be thou beloved and cherished of the gods in the highest birthplace.[1]

John Woodroffe, in his foreword to W.Y. Evans-Wentz's edition of the *Tibetan Book of the Dead* comments upon certain of its ideas:

> The dying . . . is adjured to recognize the Clear Light and thus liberate himself . . . If he does not (as is commonly the case), it is because the pull of worldly tendency draws him away. He is then presented with the secondary Clear Light, which is the first, somewhat dimmed to him by the general maya. [2]

Our Real Home

The Rigveda further states:

> Unite with the reward of thy sacrifices and good works in the highest heaven. Leaving blemish behind, go back to thy home; unite with thy form of splendour.[3]

A very succinct way of describing the fruition of our earthly life. Theosophists recognize here the causal vehicle, which

[1] X. 56. 1.
[2] p. XL, 2nd ed., Oxford, 1949.
[3] X. 14. 8.

becomes a vesture of glory when the human being is fully developed, of which the *Brhadaranakya Upanishad* says:

> Heaven is considered to be the ' body ' of mind and the sun its light-form.[1]

The rigvedic stanza [2] clearly implies that heaven is our home and that we have known this home before—a purely theosophic teaching. Furthermore, transgressions are left behind, on the threshold of the objective world, as it were. What happens to them? On this question the *Rigveda* is silent. But Theosophy, in accordance with the later development of Hinduism and Buddhism, explains that they are left as *seeds* which will bear fruit on the objective plane, once activated in another incarnation.

But beyond paradise, that stage of repose in the soul's pilgrimage, there has always been another conception, incomprehensible and unacceptable to the average person and one to which Theosophy draws attention and endeavours to clarify: the beatific union of the Christian mystic, the *atman* realization or liberation of the Hindu, the Sufi's *fana* or self-annihilation in the Beloved with its corollary *baqa* or self-perpetuation in the Godhead, the *nirvana* of the Buddhist. The very plunge of the soul into limiting conditions, into a measure (*maya*) of the immeasurable reality, is to enable it to release the boundless hidden within its depths, to cultivate that power which shall achieve the miracle: become what thou art, *thou art That*, that divinity which is not created, which does not become, but ever *is*:

> Thine own consciousness, shining void, and inseparable from the great body of Radiance, hath no birth, nor death, and is the immutable light.[3]

[1] I. 5. 12.
[2] X. 14. 8.
[3] *Tibetan Book of the Dead*, I. 1, p. 96, Oxford, 1949.

The Lord Buddha, as is well known, described *nirvana* in negative terms. But the poem of the sufi mystic Kabir is less known:

> There is an endless world, O my brother.
> And there is a nameless being, of whom naught can be said;
> Only he knows who has reached that region.
> It is quite different from what is heard or said.
> No form, no body, no length, no breadth is seen there.
> How can I tell you that which it is?
> . . . It cannot be told by the words of the mouth.

Compare the *Tao Te Ching*:

> The way that can be spoken of is not the constant way;
> the name that can be named is not the constant name.
> The nameless was the beginning of heaven and earth;
> The named was the mother of the myriad creatures.[1]

The Mahatma Letters explain:

> We call immortal but the one Life in its . . . Absolute Abstraction; that which has neither beginning nor end, nor any break in its continuity.[2]

Sentient existence with its subjection to states of unconsciousness, change, oblivion, with its ebb and flow, can have no part in the state of immortality which is beyond the web of *maya*. It is that which nought can alter, increase or decrease, build up or destroy—" desireless, self-sufficient ".[3] The ever deepening recognition of, and responsiveness to, the inner ever-blazing star, our fountain-source and our supreme goal, that glorious state of blissful, all-illuminating mastery, the

[1] p. 57, *Penguin*.
[2] p. 129; 126.
[3] *Atharvaveda* X. 8. 44.

Vedic solar splendour, is the whole purpose of human birth and death.

> I have known this mighty purusha, the divine man, refulgent as the sun beyond darkness! Only by knowing him does one overcome death. No other way is there to go.[1]

It has often been said that the message of the oriental religions is one of great pessimism. This is due to the western emphasis on " this " life as against the easterner's vision of " that " other life beyond yet within this life. In the light of Theosophy these oriental creeds appear rather to enshrine a great message of hope and glory for mankind, the glory of that eternal cosmic harmony reflected in the hearts of all creatures, leading to the ultimate victory, to that which is the Supreme—call it Brahman, Atman, Allah, God. They give the assurance that the One divine Life-breath, rooted in the ever unknown Absolute, pervades all and manifests in various forms upon every rung of the ladder of Being. It is in man " the divine herdsman, the untiring one . . . journeying continually within the worlds " [2]; the certainty of an everlasting Presence to which we can always turn. Hence the impossibility of " falling out " or erring far away since all is rooted in the one, immanent and transcendent. If Theosophy helps to bring this realization into the consciousness of distressed mankind it will achieve its great goal of unification and therefore of brotherhood.

> Where spiritual and ruling powers move together in unity that world will I know as holy.[3]

---

[1] *Yajurveda.* 31. 18.
[2] *Rigveda.* I, 164. 31.
[3] *Yajurveda.* 20. 5.

THE WISDOM IN THE CHRISTIAN TRADITION

> Thinking the deed, and not the creed,
> Would help us in our utmost need.
> —LONGFELLOW.

GEOFFREY HODSON

THROUGHOUT the first century of its existence the Theosophical Society has performed a service of incalculable value to humanity, from which the human race will benefit for centuries to come. That service is the continuing publication, in ever-improving forms, of the writings of its Co-Founder, H. P. Blavatsky.

While every aspect of the first object of the Society is powerfully supported from both esoteric and exoteric sources, the all-important part of the spiritual, intellectual and physical life of mankind, which concerns mystical experience, developed and developing creeds and organized religions, received special attention and aid from her inspired pen. World scriptures, she repeatedly stated, may best be regarded as written in a special category of literature known as the sacred language of allegory and symbol. Here are examples of her statements:

> The whole of the religious and mystical literature is symbolical. The *Books of Hermes*, the *Zohar*, the *Ya-Yakev*, the Egyptian *Book of the Dead*, the *Vedas*, the *Upanishads* and the *Bible* are as full of symbolism as are the Nabathean revelations of the Chaldaic *Qu-tamy*; it is a waste of time to ask which is the earliest, all being simply different versions of the one primeval record of prehistoric knowledge and revelation.[1]

[1] *S. D.*, V, 89. T. P. H.

For years we have repeatedly noticed that the same esoteric truths were expressed in identical symbols and allegories in countries between which there had never been traced any historical affiliation. We have found the Jewish *Kabala* and the *Bible* repeating the Babylonian myths: and the Oriental and Chaldean allegories given in form and substance in the oldest manuscripts of the Siamese Talapoins (monks), and in the popular but oldest traditions in Ceylon.[1]

Judaism, earlier and later Gnosticism, Christianity and even Christian Masonry, have all been erected upon identical cosmical myths, symbols and allegories, whose full comprehension is possible only to those who have inherited the key from their inventors.[2]

Myth was the favourite and universal method of teaching in archaic times.[3]

H. P. B. thus affirms that world scriptures were written by profoundly illumined men, whose purposes were less to write biographies of great personages than to reveal, under the veil of allegory and symbol, truths that are eternal. In this context let us consider Christianity.

The Wisdom Religion

Although Jesus the Christ appeared in Palestine some two thousand years ago, and the Christian religion thereafter came into being, it was by no means either an isolated or a new revelation. Rather was it part of a long historical development established and maintained on this planet by the spiritual teachers of the race, referred to in the New Testament as " just men made perfect ". That it was actually a continuance of an already existing religious system was recognized by St. Augustine, who wrote in the fourth century:

[1] *Isis* I, 577.
[2] *Ibid.*, II, 405.
[3] *Ibid.*, II, 493.

The identical thing that we now call the Christian religion existed among the ancients, and has not been lacking from the beginning of the human race until the coming of Christ in the flesh, from which moment onwards the true religion, which already existed, began to be called Christian.[1]

St. Paul, in a letter to his converts in Corinth, referred to the primordial existence of a divine wisdom in the following words: "But we speak the wisdom of God in a mystery, even the hidden wisdom, which God ordained before the world unto our glory".

Evidently, however, a world-wide resurgence of the one Wisdom Religion occurred between 700 B.C. and 300 A.D. During that period appeared Lao Tzu and Confucius in China; the Buddha and Shri Shankaracharya in India; Zoroaster in Persia; Pythagoras, Plato, Socrates and Aristotle in Greece; and Ammonius Saccus, Plotinus and other Neo-Platonists in Alexandria. All contributed to a great revival of philosophic and religious thought. In addition the lesser and greater Mysteries in Egypt and Greece were still continuing to attract, teach and initiate occultists and mystics. To these may be added such Jews as were studying esoteric Hebraism, known as the *Kabbalah*, and also the Gnostics (Valentinus, Basilides, Marcion and others) who contributed the concept of the "Mystery of the Kingdom". These, and other contemporary streams of thought and culture, became blended in early Christianity. This synthesis was illumined and empowered by the Christ as a living centre and source of personal inspiration and the spiritual founder of the "new" faith.

The doctrine of the Atonement may usefully be chosen as susceptible of a mystical interpretation. The attainment of

[1] *Retract.* I, xiii, 3.

Christhood or Adeptship, for example, brings full and conscious realization of oneness with the Christ-nature within every human being. The symbols of Christ as bridegroom and of the heavenly marriage are appropriately used to describe this interior unification. Oneness achieved, the ascended Master pours forth into, and shares with, every human being his own perfected spiritual power, life and consciousness. In varying degrees, according to capacity to respond, this enables the human being in bodily life to resist temptation, to renounce the " world, the flesh and the devil ", and ultimately to realize his or her own spiritual selfhood as an immortal and eternal being.

Thus viewed, the Atonement is an interior procedure, an at-one-ment in point of fact. A transmission of light is involved, rather than a transference of blood, and an inpouring of spiritualized and perfected life. It is the shedding of wisdom, not of physical blood and water from the wounds of one crucified.

One's thought is thus led to the Christ indwelling, the interior Christ principle and nature in every human being, the " Christ in you " and the " God that worketh in you " of St. Paul. The Master himself is reported as affirming to his disciples his unfailing presence in man: " I am in my father, and ye in me, and I in you "; and also to all mankind: " Lo, I am with you alway, even unto the end of the world ".

Let us now consider a further theosophical view of the gospel story. This is that the scriptures and mythologies of ancient people are composed of allegories and symbols, and are not intended to be read only as historical literature. According to this approach, the gospels do not just chronicle external events in time; they reveal eternal truths, such as the laws of being and the interior mystical experiences and attainments of nations and of men. The incidents related have both a temporal significance and at least four timeless meanings: cosmic, solar, human and initiatory, or concerning the way of holiness and its attainment.

Thus the central figure in the gospels may also represent the divine within all nature and in man, the Christ indwelling, the Logos of the soul, the divine " Voice ". The episodes in the reported life of the Christ are enacted within and by the soul of every human being, the nativity representing the beginning of a new cycle of whatever order. In the cosmos, it describes the birth of a universe at the dawn of creative day. In man, it describes his spiritual ascent to or " birth " into a new level of consciousness, and so a new and spiritual ideal of life, accompanied by the development of "gifts" of hitherto hidden powers, the Christmas of the soul.

"Which Things are an Allegory"

Let us now pass to the view that the gospels were written by men who knew the Ancient Wisdom, were skilled in the language of allegory and symbol, and wrote in that language in order to preserve throughout successive dark ages, to reveal and yet to conceal or enveil, the more power-bestowing knowledge. If this be accepted, then a dual purpose may be discerned—namely, to record in a certain manner the story of the Christ, and at the same time to reveal eternal macrocosmic and microcosmic truths. St. John, whose first five verses affirm the Logos doctrine, accentuates the cosmos, referring to the nativity, baptism, crucifixion and ascension of the Christ in such a way that they are applicable to the emanation, involution and evolution of the one Life of the cosmos as a whole (macrocosmic). The involution and evolution of the human monad (including each minor cycle of physical birth and death), the later stages of human evolution and entry upon the Path (spiritual rebirth or initiation), and the final establishment of the rule of the spirit and entry into the superhuman kingdom of nature are also described (micro-cosmic).

In this approach, the baptism of the Christ represents the further descent of spirit into matter, and the river Jordan is lifted out of time and space and seen by the inspired authors as a symbol of universal matter, into which the divine Life (the Christ) " descends " on the involutionary arc. The temptation in the wilderness indicates that the " descent " continues, and that the taint of matter is experienced. The transfiguration in its turn implies that, cosmically, spirit is still consciously in touch with the source, though the experiences in Gethsamene that followed refer to the still deeper " descent " of the one Life, and foreshadow the " death " and later " burial " in a rock tomb (entry into the mineral kingdom). From this densest point in matter the process of evolution (resurrection) begins, marking the upward turn, while ascension is emblematic of the final completion of the cycle of forthgoing and return.

This view of the gospel narrative is capable of still further application. In a possible microcosmic interpretation, for example, the human monad first projects its ray into the evolutionary field (nativity), descends deeper and deeper into matter (baptism and Gethsemane), and eventually is born into a physical body (crucifixion and burial indeed). If, in addition, the life of Christ be also interpreted as descriptive of entry upon the Path of swift unfoldment,[1] then in such a procedure the divine Self in spiritually awakened man begins to take its evolution into its own hands; or, in biblical terms,

[1] See G. Hodson, *The Hidden Wisdom in the Holy Bible*, I, Pt. 6, Ch. 1.

responds to the call of John the Baptist to " repent ". The neophyte then becomes a disciple, embarks upon the way of the cross (the Path), enters " the stream " (baptism), takes the first five great initiations (birth, baptism, transfiguration, crucifixion and ascension); and, as described by St. Paul, then comes " unto the measure of the stature of the fulness of Christ ", or attains to Adeptship.

This leads to the conclusion that it would have been of little or no moment to the authors whether what they recorded really happened or not.   In consequence, they unhesitatingly introduced into their narratives accounts of visions of people shared by no one else, and therefore unlikely ever to have been recorded; also incidents that certainly were not recorded, and indeed may never have happened.   In this, they were not in the least guilty of falsification, since their whole motive was to use the supposed history of events happening in time as a vehicle for eternal truths.

In addition, as initiates, they would be under two necessities: to reveal hidden truths, and to lead intuitively awakened readers to occult knowledge, and yet to veil it from the uninitiated.   By such means, they worked actually to bring people to readiness for discipleship and initiation, to stimulate and awaken them; and so, by self-training repeatedly advocated and described, whether by John the Baptist or Jesus, to the gateway of the Mysteries.

Drama of the Soul

This, I suggest, was their purpose, especially that of John, who did not regard himself as obliged to be an historian, but rather a revealer of the *Gnosis* and an awakener of souls. The Evangelists thus undertook the enormously important task of relating the story of Jesus so as to make available, in both openly stated and allegorical form, the mystery teaching of the nature of man, his outer and inner evolution; and, more especially, the ever open mystic way, lest these should be lost during the foreseen dark ages of " wars and rumours of wars ".

The Christ drama is thus enacted *within* the soul of man, for every individual passes through the experiences related in the gospels. All men have their conversions to idealism, however, temporary, baptisms of sorrow, temptations, upliftments, dark nights of the soul, crucifixions, and the burial of their hopes. These are common human experiences, since the life of Christ is indeed found to be a universal life.

The revelation of the existence of a sacred language of allegory and symbol, and the real interpretation of the scriptures which it makes possible, constitute the true instruments for the liberation of Christendom from the darkness of ignorance under which Christians have long lived.

What changes would be involved? Christians would learn that in his spiritual nature each man is himself a god, being thus established in his own divine right, as affirmed by both Jesus and Paul.[1]

Each human being can attain to Christhood, or salvation, by the sole power of his divine attributes. These are inherited from the dweller in the innermost, the Monad, ever existent within the solar Logos—the true and highest " Father in Heaven ".

The ministration of the historical Christ symbolises the processes of redemption and salvation, to be carried out by the individual himself, who is amply endowed with an innate interior redumptive spiritual power; the Christ is also the awakening messenger, bringing into activity that redeeming

[1] *Jn.* X, 34; I *Cor.* III, 16.

Principle within. The mystical Christ is the Christ nature within man, as St. Paul makes clear.[1]

The central message of reformed Christian theology should always have been " Christ in you, the hope of glory ". As the *Bible* assures us, neither mediator nor priest is necessary to bring about the salvation of any man.

Religion itself solely concerns the discovery by each individual of his own divine Selfhood, the Christ within him, the Logos of the soul. Abstinences are useful only when they assist the seeker to success in the discovery of the divine Self within.

Prayer is not directed to an external deity, but to the God within. It is simply a mode of conscious realization of unity with the God within (yoga), and must be shown as such.

Life must conform to profession, and conduct must be conducive to communion with the higher Self. Every day must be lived as a holy day, and so ultimately a "holiday".

Some members of the human race have already become "just men made perfect". These have entered in at the strait gate and trodden the narrow way that leads along the spiritual path and through the great initiations to ascension, Christhood, adeptship. The method by which the spiritual soul of man attains to adeptship is that of successive lives on earth,[2] or rebirth; while harmony and justice are assured by the operation of the law of cause and effect, of sowing and reaping.[3]

A mysterious law governs enduring human happiness and fulfilment. Briefly stated, it is: give to live, share to enjoy,

[1] *Gal.* IV, 19.
[2] See G. Hodson, *Reincarnation, Fact or Fallacy?*
[3] *Gal.* VI, 7; *Matt.* V, 18 & VII, 12.

serve in order to unfold. Strangely, practice of the ideal of selfless giving brings not loss but gain, not death but more abundant life. Disobedience of this law, moved by desire for exclusively personal possessions and powers, brings not gain but loss, not life but death.

This self-emptying (*Kenosis*) is practised by the Logos, who nourishes and sustains the solar system by the perpetual outpouring of his own life, and this self-emptying attitude and mode of life is a central idea in Christianity. " He that hateth his life in this world shall keep it unto life eternal ". Also: " Except a corn of wheat fall into the ground and die, it abideth alone; but if it die, it bringeth forth much fruit ".[1]

---

[1] *Jn.* XII, 24, 25.

Truth is within ourselves; it takes no rise
From outward things, whate'er you may believe.
There is an inmost centre in us all,
Where truth abides in fulness; and around,
Wall upon wall, the gross flesh hems it in,
This perfect, clear perception—which is truth.
A baffling and perverting carnal mesh,
Blinds it and makes all error; and to KNOW,
Rather consists in opening out a way
Whence the imprisoned splendour may escape
Than in effecting entry for a light
Supposed to be without.

R. BROWNING—(*Paracelsus*)

THE CONCEPT OF GOD

> There is surely a piece of divinity
> in us—THOMAS BROWNE.

WILLIAM J. ROSS

THE dictionary gives the original meaning of God to be
" what is invoked " or " what is worshipped by sacrifice ".
The history of man shows that the word God was invented
to designate the unknown cause of all effects which man
admired or dreaded without understanding them. The
storms, the cataclysms, the good or bad crops were all credited
to a force or forces which were anthropomorphized into a
god or gods. These were worshipped and sacrificed to, in
order that they might be propitiated and act favourably
toward their worshippers.

Much of this attitude or feeling is still evident today. Man
still makes his God, attributing to him human characteristics
and sacrificing or praying to the image he has created to
obtain what he wants. Although thinking man has theoreti-
cally abandoned anthropomorphism, his God, when he has
one, usually has human characteristics and is seen as a superhuman person—masculine—who has power over nature and
the fortunes of mankind.

In theosophical literature one of the most controversial
statements about God appears in Letter 10 of *The Mahatma
Letters to A. P. Sinnett*: ". . . we deny God both as philosophers
and as Buddhists ".[1] A philosopher has been aptly defined by
Kewal Motwani as one who gathers up the total experience

[1] p. 52. T. P. H.

of a culture and gives it coherence and wholeness; and this is surely the basis from which a Mahatma must speak. Further, to speak of oneself as a Buddhist is to identify oneself with a non-deistic religion.

In Buddhism there is no mention of God. One finds in it no mythological vision, no tangible creed. It is as it were a therapy, a treatment for those who recognize the pain of the human condition and are strong enough to follow the cure which is prescribed. It is not so much a religious philosophy as the advice of a spiritual physician. The Buddha diagnoses the human problem. All is sorrow, he says; and who today can look at the human condition and not feel the accuracy of the diagnosis. Then he gives the cause—ignorant craving. Man suffers because he constantly wants, and when he gets what he wants he finds it does not satisfy his craving but only leads to more wants. What is the cure? The cure as laid down by the Buddha is an operational one, a way of life, living in accordance with the noble eightfold path. It involves a commitment to doing things, to living in a certain way, to having certain attitudes towards man and the world. This frees us from our ignorant cravings and help us to find that sense of identity, that feeling of wholeness, which is the mark of a healthy human being, a being who is at once aware of his own individual uniqueness and of his oneness with the whole of nature.

None of this implies any idea of God. It is a way of life involving a feeling of responsibility, a recognition of man as the agent of his own destiny. It is in the context of this philosophical, Buddhistic point of view that we must see the words " we deny God ".

In general the denial of God is considered to be atheistic, and in a certain sense it is, but the concept that everything is divine, sacred, is quite consistent with the non-deistic position.

The three fundamental propositions which H. P. Blavatsky gives in *The Secret Doctrine* deal with certain concepts that are often referred to as God. It is well to consider them so that one's use of the word God can be more accurate and meaningful and that we know what we are trying to convey by the word.

The One Reality

The first fundamental proposition states that back of everything there is "An Omnipresent, Eternal, Boundless and Immutable PRINCIPLE ". This principle transcends the power of human conception and can only be dwarfed and limited by any expression. It is " Be-ness rather than Being " and hence beyond all thought and speculation. It is the " Rootless Root of ' all that was, is, or ever shall be ' ".[1] This principle expresses the one Reality, the Absolute, Parabrahman.

Today, when many people are trying to avoid anthropomorphism—the personification, the deification of the idea of God—this statement of the Absolute could be considered their idea of God, but if so they must be prepared to accept all that this implies.

The Absolute is, by its very nature, devoid of all attributes and is, as H. P. B. points out, " essentially without any relation to manifested finite Being ". It is this quality, or perhaps one should say this absence of quality, which is the stumbling block for most people in endeavouring to think of the Absolute as God. A God without relation to the finite beings we are is so beyond us, so out of touch with our human concepts, something which, to most of us, seems so impersonal, cold,

[1] *S. D.*, I, 14, 1st ed.; I, 79, 6-vol. ed., T. P. H.

abstract, that we do not find it satisfactory. Even if we are free of the concept of God as having skin and bone and beard we want a deity to which we can be related, a deity with attributes and qualities we can recognize and admire. The problem in our concepts of God is that while he may be infinite, we want him to be knowable in terms of our own finite life and experience.

The second fundamental proposition speaks of "The Eternity of the Universe *in toto* as a boundless plane; periodically 'the play-ground of numberless Universes incessantly manifesting and disappearing'. . .", that is, the absolute universality of the law of periodicity.[1]

This concept, involving the idea that the universe manifests in accordance with immutable law, has a wide appeal. The idea that the universe is lawful lies at the root of science and is deeply satisfying to most people, so much so that when they think of God they think of him as the great lawgiver. To such people this proposition appeals because they see in it an aspect of Deity. But there is nothing in this proposition that postulates or calls for a lawgiver. The concept is of law as inherent in and an essential, existential quality of manifestation.

Elsewhere H. P. B. says, " The Divine Thought does not imply the idea of a Divine Thinker. . ." [2] and similarly the idea of a divine creation does not imply the idea of a divine creator. The universe is a " Son of Necessity ",[3] that which needs must be by its very nature.

It is unfortunate that we tend to confuse law, absolute and immutable, with human legal systems, man-made systems

[1] *S. D.*, I, 16-17; I, 82.
[2] *S. D.*, I, 61; I, 130.
[3] *S. D.*, I, 43; I. 115.

which constantly change and which are in no way inevitable in their operation. There are frequently ways of getting round the laws of any land. This confusion between inevitable law and legal systems causes us to think in terms of evading the law, of propitiating the lawgiver in some manner. When men think of God as lawgiver they often feel that by prayer, by joining a church or organization dedicated to him, by belief in the lawgiver, or by sacrificing to him they can free themselves from the effects of the law. To recognize that law is inevitable, that the only way to be free is to realize this inevitability and work with it, is at the heart of theosophical philosophy.

The third fundamental proposition affirms " The fundamental identity of all Souls with the Universal Over-Soul, the latter being itself an aspect of the Unknown Root; and the obligatory pilgrimage for every Soul—a spark of the former —through the Cycle of Incarnation, or Necessity, in accordance with Cyclic and Karmic Law, during the whole term." [1]

How often has one heard a sigh of relief when people trying to understand what they mean by God come across the above sentence. They say immediately, " That is what I mean by God—the universal Over-soul ". The oversoul is not a personal deity, not a creator or doer; it is the aggregate of all the souls that are identified and identical with it. It is as it were, a term for the whole of that life which informs nature and of which we are a part.

Man's Responsibility

There is a further statement under this proposition, one that sums up the essence of Theosophy: " The pivotal doctrine of the Esoteric Philosophy admits no privileges or special gifts in man, save those won by his own Ego through personal

[1] *S. D.*, 16-17; I, 82.

effort and merit throughout a long series of metempsychoses and reincarnations ". The responsibility lies with man. There is no plan made by someone else, no hierarchies who rule, but only the co-operative effort of all that lives. As Shankaracharya said, the One cannot be ruler. Part of the tragedy of Christianity is that it has profaned nature, looked upon her as something outside of man over which he has dominion, something he is trying to conquer. The old pagan concept, far truer, that man is part of nature, has been lost sight of, and with it the idea that man must learn to co-operate with her. Once again to quote from *The Secret Doctrine*:

> . . . man ought to be ever striving to help the divine evolution of *Ideas*, by becoming, to the best of his ability, a *co-worker with Nature*, in the cyclic task. The ever unknowable and incognizable *Karana* alone, the *Causeless* Cause of all causes, should have its shrine and altar on the holy and ever untrodden ground of our heart—invisible, intangible, unmentioned, save through the "still small voice" of our spiritual consciousness. Those who worship before it, ought to do so in the silence and the sanctified solitude of their Souls; making their Spirit the sole mediator between them and the Universal Spirit, their good actions the only priests, and their sinful intentions the only visible and objective sacrificial victims to the *Presence*.[1]

This, I think, is the key to the understanding of the concept of God. It helps to free us from the dichotomy of the religious and the secular, of God and man. It brings us to a sense of wholeness, of unity, to the understanding that the fundamental law of our system is the one homogeneous divine substance-principle. This is the "omnipresent Reality; impersonal, because it contains all and everything."

[1] *S. D.*, I, 280; I, 322-23.

But the austere impersonality of this idea often appears quite inhuman, and so man creates his own God nearer to his own image. He sets up an ideal man with the qualities and attributes he would like to possess. This does no harm so long as what is being done is recognized. Such projections are frequently a useful focus for meditation and contemplation, part of the mythology of our culture. But it is all too easy to lose sight of the projection as symbol and to think of it as an objective reality which guides and controls, and so we forget " personal effort ". What is needed is not a belief in a God but a sense of Godness, not the idea of a deity but the recognition of the divinity, the sacredness of all nature.

When saints and sages, past or present, try to describe their mystic or peak experiences they speak of being, of the perception of one-ness, of absoluteness, of transcending time and space, of effortlessness, of order, of simplicity. Awareness of this sense of being in ourselves brings about a similar view of the world. We become free of the dichotomy of the inner and the outer, we no longer need to create God, for we discover that all is divine.

A man can have no god that is not bounded by his own human conceptions. The wider the sweep of his spiritual vision, the mightier will be his deity. But where can we find a better demonstration of Him than in man himself; in the spiritual and divine powers lying dormant in every human being?

Call the phenomena force, energy, electricity or magnetism, or spirit-power, it will ever be the partial manifestation of . . . that intelligent, omnipotent and individual WILL, pervading all nature and known, through the insufficiency of human language to express correctly psychological images, as—GOD.

—ISIS UNVEILED

A MESSENGER AND A MESSAGE

To unmask falsehood, and bring
truth to light—SHAKESPEARE.

BORIS DE ZIRKOFF

THE writings of H. P. Blavatsky and of her Adept-Teachers
are the cornerstone upon which the modern Theosophical
Movement rests. They embody in present-day language the
essence of the trans-Himālayan esoteric knowledge which has
been from time immemorial the fountain-head of all genuine
occultism on this earth.

Upon this cornerstone has been erected a superstructure
which, although imperfect in many respects, has nonetheless
withstood the attacks of entrenched materialism, and of the
forces of obscurantism which have attempted from time to time
to obliterate or disrupt the Movement as a whole.

The literary heritage of H. P. Blavatsky is of primary
importance because it contains in systematic form the ageless
tenets held in custody by the most advanced individuals of
the human race whose school of esotericism is the source of
all true knowledge. These tenets are the foundation-principles
which will, in due course of time, serve as the basis for a new
philosophy of life the world over, and will give rise to new
currents of inspiration for bewildered humanity.

Today, in the latter part of the twentieth century, we find
the age-old teachings of Theosophy, which is the universal
spiritual tradition of mankind, confirmed and supported by

every major scientific discovery. As we observe the developments in the world of human thought, we sense that the vindication of the mission and work of H. P. Blavatsky is close at hand. The continued publication of her writings in many different languages contributes vitally to this ultimate objective.

Apart from the scholarly nature and the important occult factors revealed in her literary output, what strikes the earnest student in his study of H. P. Blavatsky's writings is her profound insight into the psychological and intellectual characteristics of our era, her prophetic analysis of our recurrent mental and emotional crises, and the amazing timeliness of many subjects on which she wrote close to one hundred years ago, as if she were dealing with the conditions of the present era.

Three Phases

A careful study of H. P. Blavatsky's writings reveals at least three distinct but inter-related levels in them.

The least important of these from the occult standpoint—however interesting and entertaining it may be—is the level or phase which relates to H. P. Blavatsky as a mere person, an individual endowed with a forceful style of writing, with singular ability for controversy and argumentation, and with sudden flashes of humour. She draws from an arsenal of sharp weapons, and is never on the defensive. Her enemies, engaged in mounting an ill-advised attack, find themselves laughed to scorn or ridiculed in a sort of good-humoured way. Occasionally, some little suspected fact of occultism is thrown at them in an offhand manner. At other times, Blavatsky clears the ground temporarily occupied by the intruder, and uses it quite unexpectedly as a basis from which to send a new salvo of challenges, none of which can easily be met or faced.

To this phase or level belong also her travel stories, such as *From the Caves and Jungles of Hindostan*, *The Mysterious Tribes of the Blue Hills*, *The Durbar in Lahore*, and other shorter pieces, all of which, written in her native Russian, are of high literary value, couched in the best style of Russian language and revealing here and there some occult truths well worth pondering over. A complete English translation of these Russian writings is ready in manuscript, and will eventually be published as an integral part of Blavatsky's *Collected Writings*.

Some curious peculiarities may be noted so far as the English writings of this particular phase are concerned. They exhibit interesting characteristics. In many places, it is quite obvious that H.P.B. was thinking in Russian and translating her thought into English, with the result that her English shows a Russian construction of sentences. In other places, she must have been thinking in French, as her English is typically a translation from that language. One other peculiarity is worth mentioning; it is that, both in her English and in her Russian texts we are now considering, she uses at times words which had become archaic even in her time, and which can hardly be expected to occur in either English or Russian writings of her day. It is not easy to explain exactly how this happened to occur.

The other phase or level of H. P. Blavatsky's writings is of a totally different character. It has to do with magnificent, inspired passages on very lofty subjects, written in perfect English and obviously backed by spiritual power and intellectual force of an exceptional kind. While an outside source of inspiration cannot definitely be denied, it would be wiser to attribute this type of writings to a direct inspiration from her own higher Self, the centre of power and spiritual knowledge residing in her own higher consciousness—the reimbodying Ego illumined by the monadic Individuality. Such passages occur here and there throughout her writings, and may be encountered both in her best known works and occasionally in her ephemeral articles, where we might expect to find nothing of this kind. It stands to reason that our rather limited understanding of her real occult status, and of the mysteries connected with human consciousness, makes it difficult for us to distinguish the real source of this inspiration from that other source which is directly related to the third level or phase of her writings.

That third phase, in the viewpoint of many students, is the most important, and concerns her unusual occult nature and real mission. We have in mind now the fact of her being at times the channel of a higher consciousness—the mind of her own teacher or of one or another initiate whose direct agent she was during her life-time. It should be carefully observed that this transmission of a higher consciousness has nothing to do with mediumship of any kind; in fact, it is the very opposite. A trained disciple, an occult student of considerable advancement along the Path, is taught how to set aside for a time his or her own personal consciousness, and permit a higher consciousness or mind to channel through ideas and teachings which that disciple is expected to convey to the world at a certain specific cyclic time in the history of the human race. This process has nothing to do with trance and is engaged in by the disciple in complete self-consciousness. Large portions of both *Isis Unveiled* and *The Secret Doctrine* were written in this manner. Passages of that type can best be identified whenever H.P.B. says: " Occultism teaches," " the Secret Doctrine states," " the Esoteric Philosophy affirms," " Occult Science declares," or other expressions of the same kind, followed by a succinct, positive and authoritative outline of one or another aspect of the occult doctrine. When such passages are linked together, it becomes obvious that they present (wherever they may occur) an outline of the heretofore secret science or philosophy of occultism, publicly given out by at least two Initiates of the Brotherhood of Adepts through the intermediary of their direct messenger, H. P. Blavatsky.

This difficult subject, which is of paramount importance in the life and work of H. P. Blavatsky, is thoroughly gone into in Geoffrey A. Barborka's remarkable work, *H. P. Blavatsky, Tibet and Tulku*,[1] which is commended to the careful attention of all serious students.

Among the works of H. P. Blavatsky, *The Key to Theosophy* is the one most suited for the general inquirer who wishes to acquire a bird's-eye-view of the main theosophical teachings. It is written in question and answer form, and the replies are definite, clear-cut and brief, even though at times not too simple. The presentation of the teachings is challenging, and the reader acquires after a while the desire to read other works by H.P.B., and to delve deeper into the theosophical philosophy.

As to the devotional and ethical aspects of the teachings, *The Voice of the Silence* remains a classic in that sphere of thought, a fact which a very large number of people, otherwise unrelated to the Theosophical Movement, have acknowledged through the intervening years. It establishes, better than anything else from H. P. B.'s pen, the close interrelation between the teaching of Theosophy and the Mahayana School of Buddhism by means of the strong emphasis placed on the ideal of the Bodhisattva who renounces nirvanic bliss in order to stay among men and help their faltering steps towards spiritual knowledge.

[1] T. P. H.

Mainly in English

It is interesting to note that the greater portion of H. P. Blavatsky's writings was produced by her in English—a language which she learned to speak only later in life. She wrote a number of essays, some of them fairly long, in French—a language which she spoke fluently and used in her many travels prior to her theosophical mission. We also have a couple of articles from her pen written in Italian. There seems to be no definite indication anywhere of her speaking or writing in German. Her travel stories (mentioned above) are the only writings in her native tongue and published in Russian, both in her cwn time and a few years later. Of course, these early editions are long out of print and are not easily available even in university libraries.

Whether the authorities in Russia would be interested in ever reprinting them is anybody's guess, although their literary value would easily be recognized, side by side with travelogues and novels of other nineteenth-century writers.

Essays written by H. P. B. in French deal mainly with the origins of Christianity, the concept of the Christos, the traditions of occultism throughout past ages, alchemy and mediumship from the spiritualistic standpoint, as contrasted with occult facts. All of those essays may be found in the series of her *Collected Writings* now in production. However, if they were gathered together and published in their original French, they might be a useful, small-sized book for French-speaking Theosophists and other readers.

Important among H.P.B's writings are her personal letters written to a great variety of people. Those written to A. P. Sinnett have been published; a few others have appeared in print here and there, such as her letters to Professor Hiram Corson and others. But there are scores of other letters in the archives of the Theosophical Society which have never yet been published. All of them, so far as we have been able to ascertain, are now fully transcribed, translated into English in the case of those written in French or (to her relatives) in Russian, and collected in chronological order. They await eventual publication as part of the *Collected Writings*. These letters present less known aspects of H. P. Blavatsky's character, and give an intimate glimpse into the many difficulties she had to face and overcome, in dealing with other people. While only casually concerned with teachings, they nevertheless contain many hints along occult lines, sometimes even ideas which cannot be met with in her other writings.

Mention should be made of the *Transactions of the Blavatsky Lodge* in London, which are transcriptions of discussions on various difficult points in the text of *The Secret Doctrine* elucidated by H. P. B. during the sessions of the Blavatsky Lodge. They are available both as a separate work and as part of Volume X of the *Collected Writings*.

In the last year or two of her life, H. P. B. assembled a large number of passages from the Eastern writings and arranged them in chronological order through the twelve months of the year. This was published in 1890 as a Birthday Book of Precepts and Axioms under the title of *Gems from the East*.

Another work from her pen bears the title of *Nightmare Tales*, and was published posthumously in 1892. The five stories included in this little collection show H.P.B. as a vivid, graphic writer, gifted with brilliant imagination. She has embodied in these often blood-curdling tales profound hints along occult lines. Three of these stories appeared many years earlier in the New York *Sun* and the Boston *Banner of Light*. One of them was translated into Russian by H. P. B.

herself. Only one of them appears to have been written in the last years of her life. However, she wrote several other stories of a similar nature; apparently these were overlooked by the editor and were not included in the *Nightmare Tales*.

"Isis Unveiled" and "The Secret Doctrine"

It is almost impossible to assess in a few brief paragraphs the nature and contents of H. P. B.'s larger works, without doing injustice to them. Her first master-stroke in the cause of Occultism was, of course, *Isis Unveiled*, published in 1877, and spoken of by an American author as "a book with a revolution in it." This work is not what some people imagine it to be, namely, a textbook of occultism. It is rather a bird's-eye-view of the history of occultism in its many aspects, and of the universal presence of its basic tenets in all ages and among all the peoples of the earth. It traces the golden thread of occult tradition, and is, confessedly so, a first attempt to present, as cautiously as possible, certain principles of the occult science to a western public unaccustomed to this type of thought. *Isis Unveiled* has been published and republished through the years, and has remained practically on the best-seller list of occult literature.

The Secret Doctrine, on the other hand, is a fairly systematic presentation of the heretofore secret teachings concerning the origin and evolution of both mankind and the planetary system to which we belong. It is not a textbook either, but a student can make of it something similar to a textbook by underlining certain passages throughout its volumes, and finding hereby that they embody an unfolding picture of the gradual development and growth of worlds and the life-waves inhabiting them. It is almost like having a book within a book, as the method indicated above brings out various additional thoughts by juxtaposition. In regard to this *magnum opus* of H. P. B., it might be said that, had she never written anything else in her entire life-span, she would have nevertheless carried out most of her mission by delivering to the world the basic foundation-principles of occult science through the pages of *The Secret Doctrine* alone.

The entire literary heritage of H. P. Blavatsky has been in process of publication for many years under the general title of *Collected Writings*. Eleven volumes and a new edition of *Isis Unveiled* are now available in that series. Eventually, it is hoped that everything she ever wrote will be part of this uniform edition. Work is proceeding now on a new edition of *The Secret Doctrine* and on at least two more volumes of her miscellaneous essays written mainly for the pages of her London magazine, *Lucifer*. The entire text of her Russian articles in English translation is ready to be set up and printed when arrangements can be made. Several hundred of her letters are also carefully filed with unpublished material; they require, however, many explanatory notes and elucidations before they can be published.

The vast literary output of H. P. Blavatsky in a little over sixteen years, and the astounding contents of the greater part of her writings, appear today, in retrospect over her mission and work, as one of the most remarkable achievements of human genius.

THE MAHATMAS OR ADEPTS

Be ye therefore perfect.—The Bible,
Math. V, 48.

N. SRI RAM

A. P. SINNETT, then the editor of India's foremost newspaper, relating the beginnings of his correspondence with those who have come to be known as Mahatmas, dedicated his first book to one of them in the following words: " To one whose comprehension of Nature and humanity ranges so far above the Science and Philosophy of Europe that only the broadest minded representatives of either will be able to realize the existence of such powers in Man as he constantly exercises."

Many years later, after Sinnett's death, the letters received by him were published under the title *The Mahatma Letters to A. P. Sinnett.* There are references in those letters to some belonging to the same fraternity or hierarchy with even greater knowledge and powers. The world at large has thus, and through other books written about them since, become familiarized with the idea that there are such beings, human like ourselves, but far beyond humanity in the evolutionary scale.

The Mahatmas or Adepts—a word used by H. P. Blavatsky and Sinnett to indicate their occult knowledge and powers —repudiated the idea that they were mere wonder-workers, or such " spirits " as appear in spiritualistic séances taking various forms. They are human like ourselves but represent the efflorescence of the human tree. There are many indications in the Letters as to the nature of their attainments, interests and work. The fact that they are human, living in physical bodies as ours, unrecognized and unknown, for purely altruistic ends and as co-workers with nature, is brought out clearly. What those ends are and what kind of development or change from the common run of mankind is connoted by Adeptship, can be gathered, but even then somewhat vaguely, only from a study of nature and man and the whole process of evolution from the occult standpoint. There are theosophical books dealing with this subject. It is not possible for the human intellect, said the Lord Buddha, to conceive the state he called Nirvana, although all Buddhists regard it as the highest and ultimate goal attainable by man, and there are indications of its nature in Buddhist books in such general terms as a state of transcendent peace, blessedness, freedom from all stain and sorrow, and so forth. Similarly we can know the nature of an Adept, from which spring his knowledge and powers, only in very general terms. The terms that have been used to refer to them indicate the type of beings they are and bring out its outstanding aspects so far as we can comprehend them.

The word Adept denotes proficiency or skill, particularly in the occult sciences. H. P. B. used this term rather loosely in the early days. She speaks in certain places of initiated Adepts, implying that there might be men who may be termed Adepts but who had not yet come to the stage of initiation, a word which has the meaning both of an induction into the occult mysteries and the beginning of an expansion of consciousness along the lines that result in a complete transformation of the inner being of the person. She also speaks of the Adepts on the right-hand path, which suggests that there may be others who may be adepts at certain things, for instance magic, but may be on the wrong road. So the word Adept as used in the early days falls short of the meaning which it bears in later theosophical literature. We now understand by that word something more than and different from one who is merely versed in occult lore or is able to manipulate certain occult forces.

Another word which has been used particularly in India is Mahatma. Literally it means " great soul "; but this term has been applied to persons who have betaken themselves to an unworldy outer life even though they may have marked personal defects. So this word also has acquired a different signification from what perhaps it bore originally. Various quite ordinary people, who may in some cases be unattractive and uncultured, pass for Mahatmas in India. The term is a Sanskrit word and it has somewhat the same signification as a saint. The generality of saints—there were some exceptions—were far from being perfect men; they were all the time struggling with temptations of one sort or another, and some of them have spoken very candidly about their struggles and weaknesses.

When we use the word Master, it means one who has a disciple. It was used in connection with the Christ, who was spoken of as the Master. It has come to mean an exemplar or guide. In theosophical literature it has the same meaning as the Sanskrit word guru, which indicates a spiritual teacher or guide. When we refer to someone as a spiritual teacher the question arises: What is meant by spiritual? Is the person one who can show the way to Reality or Truth in the highest sense?

The Perfect Man

We may use any term—Adept, Master, Mahatma or any other. What is meant is really the Perfect Man, one who is inwardly, spiritually perfect. There is another word used in India, *Mukta,* which means a liberated being. This description denotes the nature of the accomplishment that the person has come to; it indicates also the nature of the being that he is. In such a case one prefers to use the word being rather than person. The being is the indwelling Life, the real man, the outer person just an expression or mask, as the very word indicates. A liberated being is one who has liberated himself from the bonds of flesh; that is to say, although he may wear a body, he is untrammelled by it; he is able to transcend its limitations. Not only can he put away the body at will but he is not dependent upon the condition of the body so far as his inner state is concerned. The word *Jivan-mukta* signifies that he is free even while living in a physical body; he is free from the necessity to be re-born.

Some of those who have become Adepts do not have a physical body but remain on the inner planes helping mankind by the forces they evoke and use or pour out. They are spoken of, particularly among Buddhists, as *Nirmanakaya,* a term which occurs also in *The Secret Doctrine* by H. P. Blavatsky. Though not wearing a physical form, they can be contacted on the inner planes, the astral or the mental in theosophical parlance; they can create at will a subtle form suited to themselves, expressing their nature, as necessary.

The liberated man is one who has finished with karma. He has liquidated all accumulated or existing karma and he makes no more although he is active in various ways. That is something which may be difficult to understand because he is active on the planes of thought, emotion and even outer affairs; yet somehow his action does not create karma. From an inner point of view all action has the aspect of releasing forces which are either sent out deliberately, or merely radiate.

When we think, certain forces are liberated; when we feel
or have certain emotions, that also sets up vibrations in the
inner realms; and of course when we act outwardly in relation
with people we liberate forces that move outward and affect
others. But these forces that emanate from the liberated
being do not return to him. That is the beauty of it; they do
not return to his self because there is no self. When the action
is performed just because it is right to perform it and there is
in it no element of self, then the forces which proceed from
such a being or centre move along a curve or curves which
rise upwards into the more subtle realms and do not return to
the point on the lower levels from which they emanate.

This is explained by C. W. Leadbeater in *The Inner Life*
and in other writings. Such a person is merely a force in
the direction of evolution, to use the language of that theosophical manual, *At the Feet of the Master*. What we have to
understand is that when he has reached the summit or goal
of human evolution, he is just such a force in reality, even
though he may have a distinct personality and a physical
body, and dress, eat and perform various other acts like other
people in physical bodies.

There is another word, used in Buddhist books, which is
also full of meaning, and that is *Asekha* which means " nothing remaining ". There is nothing to carry over; nothing
left of karma because it has been exhausted; nothing left of
lessons to learn through earthly existence. He is one who has
completed " the good journey " or " has crossed over to the
other shore," phrases which have been used of a person who
has come to that attainment. *Asekha* has also the meaning
that at any given moment there is in such a being's own inner
condition no forces impinging from the past. He does not
carry over any residue from the past into the present, so that

at every moment his cup is filled with the purest wine of life
with no dregs at all. Every moment is a new moment, because
memories from the past do not thrust into the present to
make him desire experiences he has previously had. If
there has been a relationship with a person in which he had
experienced some sensation, some pleasure, he is not attached
to that sensation and does not seek it; nor has he any feeling
of hatred or dislike towards any person that would prevent
him from helping that person. One who is a Master or an
Adept always helps everyone whom he encounters. Even if
in relation with a certain person there have been incidents in
the past of an unpleasant nature, they have all been washed
out; and the Master meets this person as though for the first
time. That means that every relationship begins freshly;
there is nothing carried over to embitter or sour it.

Enlightenment and Wisdom

There is also the word *Bodhisattva*, used in Buddhist books,
which has a cognate meaning. It means a being whose
nature is full of enlightenment and wisdom. *Sattva* means
either " strength " or " substance " and *bodhi* means " enlightenment ". Such a being is one who lives in Truth, not
in illusion or shadows. In one of the Mahatma Letters the
Master says that " the Adept lives in truth", which means
that his inner consciousness is centred in the truth of things
and not in something projected or invented by a mind prone
to wishful thinking. There is in his nature no shade of
falseness.

" Truth " is a word which has a much deeper, subtler and
fuller meaning than the facts of the external world, with regard
to which also we use the same word. Truth, as distinguished
from concrete facts, refers not so much to the outer form as to

the soul of things, so that when you go inwards into what the outer form imperfectly represents you come to a different nature from that of the material form; and that nature is a nature of harmony and beauty.

In this connection one might mention the word *Rishi*, often used in Hindu books. Each of these terms describes some point to be noted with reference to the nature of an Adept. All these terms have been used by the persons who invented them because they must have thought of some particular characteristic that the term expresses. *Rishi* means " seer " but it is not just ordinary clairvoyance, extrasensory perception of some sort. One who is clairvoyant or psychic may see rightly or wrongly; he often sees his own thought forms. There are many people who think that if a person is reputed to be a clairvoyant, whatever he says must be correct; but that is not so. In *The Voice of the Silence*, also by H. P. B., there is this sentence: " Seek not thy guru in these mayavic regions", that is, the region of the deceptive mind influenced by its memories, where very often a person is apt to see a form projected by his own subconscious mind and to mistake it for the truth. He may see something which seems real, but what he sees is shaped by preconceived ideas or his suppressed desires, by what he expects that appearance or form to be. A *Rishi* is one who sees the essence of things, the inner quality of a thing, whatever that thing may be. He sees into its true or inmost nature, the spiritual core that lies within the material form. His seeing is really a spiritual seeing. When you see the *soul* of the thing, not its psychic counterpart, then however crude and unshapely it may be outwardly, what you see is the divine idea, the perfection-to-be, embodied in it. He who sees it is the true seer.

10

There is the idea that all things are evolving towards their archetypes. The perfection which each distinct thing will ultimately attain, which will be revealed as a result of the evolutionary process, is already present in the thing in some subtle manner, or hovering over it invisibly, influencing the direction of its evolution. The whole object of this movement is ultimately to release or reveal what has been hidden all the time within it.

All these different meanings really coalesce and are present in what might be termed spiritual perfection. That perfection is a natural flowering of the divine seed that is in each human being. We learn that there is this divine spark or seed and at a certain point, when the way is clear, it begins to manifest itself. This manifestation can most truly be described as a kind of flowering

H. P. B. speaks of evolution as being triple. Three strands run through it. There is the evolution of the material form, the evolution of the intellect or psychic evolution, and in addition spiritual evolution which is an unfoldment of what is already present, the spirit being a fullness that exists always.

Flowering of Divinity

The flowering of the divine seed cannot be forced; it has to take place by itself in absolute freedom. It is not possible to use one's will to bring it about. That seed which has infinite potentiality manifests its nature in forms of harmony, and the flowering of it in each individual manifests a different type of harmony. The spiritual man is flowerlike in his inner nature, along with all the power that he may radiate—flowerlike with many petals which may either unfold like an open blossom or fold up as does the lotus flower, which is regarded in the Indian books as a symbol of spiritual beauty and wisdom.

One Adept differs from another in his appearance and in some ways in his nature. Although all alike may have the same wisdom, beauty and strength, yet each one is distinctive and different from the others. One average man is like another in his general shapelessness so far as his inner nature is concerned; but each Adept has a quality of his own, an influence which is like a fragrance, but unique, not reproduced in any other. It may be difficult for us to comprehend the nature of this uniqueness, but one can imagine how extraordinary it can be, and it represents the truth with regard to those who are called Adepts.

In some of the ancient Indian books there are references to this spiritual quality in an evolved being, and it is thought of as shining through every aspect and expression of his being. This fact is referred to in peculiar terms which may strike us as odd. They speak of his lotus eyes, his lotus feet, his lotus hands, his lotus throne and so on. The word lotus is used as an adjective for every aspect, feature and expression of his personality. All this means that his whole being or personality becomes the crystallization of an unearthly beauty; and the comparison is with the lotus which springs from the mud, rises through waters that may not be clean but muddy, and unfolds its beauty in the region of air and light. That is regarded as symbolic of human evolution and existence. Each human being starts his career as a germ of consciousness which expands, and very many changes take place. It is only when the active being of man rises to the plane which is beyond the muddy waters that the inner beauty and fragrance are revealed. But no symbol should be applied too literally. It should be regarded as an illustration of certain facts, designed to help our understanding.

The nature of the spirit or the spiritual nature has in it very great depths. It is also vast like the sky. This may seem to be a poetic comparison, but it represents the possibility as well as the truth with regard to spiritually perfected beings. One might speak of it as the poetry of truth. When you speak of truth in the spiritual sense with all its subtleties and beauty, it necessarily takes on a poetic colour. In that nature of truth and beauty what we may regard as opposites are perfectly blended. There is in it an extraordinary delicacy and refinement and there is also firmness and strength. The petals are soft like those of a rose, yet you cannot break or modify their shape or texture. It is responsive to the will that acts within, which we may call *its* innate will.

The seed of this extraordinary nature is also in ourselves. In trying to understand someone who may be called an Adept we are really trying to understand a nature which is latent in ourselves, to which we refer—without comprehending the reality of it—as the spiritual nature of man. There is in the book *Light on the Path* a sentence that speaks of " the glorious moment when perception awakes ". It refers to the awakening of the spiritual nature of man. The possibility of such perception is in everyone of us. Though that nature may be dormant at present, there comes to each one a point at which it awakes; and he begins to see something of the true, the hidden beauty in all beings and things. The Adept is one whose spiritual nature is fully awake and the rest of his being has been brought into complete harmony with it.

TOWARDS A SCIENTIFIC METAPHYSIC

> I have taken all knowledge to be
> my province—BACON.

CORONA TREW

ONE of the most notable changes in the one hundred years since the Theosophical Society was founded has been in the relationship of Theosophy and science. This is largely due to profound changes in the scientific view of the ultimate nature of matter, which has led to changes in the philosophy of science. This can no longer be termed materialistic in the sense used when theosophical literature was first being formulated by H. P. Blavatsky. With the discovery of radioactivity, the analysis of the structure of the atom, the identification of a multiplicity of sub-atomic entities which are manifestations of electro-magnetic energy, and the recognition of the role of energy force-fields in forming atomic and molecular patterns, the materialistic basis of scientific philosophy has been removed. Science is increasingly probing into the realm of the non-material. The newer sciences of psychology and sociology, which are beginning to accept paranormal phenomena as suitable material for scientific study, have led to a widening and deepening of the horizons of scientific thought.

Theosophy, the ancient Wisdom teaching, affirms the existence of non-material states of being and fields of conscious experience within the cosmos—psychic, intellectual and spiritual. These are within the range of human conscious-ness, and many thinkers recognize their existence and importance for the future progress of the life evolving in the universe. Some measure of the progress made is shown by the following passage from *The Imprisoned Splendour* by Dr. Raynor Johnson, physicist and psychical researcher: " We can see Man as a synthesis of principles or vehicles of growing significance and widening powers as we approach towards his essence which is one with the ultimate reality ".[1]

It is one of the basic postulates of theosophical philosophy that the investigations of the inner fields of conscious being can be attempted by the same scientific methods as are used by exact science in the study of the physical universe. Only the fields of study are different, and the task is a more exacting one for those who would attempt it.

Theosophy, in common with all great religions and philo-sophies, derives the universe and all in it from a pre-manifesta-tion state of latency and being, in which is contained the potentiality of all that ultimately emerges into manifestation. In the Proem of *The Secret Doctrine* of H. P. Blavatsky this state is termed " be-ness " rather than being, within which all is in a state of potentiality rather than actuality, since it is a latent undifferentiated spiritual state.[2] The word spiritual, often used in a vague verbal sense, is defined in *The Oxford Dictionary*: " of spirit as opposed to matter; inner nature of man; having the higher qualities of the mind ". In philo-sophical writings it concerns all that lies within and behind the ordinary reaches of the mind and the outer phenomena of the material objective universe. It represents that which sustains the phenomenal world.

[1] p. 262. Quest Book reprint. T. P. H.
[2] *S. D.*, I, 14-19 1st ed; I, 79-82, 6-vol. ed.

In the process of emerging into its present manifested state, the vast evolutionary scheme has passed from latent unity and be-ness into a conditioned duality or polarization of opposites. These are termed spirit and matter, and are represented in the contrasting states of subjectivity and objectivity. Subject and object are the root antitheses of human experience in the vast evolutionary scheme. What we term consciousness is a state of being or awareness born of the tension or polarity that exists between the polar opposites, spirit or subject (the inner pole of unity) and matter or object (the outer pole of manifoldness and diversity). This has been expressed as the pattern of existence woven between the " eternal poles of spirit and matter ", between the " One and the many ".

Spirit and Matter

Modern Theosophy has in the past 100 years developed a coherent metaphysics and philosophy of relationship between spirit and matter and the universe and man. During the past century, also, scientific thought has changed radically. An increasing number of scientists is now exploring the deeper metaphysical implications of scientific thinking about man and the universe. Metaphysics is now becoming acceptable to many progressive thinkers in its primary dictionary meaning of " theoretical philosophy of being and knowing: a philosophy of mind ". As illustration, an essay by Dr. Ervin Laszlo, Associate Professor of Philosophy, New York State College, on " The Recovery of Intuitive Wisdom in Contemporary Science", appeals for a recognition of unity within the framework of scientific thinking, if we are to reap the full philosophic implications of modern field-theories and the quantum mechanical revolution in contemporary physical theories of the nature of matter. " Through the deductive postulate of a universal space-time structure, physical science recovers a high degree of unity within its own design of investigation ".[1]

Laszlo further points out that this " transition from metaphysics to a unitary scientific framework " (i.e. bringing metaphysical thinking into a scientific framework) was foreshadowed in the writings of A. N. Whitehead. Writing in the 1920's and 1930's, his brilliant thought on the philosophy of science has hardly yet been fully comprehended or applied. In *Process and Reality* Whitehead affirms that speculative philosophy is " the endeavour to frame a coherent, logical, necessary system of general ideas in terms of which every element of an experience can be interpreted ".[2] Since all general truths condition each other, " the systemization of knowledge cannot be conducted in watertight compartments". Although courses available to university students are already becoming more broadly based and cover more than one specific scientific discipline such as biology, chemistry, physics, etc., the full philosophic implications of a unified field behind all phenomena is only now beginning to be recognized; the application of force-field concepts to our thought systems has only just begun.

The concept of organic unity, linking man and all living organisms with the universe, is the basic postulate of the Wisdom philosophy called Theosophy and it is the root doctrine of most of the great religions of mankind. As the dogmas of institutional religions lose their hold on men's minds and the pattern of organized religious practice breaks down in all religions, some understanding of the unity of human consciousness within a framework of universal mind is required if we

---

[1] *Main Currents in Modern Thought*, Vol. 25, p. 115, Foundation for Integrative Education, New York, 1969.

[2] Part I, Ch. 1.

are to preserve civilization and ennoble its cultural values. Progressive social scientists are in fact recognizing the complementary nature of religion, art and science regarded as " man's attempts to communicate with the universe ".

Laurence K. Frank, a social scientist in America, points out that " the assumption that the universe is orderly and meaningful is common to all three ".[1] Although science may be unable to explain the whys, as theology has attempted to do, or to provide values, images and patterns as art does, it " may help us to gain a feeling of belonging to the universe in which man exists as an organism that lives as a personality in a symbolic cultural world ". Furthermore, science has expanded our possibilities for knowing and communicating with nature and with man himself; it is this which theosophical theory attempts to do, and so it can be claimed as a science in this respect. It is thus timely to examine some of the basic advances in recent scientific thinking on man and the deeper aspects of the cosmos within which he is developing as both an organism and a personality.

Wheel of Life and Death

An attempt to correlate the philosophic implications of modern scientific thought with eastern philosophic teachings about the nature of human consciousness has been made in an essay in *Main Currents*. The author, Lawrence Le Shan, a research and clinical psychologist, presents this material as the result of research into the problem of human survival after biological death. He makes use of the concepts of modern field-theory in physics to find an answer to the age-old question " what is the nature of the relationship between the human being and the rest of reality and how does this

[1] *Main Currents*, Vol. 25, p. 45, 1968.

change with biological death?"[1] The problem as thus stated is that of every man who has, following the terminology of the Neoplatonist Plotinus, been described in theosophical literature as " the pilgrim in the cycle of necessity ", the cycle of necessity being the universe, in which the natural order of law controls the evolution of all forms. It is the wheel of life and death of Indian thought. Le Shan's solutions result in concepts similar to those of theosophical and religious philosophy.

Starting with the historical fact that we have " two quite different approaches in our attempts at solving the problems of what is the nature of things ", he develops a two-tier structure for our thinking about ourselves and the universe. The two approaches are those of classical physics or Newtonian mechanics and that of modern physics, field-theory or quantum mechanics. These are not as forbiddingly remote for the non-science thinker as they might seem. The approach of Newtonian mechanics or classical dynamics is based on the concept of the existence of unique units (things and events and indeed people); of atoms as particles existing in a real world. Le Shan terms this the commonsense approach, " where the focus is on the individual unit of being, separate in recognition from the rest of reality, and this individuality is considered most real; the placing of it in classification is only for the purpose of making it easier to think about and to remember ". It is this view that has enabled us to develop modern science and all its technological applications; it is the viewpoint of commonsense, individuality first, classification second.

The more recent quantum mechanical theory, however, which has had such widespread success in solving problems of physics and chemistry, is quite otherwise. In the words

[1] Vol. 26, p. 35, 1969.

of Le Shan, "the primary most real aspect of an entity is its part in the larger pattern and our perception of it cannot be responded to by ' oh, that is a so-and-so '. To perceive it at all apart from the total field is to perceive it as a sub-system, an artificially separated aspect of a field of stresses, a pattern ". A simple example which helps one to understand this viewpoint is that of watching the wind blow over a field of corn; here we perceive the changing pattern of the waves set up in the total field as the wind pressure shifts and changes direction. Only secondarily do we realize that individual ears of corn are moving about and shifting their position and varying the amplitude of their displacement from a mean point. This approach is that of " *Gestalt* first, individuality second ". *Gestalt* is defined as " an organized whole in which each individual part affects every other, the whole being more than the sum of its parts ".

These then are the two approaches forming a two-tier structure in our thinking that demands a synthesis if harmony is to be maintained. To resolve this paradox of complementary concepts, Le Shan follows earlier scientific thinkers, such as Erwin Schrödinger [1] and the metaphysicians, philosophers and mystics of all ages. He shows that by a simple intuitive jump an extension of the field approach involves the recognition that the " individual 'I' which can cognize both these conceptual approaches is also the totality of the field, of the whole. We can only fit our construct of the 'I' into the field-theory viewpoint by conceptualizing the 'I' as boundaryless in the continuum (the underlying space field); as not being separate from or isolated from the rest of what is; as not being limited by specific events such as the perceived ceasing of biological activity (i.e. death) ".

[1] *What is Life?* p. 87, Cambridge, 1944.

States of Consciousness

At this point in the logical development the author stresses the very real importance of both approaches, and that we should not underestimate the significance of the view of total Reality which each of them gives us. He goes on to ask a second question: " What can we say about consciousness and self-awareness in a cosmos structured from a field-theory viewpoint? ". To answer this he turns to the writings of the mystics, such as Evelyn Underhill, Meister Eckhart; to Zen Buddhist masters and the Vedantists; to teachers such as Sri Ramakrishna for a description of " progressions of mental states in which . . . our concepts of reality progress from the everyday view of commonsense and classical physics to the field-theory viewpoints ".

States of consciousness, from ordinary consciousness through various deeper levels to the complete mystical state, that of paranirvana, " have been described by thousands of individuals who have participated in each state ". All attest that the deeper states are accompanied by a retention of the state of self-awareness, but it is secondary to the " basic sense of being part of and totally in harmony with, the rest of the cosmos ". There is a sense of peace and harmony, knowledge of transcendence of space-time and of joy in these deeper states in which consciousness IS and IS the ALL.

Here we have a highly significant contribution from a modern psychologist showing that the new physical theories of the structure of the universe can be related to the higher states of consciousness recognized by mystics and philosophers of all ages. The universal substratum of this highest state of conscious being described in Le Shan's article is recognized as the ultimate in Buddhism, Hinduism, Taoism, Chaldean literature, the writings of Plotinus, Dionysius the

Areopagite, Meister Eckhart, Ruysbrook, St. Teresa of Avillia and St. John of the Cross, to name but some of the philosophical and mystical writers who have considered this supreme state of being.

Modern Theosophy presents an exposition of the perennial wisdom-teachings on these deeper states of consciousness. Its statements are based upon the *a priori* or deductive method used in ancient philosophy and are nonetheless scientific in the wider sense defined above. H. P. Blavatsky states in *The Key to Theosophy* that these have been checked and tested by untold generations of seers who only accepted as fact that which stood the test of developed spiritual senses far more reliable than the instruments of modern science. In a chapter on the " Unity of ALL in ALL " we find the answer given to the question, What are the theosophical teachings on God, the soul and man?

> In their origin and in eternity the three, like the universe and all therein, are one with the absolute Unity, the unknowable deific essence. (i.e. unknowable since knowing is a limited activity of consciousness) We believe in no *creation*, but in the periodical and consecutive appearances of the universe from the subjective on to the objective plane of being. . . .[1]

In his book *Mysticism*, T. C. Happold summarizes the chief characteristics of enlightenment which mystics of all times have spoken of as the ultimate state of consciousness.[2] It is characterized by a number of qualities. These are, first, irrationality, that is, it comes unexpectedly, suddenly, not by reasoning about it; secondly, it has a nöetic quality, that is, it is intuitive and of the nature of insight (to see the

[1] p. 83, T. P. H.
[2] pp. 45-48. Penguin.

inner meaning, essence or nature; to perceive); thirdly, it is authoritative and has a compelling certainty. Further, it is affirmative and accompanied by a sense of illumination. In addition, it gives the sense of beyond; it is also impersonal in tone, conveys a feeling of exultation and serenity, and it is characterized by momentariness, that is, abruptness and suddenness. This ultimate state of consciousness is recognized at the heart of Being in theosophical philosophy, as in the deeper religious philosophies of man. It is perhaps described in its purest form in the Buddhist literature of the Mahayana, or Northern, Buddhist School. Here it is termed variously satori or enlightenment; the attainment of Nirvana or union with the essence of mind; sometimes quite simply " suchness " and " sunya ", or " void ". Differing schools use slightly different terms.

Thus Mrs. Suzuki, an authority on Mahayana Buddhism, says that the Madhyamika school of Buddhist philosophy

> calls the highest truth " Void " (sunya) in that nothing connected with relativity can be predicted of it, but Void does not mean nothingness; it is only void or empty of all relative terms and descriptions. In other words it is absolute, that is, all that can be said of it fails to give any correct idea of it. In fact, it is no idea at all, for it is to be intuitively grasped and not logically represented. The intuitive understanding of void constitutes enlightenment.[1]

In Buddhist terminology enlightenment " is knowledge of the absolute which is absolute truth ". It is the knowledge of " suchness " (Tathata in Sanskrit and Shinzo in Japanese). We may compare this with H. P. Blavatsky's coined word be-ness, another attempt to describe the indescribable deeper states of consciousness.

[1] *Mahayana Buddhism*, A Brief Outline (with foreword by Christmas Humphreys) pp. 24-25, David Marlow, 1948.

Realms Beyond Thought

What is this state termed " suchness " or enlightenment?

> It is to see things as they are in themselves, to understand them in their state of self-nature, to accept them as themselves. To see things as they are, that is, in this state of suchness means to go back to a state of mind before such decisions of the knowing and the known take place.[1]

This from *Mahayana Buddhism* may be compared with a similar description by N. Sri Ram in *Life's Deeper Aspects*:

> When the being of consciousness which is in reality man sheds the limitations imposed by its dependence on the body ... there is a new consciousness which is consciousness in its pure nature. Being the pure subject, it perceives every object as it is and responds to it not only with freshness but with its full potential which far transcends mere mental knowing but includes that mode of sensitivity which is feeling and love. It is this utterly innocent, pure, fresh, ever-new state of mind and heart, which alone is open to the subtle nature and the heavenliness of things.[2]

It is increasingly being accepted that some realization of this state within our deepest being can be attained by human consciousness; that there is a state in which individuality can be united with a transcendent all-comprehensive unity. If, then, infinite space is the very substratum of consciousness, there being no differentiation therein, no *separate* individualized consciousness can exist there. All individualized consciousness is transmuted into the universal. Any attempt to define this state of awareness in rational terms can lead to a conceptualization of it which will destroy its essential nature. So each of the writers who have touched upon it, and lived

[1] p. 106.
[2] p. 88, T. P. H.

from it, use negatives or paradoxical statements. Plotinus spoke of " the flight of the alone to the alone ". The Zen Masters speak of the return of " no-thing " to " no-thing-ness ". The Buddhist Lankavatara Sutra tells men that " if they only realized it, they are already in the Tathagata's Nirvana, for in noble wisdom all things are in Nirvana from the beginning ". Such a state is to be experienced and realized, not thought about or conceptualized. Meditation and deepest contemplation aim at raising human consciousness to this state, for it is possible of attainment if one sets the right way about it. Man here passes from a condition of be-coming to be-ness or be-ing; from separation to unity. All who have touched upon this state attest that it is simply attained when the time is ripe by the "turning about" of the entire personality so that the light of the supreme Self reveals itself. It has been described as a spiritual revolution leading to enlightenment. Although it is a state of unity, self-consciousness is retained. When enlightenment comes, the qualities of the spiritual Self shine forth. The higher qualities of truth, integrity, love and compassion irradiate the centre of consciousness and stream thence to all around, as the sun shines on all. Only as men attain this transformation can we hope to resolve the problems which beset our age.

Many deep thinkers who are trained in scientific methods are perceiving this truth. The one universal mind that some modern scientists recognize as the sub-stratum of all phenomena is the basis of this state of unity. In the Theosophical Movement the attainment of this state of enlightenment, contemplation and meditation is seen as the next step for humanity.

RELATION OF CONSCIOUSNESS TO THOUGHT

> Consciousness the Will informing,
> till it fashion all thing fair—THOMAS
> HARDY, "The Dynasts."

PETER SEDGWICK

THE word consciousness is etymologically a compound of two Latin words, *con* and *scire*, which mean respectively " with " and " to know ". It has been suggested that this originally signified " knowing things together ", probably in the sense that several things are known simultaneously. The first to adopt the adjective conscious is said to be Francis Bacon (1601), who used it in the sense of " aware ", speaking in that particular case of someone who was " conscious to himself " that he had performed a duty satisfactorily. The noun consciousness is thought to have been first employed by John Locke (1690), who explained it to mean " the perception of what passes in a man's own mind ".[1]

In the nineteenth century, psychology, which only then began to come into its own as a separate science, was often called the science of consciousness; and psychologists have been disputing ever since as to the exact meaning of this term.

The so-called behaviourist school, having rejected introspection and anything subjective as alien to scientific study, rejected also the abstract word consciousness. This brings us to a point of primary importance. A materialist is normally

[1] *Encyclopaedia Britannica.*

11

understood to be a person who maintains that nothing exists outside of matter and thus denies, for instance, the reality of any such concept as soul or mind as distinct from matter. If consciousness is the " totality of the processes of being aware "[1] then, according to the materialist, these processes are purely material and cannot be anything but a function of the physical brain. Mind, therefore, is identical with brain. There is, it is affirmed, no such thing as a separate mind working through, or independently of, the physical brain.

Not a few modern writers, however, incline to a contrary opinion. " It seems to be fairly certain that one is able to be conscious apart from the brain, hence that consciousness is primarily in the *mind* and not in the body. The body is the mechanism through which mental consciousness penetrates into the physical world as far as the brain permits, and no further." [2] The theosophical hypothesis, which is supported by the general climate of present day thinking, definitely claims that mind is not the same as brain.

It is interesting to note the concept of matter that appears in *The Mahatma Letters to A. P. Sinnett.* One of the Tibetan Masters of the Wisdom writes that the philosophy of the brotherhood to which he belongs " falls under the definition of Hobbes".[3] Thomas Hobbes (1588-1675) was a thorough-going materialist (although to avoid difficulties he somehow managed to pay lip-service to the existence of God). The letter further states:

> When we speak of the one Life we also say that it penetrates, nay is the very essence of, every atom of matter . . . hence,

[1] *Collier's Encyclopædia*, Vol. 7, p. 196.
[2] L. J. & P. D. Bendit, *The Transforming Mind*, p. 28, T. P. H.
[3] Letter 10, p. 52, T. P. H.

is material, is *matter itself*[1]. . . We believe in matter alone, in matter in visible nature and matter in its invisibility as the invisible omnipresent omnipotent Proteus with its unceasing motion which is life and which nature draws from herself since she is the great whole outside of which nothing can exist.[2]

This leads to the postulate that there are numerous states of matter besides the physical. The letter does not state a belief in physical matter alone: indeed the word invisible makes clear that this is not meant. The term materialist in this use thus loses its usual connotation. This then is no denial of spirit—far otherwise. The theosophical philosophy is based on the notion of spirit in matter manifesting as activity throughout the universe. This accords with the theory (or is it perhaps fact?) that at the beginning of the manifested universe, the dawn of the "Day of Brahma", spirit and matter were unmanifest, being two inseparable parts of one whole. This idea, which finds expression also in other Mahatma Letters, has been formulated thus:

> In the theosophical concept there is postulated a First Great Cause, an Infinite Reality, within which all manifestation has its source. From this Root Cause of all there arise two fundamental and opposite polarities, "Spirit" and "Matter". Between these two a relationship springs up. This is the field of future manifestation, a tension between the two polar opposites which, having been divided, tend always to reunite. As that reunion takes place it gives rise to the phenomenon we call consciousness.[3]

Again, " The evolution of life is really an evolution of consciousness plus the evolution of the organization or form needed for its action." [4]

[1] *Ibid.*, p. 53.
[2] p. 56.
[3] E. Norman Pearson, *Space, Time & Self*, p. 6, T. P. H.
[4] N. Sri Ram, *Consciousness; its Nature & Action*, p. 9, T. P. H.

Consciousness and Life

The theosophical doctrine is that consciousness is one, undivided and universal. Psychology and psychoanalysis tell us of various subdivisions of human consciousness on the physical plane, and workers in this field have provided highly useful insights into the realm of the unconscious and its importance for mental health. All this, however, belongs to an extremely restricted field.

> The history of consciousness and its place in the world remain incomprehensible to anyone who has not seen first of all that the cosmos in which man finds himself caught up constitutes, by reason of the unimpeachable wholeness of its whole, a *system*, a *totum* and a *quantum*: a system by its plurality, a totum by its unity, a quantum by its energy; all three within a boundless contour.[1]

Consciousness, born of the One from which spirit-matter first came forth, permeates the universe and indeed all the universes in the ever-evolving scheme of manifestation. " Consciousness and life are identical. There is no life without consciousness, there is no consciousness without life." [2]

Consciousness evolved through matter, which paradoxically is said itself to be consciousness. " The densest matter, the physical, has its core of consciousness; the gas, the stone, the metal, is living, conscious, aware." [3] This may sound nonsensical to some; but the noted biologist J. B. S. Haldane wrote in this connection: " We do not find obvious evidence of life or mind in so-called inert matter . . . but if the scientific

---

[1] P. Teilhard de Chardin, *The Phenomenon of Man*, Bk. I. Ch. I. " Total Matter ".

[2] A. Besant, *A Study in Consciousness*, Ch. II, T. P. H.

[3] *ibid.*

point of view is correct we shall ultimately find them, at least in rudimentary forms, all through the universe." [1]

N. Sri Ram, as if elaborating on the words of Annie Besant quoted above, wrote:

> Although life and consciousness are in essence the same, there is an important difference between them, as between water and air. Both are plastic; life adapts itself to the body as water adapts itself to the configuration of the river-bed, a simile used by Bergson, but loses its freedom in so doing. Consciousness is infinitely more plastic, not bound to the organization as life is . . . Consciousness . . . can assume any form, mould itself into any image.[2]

Consciousness then is, in Teilhard de Chardin's words, a " vibration on a wide front ".[3] The wideness of the front is indeed inconceivably immense, particularly in the theosophical concept of it. It notes the doctrine of the numerous planes* of spirit-matter of which the cosmos is composed. Physical matter is the " lowest " of these planes of which we are conscious: the physical brain is the lowest instrument through which consciousness manifests in the human kingdom. Here we return to the question of the identity or non-identity of mind and brain. Theosophy contends that mind (a word with many meanings, difficult to define) is an aspect of universal consciousness, which in man has its abode on a different plane from that of the physical. This plane is nonetheless real, as are also the several spiritual planes " above " it; all

---

[1] Quoted, *Phenomenon of Man*, Bk. I, Ch. 3, " Existence ".

[2] *Consciousness*, p. 12.

[3] Bk. III, Ch. i, A(d).

* The use of the word " plane " is common in theosophical literature. *The Theosophical Glossary* states: " As used in occultism, the term denotes the range or extent of some states of consciousness, or of the perception of a particular set of senses, or the action of a particular force, or the state of matter corresponding to any of the above ". (p. 255)

are composed of matter which we are accustomed to describe as " subtler " than the matter of the physical world. The mental plane is the abode of the higher Self, the individuality or ego,* which is a fragment of the real Self, the Spirit. This, the monad, is a spark of the one universal divine fire of Life.

In the everyday field of human consciousness, the mind works through the physical brain as its only instrument for contact with the physical world and thus enables us to perceive with our senses. But on its own plane it is the thinker. Our thoughts, therefore, are mental stuff in the fullest sense of these words and as such they have their own life on their own plane. It has been said that " thoughts are things—have tenacity, coherence and life—they are real entities ".[1] Thought is a function of the mind, a product of matter certainly, but of subtler matter, not of mere physical molecular combinations. Thoughts being things, they dart in all directions and form patterns, peopling and filling the mental plane and impinging and interacting on other thought forms. Most people's thoughts are a kaleidoscopic medley; system and concentration are the exception rather than the rule. Other people's confused, trivial, and sometimes evil thoughts surround and attack our own, and vice-versa, and the result is a general scramble with a deplorable effect on mental equilibrium and peace.

Since no action can take place unless it has been previously thought, our thoughts are, in a way, more important than our actions. Hence Jesus is reported as saying that an evil action is already committed when the corresponding thought is harboured. It can thus readily be understood that schools

* See footnote p. 15.
[1] *M.L.* 9, p. 49.

of meditation and yoga attach great importance to the control of thought, not only as a means of progress along the individual path of enlightenment but as a way to influence our environment and our fellow men. Many people are inclined to regard contemplative monastic orders, for instance, as anti-social because they " do " nothing. In the light of what has been stated, however, it should be clear that their individual and collective thought-forms, in so far as they are conducive to spirituality and peace, could greatly influence, in concrete fashion, the entire neighbourhood. The same applies, of course, to individual contemplatives such as the Indian Sannyasis.

Power of Thought

Thought, then, is a real and tremendous force. From the occult point of view, the significance of the statement is immediately manifest. But there is concrete (or analytical) thought and abstract thought: there is thought that dissects and thought that synthesizes. These two modes of thinking have sometimes been considered as subdivisions of the mental plane, the lower and the higher. The latter, the world of the Ego, is said to be linked with the intuition, a word that is an imperfect translation of Buddhi, a term that occurs often in Indian philosophy. But, superior as Buddhi may be, it would be a mistake to regard the lower-mind, the intellect, the mind of analysis and logic, as of minor importance in the search for truth. At the present stage of human development it is essential to think clearly, logically and analytically on this lower plane before one can hope to transcend it. It is not necessary to be clever in order to be good. But analytical intelligence and clear thought are highly important qualities in comparative religion, philosophy and science, the study of which is one of the objects of the Theosophical Society. Obviously also we must think in our daily life. Yet this very thinking conditions us, and all conditioning blocks an approach to truth or reality.

What is the effective connection between consciousness and thought? Consciousness can exist without thought in sub-human kingdoms, but in man consciousness is nearly always bound up with thought. N. Sri Ram writes:

> In man consciousness has a range beyond that of any animal and, further, he is capable of thought, which is a sort of superstructure raised on the ground of his basic awareness. . . . We hardly know what it is to be aware without thought, with consciousness free from superimpositions and at peace with itself.[1]

This is a theme that has been exhaustively treated by J. Krishnamurti, who has constantly affirmed that in order to attain basic awareness and thus to come face to face with reality and truth, all thought must be eliminated; because thought is always old, always conditioned. In the very moment when thought is born it is of the past.

This does not imply a sort of hypnotic lethargy, but the exact opposite. Basic awareness without the interference of thought is a state of the most intensely active *Being*. In describing this state as negative Sri Ram writes:

> The word negative is to be understood in the sense of being highly sensitive and not as unsusceptible and indifferent . . . Such a state of mind and heart is open to the actual, to the truth. In this state there is no attempt or desire to escape from reality, no subjectivity that spells withdrawal of contact from the actuality of things.[2]

[1] *Consciousness*, p. 3
[2] *ibid.*, p. 4.

We might almost say, with Kant, *das Ding an sich*—the thing in itself—and Krishnamurti would say "what *is*". The "actual" is here Reality itself, uncoloured by the super-impositions caused and projected by the conditioning of the mind. We are all conditioned by what we have learnt, by what we have experienced, by the way we were brought up. Although it is almost impossible to eliminate this conditioning, awareness of it can neutralize its psychological results, so that we may experience the real. In this sense then, thought must be transcended if reality is to be apprehended.

Consciousness works through all the planes of nature, and it is possible, by developing the faculties latent in man, to expand consciousness and raise it to higher levels. The unfoldment of these hidden powers is one of the objects that now occupies the attention of many research workers. This, however, is just the fringe of the powers latent in man. Theosophy goes much farther than the tentative steps undertaken by the majority of these workers. It indicates the various planes of nature on which consciousness can operate.

H. P. Blavatsky said that psychic powers " are comparatively easy of acquirement by artificial means, but fade out as soon as the nerve stimulus exhausts itself. Real seership and adept-ship, which is accompanied by true psychic development, once reached is never lost ".[1] So, although a certain expansion of consciousness can be attained by means of drugs, the results so attained are regarded as largely spurious and trivial from the deeper point of view; not justifying the means. This is no royal road and leads only a little way, often in the wrong direction.

All genuine mystics throughout the ages have known that the goal is the uniting of the fragmentary human consciousness

[1] B. C. W., VI, 334. T. P. H.

with the glorious divine consciousness in which it has its root. This unity is real and present; it is there. All we have to do —and this is our major task—is to become aware of it. It is not, in other words, a question of forging this unity; it is a question of opening our eyes and seeing it.

To sum up, consciousness (or life) and matter are inseparable; two parts of one whole. Thought is the action of consciousness working as mind, which gives rise to thought-forms on a normally invisible plane described as the mental—a plane consisting of its own subtle but none the less real matter and, incidentally, only one of the many planes on which consciousness can be active. The brain is the instrument through which thought filters into the physical world.

The higher planes of consciousness can be discovered and experienced through the unfoldment of man's hidden powers. The various schools of yoga throw light on these possibilities.

There is one universal Consciousness—call it, if you like, a world Soul. The final human goal is the linking up or union of man's fragmentary consciousness with this. Mystics, in various ways and using differing terminologies, are agreed on the reality of this experience. H. G. Wells wrote some fifty years ago that man will " reach out to his realm among the stars ". Man has already begun to do this. But if the science of the future concerns itself with the exploration of the higher planes of being, man may set out to explore, in higher states of consciousness and in subtler bodies, the starry immensities of the divine.

MYSTICAL QUEST FOR REALITY

. . . to know ourselves Parts & Proportions of one wondrous whole—COLERIDGE

HUGH SHEARMAN

IN the early days of the Theosophical Society mysticism was not regarded, as it was at a somewhat later period, as standing in antithesis to occultism. H. P. Blavatsky used the word mystic quite loosely to refer to anybody who had experience and knowledge of " inner " things. Indeed in many passages where the word mysticism is used in *The Secret Doctrine* a later generation would see little reason why the word occultism should not be substituted for it.

Equally, her definition of occultism or Theosophy sometimes implied a spirit of surrender which, expressed in only slightly different words, might not have seemed inappropriate to describe the attitude of some acknowledged mystic such as St. John of the Cross. Thus, in one of the essays subsequently published in *Practical Occultism*, she wrote:

> True Occultism or Theosophy is the " Great Renunciation of Self ", unconditionally and absolutely, in thought as in action. It is Altruism, and it throws him who practises it out of calculation of the ranks of the living altogether. " Not for himself, but for the world, he lives ", as soon as he has pledged himself to the work. Much is forgiven during the first years of probation. But no sooner is he " accepted " than his personality must disappear, and he has to become a mere beneficent force in Nature.[1]

[1] pp. 50-51. T. P. H.

In the early years of the twentieth century, however, mysticism tended to be seen, both inside and outside the Theosophical Society, in a largely Christian and certainly in a devotional context; and some of the most influential writings on the subject came from prominent Christians, such as Baron von Hügel, W. R. Inge and Evelyn Underhill. Within the Theosophical Society, G. R. S. Mead published a series of works making available the literature of western traditions of mysticism outside as well as inside Christianity, including the early Gnostics and the teachings of Plotinus and his successors.

With this background, Annie Besant often described the mystic and the occultist as two temperamental types, taking two different paths, the mystic aspiring through ardent feeling and the occultist advancing through intellect and will.

Later, however, probably partly as a result of the pervasive influence of J. Krishnamurti in breaking down fixed concepts, there was a growing tendency in the Theosophical Society to see mysticism and occultism as two aspects of one human experience. Rohit Mehta states in *The Intuitive Philosophy* that in mysticism we commune while in occultism we communicate. This very fairly defined the use which had been made of the term occultism to refer to what was descriptive and what was concerned with method; but it also carried the implication that without some indescribable motivation, some wordless intuition of purpose from within, all descriptions or techniques could be in vain.

The words mystic and mysticism are derived from the Greek verb μύάω meaning to close the lips. The implication of this extends to the closing of the eyes and other sense organs and hence the seeking or experiencing of a truth that is not dependent on communication or sense data. The very notion of such an experience demands that human nature should be capable of outpassing in some way the Cartesian dualism of subject and object, knower and known. In the *Yoga Sutras* of Patanjali it is said (1:41) that, for the enlightened yogi, the knower, knowledge and the known are one. And it is significant that today there is some tendency among academic students of philosophy to revolt against the once apparently ineluctable dualism which Descartes seemed to impose upon epistemology.

Madame Blavatsky in *The Secret Doctrine* saw *advaiti* or non-dualistic Vedantism as the truest and most deeply based philosophy and saw Buddhism as being fundamentally just another interpretation of the same view of truth. An early contribution to western understanding of Vedanta was the translation, by Mohini M. Chatterjee, a prominent member of the Theosophical Society and of Madame Blavatsky's immediate circle, of the *Viveka Chudamani* or *Crest Jewel of Wisdom* of Sri Shankaracharya, a classical exposition of the unitive basis of Vedanta. Whether expressed in Vedantic terms, as the oneness and partlessness of Brahman, or in Buddhist terms as Nirvana, or in Christian terms as that state in which " God shall be all in all ", the basis of all expositions of Theosophy has at all times been, in fundamentals, uncompromisingly unitive.

The descriptions of existence and the universe, which are set out in various forms in the literature of modern Theosophy, all imply that we come forth from unity and return to unity and that an underlying unity is the only reality giving meaning and purpose to evolution or to any other process. Evolution is seen as a change from a state of being unconsciously grounded on unity, through a state of conscious disunity, to a state of being consciously grounded on unity. The middle phase of apparent disunity has a mysterious transforming function between the unconscious unity of our origin and the conscious unity of our goal and achievement. The middle phase is summed up in the fact that we are human.

One Mind and Heart

It is possible to suppose that there is in nature one mind and one motivating heart, providing every organism and every creature with a pattern of instinctual response upon which it unconsciously depends. In our human condition, which has often been seen as one of alienation from nature, of exclusion from a Garden of Eden, mind and heart are consciously asserted as separate individual possessions. This is the state in which we are deeply concerned with the dualism of subject and object and it is that state of consciously divided selfhood which gives rise to tragedy.

But all the great religions put before us the notion of a rediscovery of our unified condition, when conflict is outpassed, when we are integrated once more, when we can become " as a little child ", our robes washed white, our innocence restored. In its etymological sense, religion is a re-linking. It implies a restoration of our rootedness in the one reality, a rootedness which we lost, by turning our backs upon the instinctual uniformity of response which is seen in wild nature, and becoming human.

In the human condition, mind is made individual. It is associated, or indeed identified, with a particular individual organism, with its memories, defensive reactions and all that segregates us from others. It is no longer that universal mind, the " mind of God ", which those who pursue natural theology or certain traditions of nature mysticism, claim to find in nature. It has become " your " mind or " my " mind. But when the segregated mind has exhausted the pursuits of

competitive separateness that constitute so much of human life,
it can rediscover its unity with universal mind. Some would
say that it is as if universal mind rediscovers the individual
and takes him once more to itself.

The experience of one in whom this discovery has been
made is described in the following words in H. P. Blavatsky's
little book *The Voice of the Silence*: " His mind, like a becalmed
and boundless ocean, spreadeth out in shoreless space."
This is saying in rather different words what must be meant
by Edwin Arnold's line, " The dewdrop slips into the Shining
Sea ." It has been said of this that, in effect, the shining
sea flows into the dewdrop and the latter remains, retaining its
individuality as a natural function or facet of that unity with
which it is now discovered to be at one. In many mystical
literatures, too, the metaphors or similes used to describe or
at least to point to the possibility of a surrender of the particular self to the universal are sexual, merging again into those
descriptions of seas and fluidic things.

In the traditions of the great religions, those who consciously rediscover reality as one and universal—or, as some
would put it, are rediscovered by reality—are said to find
themselves in a great company of others who have made the
same step. In all human life, what most unites us is shared
experience, and this supreme experience creates a brotherhood,
a communion of saints, a unanimity of the wise. Those who
have, to a greater or lesser degree, entered this brotherhood form
the higher self-consciousness of humanity, the spearhead of
advancing collective human evolution. Of this shared consciousness of those who have entered what may be regarded as the
stage of evolution beyond the human, C. W. Leadbeater wrote:

It is like a great calm shining ocean, so strangely one that
the least thrill of consciousness flashes from end to end of it

instantaneously, and yet to each member it seems to be absolutely his own individual consciousness, though with a weight and a power and a wisdom behind it that no single human consciousness could ever have... There is nothing down here to which this consciousness can be adequately compared; to touch it is to come into contact with something new and strange, yet inexpressibly wonderful and beautiful, something which needs no evidence and no comparison, but asserts itself to be of a higher and unknown world.[1]

When so much is said about " mind " in the literature of Theosophy, it is easy to miss the essentially mystical implications of a good deal that is propounded in that literature. Though it can do wonderful things, the discursive mind is usually seen by exponents of Theosophy as a neutral faculty, to be set in motion by something other than itself, much as Hume said that the mind has to be the slave of the " passions ". It can be stirred and put to work by the desires of the outer personality or by the unitive wisdom of our deeper nature. Thus in the *Bhagavad Gita* mind or *manas* is not referred to by itself. It appears either as *kama-manas*, which is mind set in motion by the desires and repulsions of competitive personality existence in the world, or it is *Buddhi-manas*, illumined mind, mind activated by wisdom, or by what is sometimes called pure reason, the innate and unitive wisdom of reality, when reality has not been evaluated by the greedy demands of a competitive personal self and is therefore able to make its whole and direct impact upon the mind.

In either case the activating source is non-rational. With mind set in motion by desire and passion of a personal and compulsive nature, it may be called a sub-rational motivation, even though this would apply to many of those complex

[1] *The Masters and the Path*, " The First Initiation ", T.P.H.

intellectual achievements in which mankind takes a considerable pride. And when mind is set in motion and given
its pattern by inner wisdom and the unmediated impact of
reality, it may be called a supra-rational motivation.

The literature of modern Theosophy is largely oriented
towards mankind's rediscovery of a supra-rational purpose
in life. And this is necessarily a mystical pursuit. It cannot
be translated into terms of sense data or of any objects with
which the discursive mind can be concerned, not even with
those packagings of thought which we call concepts. Being
unitive, it is, as Patanjali noted, beyond even the duality of
subject and object, knower and known, on which most of our
processes of scientific observation very properly rest.

Most of that theosophical literature, however, addresses
its initial appeal to the ordinary personal mind by attempting
to demonstrate in various ways that this can indeed be so
and that behind and underlying all this apparently discordant
diversity there can be a harmonizing transcendent unity.
This has been attempted in many different ways. Often it
has been done by presenting a descriptive system which, if it
were true, would have to presuppose an underlying unity.
Such descriptive systems or models, which form an important
part of theosophical literature, have to be studied with a
background recollection that, since truth and unity refer to
what must be supra-rational, no system devised or expounded
by the discursive mind can contain the truth.

Beyond the Mind

Theosophical study, therefore, is not primarily for the
purpose of getting information but rather for leading the
mind to a condition in which a deeper intuition can come awake
and something that is " beyond " the mind find expression in

12

our lives and experiences. And some mutual inconsistency in the details of the various systems or models or ontological descriptions studied is unimportant. As in the case of the many disparate cultures and the religious images and beliefs of mankind, the point of convergence or of reconciliation is not at the level of the factual mind but in a certain intuitive recognition and response within the individual.

The study of religions within the modern Theosophical Movement has tended, too, to be pursued in terms of their psychological and mystical implications rather than in terms of their theological systems. Their stories and mythologies have been seen as dramas which objectify symbolically things of the inner life and the subjective world. The Christ of theosophical Christian studies has been less the historic teacher and more the " Christ in you the hope of glory " referred to by St. Paul.

Most descriptive theosophies have a characteristic in common that they offer a model of the invisible anatomy of man, a description of human nature in terms of analysis into a number of " principles ". And nearly all of them make clear in their explanations or diagrams that the fundamental principles in our make-up, and those which establish our true rootedness in the real, are those which are " above " or " beyond " the discursive, analytical and factual mind. By implication, the awakening of those principles within us would have to be a mystical event, beyond the scope of analysis or comparative thinking and not the end product of any synthetic or syllogistic process.

Madame Blavatsky is reported, by one who took notes of some of her oral comments, to have described as follows the rediscovery of reality, with its need to refrain from clinging to particular systems:

As one progresses ... one finds conceptions arising which, though one is conscious of them, one cannot express nor yet formulate into any sort of mental pictures. As time goes on these conceptions will form into mental picture. This is a time to be on guard and refuse to be deluded with the idea that the new found and wonderful picture must represent reality. It does not. As one works on, one finds the once admired picture growing dull and unsatisfying, and finally fading out or being thrown away. This is another danger point, because for the moment one is left in a void without any conception to support one, and one may be tempted to revive the cast-off picture for want of a better to cling to. The true student will, however, work on unconcerned, and presently further formless gleams come, which again in time give rise to a larger and more beautiful picture than the last. But the learner will now know that no picture will ever represent the Truth. This last splendid picture will grow dull and fade like the others. And so the process goes on, until at last the mind and its pictures are transcended and the learner enters and dwells in the World of No Form, but of which all forms are narrowed reflections.[1]

Rediscovered unity reveals itself in stages to the individual, each enlargement of experience seeming to be beyond any possibility of being superseded by anything more beautiful and splendid and yet each in turn being superseded.

Within the Theosophical Movement, though not within the framework of any theosophical society, some have pursued efforts to still the mind and open human nature to deeper reality from within by establishing specialized fields of experience in terms of ceremony or sacrament. One finds in the structure of ceremonial and related procedures a reflection of the principle, declared by Giordano Bruno and developed in some detail by Madame Blavatsky, that man is the microcosm

[1] *How to study Theosophy* by H. P. B., pp. 10-11. T. P. H.

of the universe. What is aimed at in the theosophically oriented ceremony is the attuning of the particular to the universal, the mystical opening of the individual consciousness to that which " spreadeth out in shoreless space ".

The Theosophical Society, which places no restriction upon belief or the expression of experience, gives recognition to the infinite variety of human temperament as revealed in the pursuit of living truth. And many of these pursuits are clearly mystical in their goals and insights.

There is, of course, a danger in the fact that much that is spurious, exploiting, atavistic or simply silly can clothe itself in the language of the traditional forms of mystical pursuit. The source and criterion of safety that Theosophists have always found lies in the service of humanity. If a pursuit involves sacrifice and the abandonment of the personal self for the welfare of humanity, without distinction of what sort of humanity we are concerned with in terms of race, sex, creed, caste or colour, that pursuit probably has a validity and a potentiality of fruitfulness. Otherwise we are probably looking in a wrong direction and inviting frustration.

A former President of the Theosophical Society, C. Jina-rājadāsa, in *The Nature of Mysticism*, reviewed the main patterns of mysticism and claimed to find among them a distinctive theosophical mysticism. He saw it as a mysticism of work and service.

One mighty Divine Thought is building and unbuilding according to a Plan alike the atom, the human soul and the stars. This Thought which is at work, this Plan which is being carried out, is a radiant Love, an omnipotent Power and an entrancing Wisdom. . . The Maker of the Plan is Himself the Plan; and therefore to work for the Plan, to cooperate with it ever, is the way to communion with Him and to the discovery of the God that we are.[1]

And he went on to say that the Plan "is not a mechanical working of the forces of nature" but "a wondrous Personality . . . beyond all personality and yet a Person of Persons."

The philosophical possibility or impossibility of retaining within a unitive view of reality any kind of God-image is a very delicate one. Obviously any such image in the mind of the individual is bound, according to its own presuppositions, to be transcended and outpassed, perhaps by a different and more splendid image. Yet a specific God-image is a deeply felt need for some temperaments, a poetic need and a means by which certain qualities of the whole can be concentrated as through a lens. At certain stages of the mind's adjustment to the notion of ultimate reality, it may even seem to be a logical need and the only possible interpretation of certain experiences. And that need, of whatever nature, is not removed merely by the destruction of a particular image. It is evident that some images are limited and limiting, and their imposition upon the minds of others is likely to be resisted. But the rightness or wrongness of anybody responding to a God-image in the course of the quest for a mystical reality beyond personal reason is not a matter on which a Theosophist will wisely attempt to pronounce.

It is to the infinite untapped resources of nature, particularly human nature, that the Theosophical Movement looks for its renewal down the centuries. Descriptive literature and things that are put into words can steady and prepare the mind; but growth and renewal come from the fresh, and at first formless, upwelling of "life" itself, the insight that is not contained by the reason of the discursive mind but springs

[1] pp. 69-70. T. P. H.

from a certain artistic innocence, a certain experience of frontierless love.   Every such insight, though formless in its beginnings, inevitably gives rise to forms in the world of the discursive mind, perhaps breaking up old forms while it inspires new ones; but such a movement as the Theosophical Society, however much involved in institutions and concepts, depends for its life on this fresh vitality from within, the fountain of healing water, the song of undiscovered things in the human heart.   If it is to remain alive it cannot escape being to an unpredictable extent a movement with an inner core of living and actual mystical experience.

AN INVOCATION

O hidden Life, vibrant in every atom,
O hidden Light, shining in every creature,
O hidden Love, embracing all in Oneness,
May each who feels himself as one with thee
Know he is also one with every other.

ONE'S OWN PATH TO THE WAY OF ALL

I am involved in Mankind—
JOHN DONNE

CURT BERG

ONE of the paradoxes of life is that uniqueness is a key to unity.

We know that every human being is unique, at least not like any other we have met. Yet usually we have only perceived that uniqueness in a superficial way. Often we meet other people with our inner reactions, with preconceived ideas about someone, or about that type of person, with expectation, or fear; or perhaps associating him with some other man or some other situation; or we do comparisons of various kinds.

This means that we do not perceive so much the man we meet, as a picture of him formed and coloured by the content of our own minds. If we watch ourselves, we shall find that almost always there is such an element in our meetings with our fellows. We have not met the real man, not seen truth, reality, on this point of life.

It is often the recollection of past experience—what has been called psychological memory—that inhibits us from seeing people and things and events as they really are. Moreover, we tend unconsciously to project on to others aspects of our being that we do not like. In doing so we create a mirror, as it were, in which we do but see our own imperfections reflected. Both these factors distort our sight, and prevent us from seeing correctly.

The first step towards removing these limitations is to become aware of them. We can then observe them objectively, and start to deal with them. For it is possible to see another person as he is, free of preconception and misconception, at least to a greater extent than usual. It is possible to be quiet inwardly, open to the person in front of us, with no attitude of defence or suspicion; to meet the other man or woman quietly, without reactions in our own consciousness, and to perceive something of his being in ourselves.

In doing this, we also see that our fellow man is an entity of life and consciousness, and that he is in the process of development, like ourselves. We come to understand that there is the same life in all, expressing itself uniquely in each case. We can extend this to flowers, birds, animals; and gain some understanding of the one Life having an infinite variety of expressions.

The one Life behind all is often referred to by the term unity, which is perceived when we accept diversity as so many manifestations of that Life. Unity is a reality at the root of existence—there is much testimony to that throughout the ages, which shows its deep significance for the individual. Unity, then, must surely be the true source of man's life and of a right way of living; and ultimately the purpose of life has to be realization of this unity. Further, it must be of the utmost importance for the relationship between individuals, groups, nations.

Many people have had a faint glimpse of unity, vaguely perceiving that they have that dimension in themselves. This should mean a new and ever fresh way of meeting others; but the small glimpse is too easily swallowed up or repressed by the thought processes constantly going on. The mind, the thought process, is a most valuable and necessary tool for man; but if the forces of the mind are so strong that he does not master them, then his inner possibilities are inhibited.

Let us think again of how we mostly meet other human beings —with preconceived ideas, comparisons, expectations, fears. On looking more closely, we find that we are living, thinking, acting, in a very well established set of ideas and emotions; well established, but capable of variations and different expressions within its own sphere. This pattern is often so firm that we never get outside it. One contributing factor to this imprisoning is that we never get the idea that we could go outside it. Another factor is that we should lose some of our security if we went outside this sphere. So we seldom or never break through the shell to contact life nearer its source —as indeed it is to be found within us. Pursuing this examination a bit farther, we shall probably find, for instance, that a natural trust in life is replaced by reliance on knowledge and the false security of possessions; and that, lacking union with Life, we depend on the love and acceptance of others.

This means that we mostly think and act in a mechanical, automatic way; a certain sense impression, or a word, sets our psyche going along a well-trodden track.

Let us suppose, however, that an individual who is still to some extent subject to these limitations has yet got a vision of unity and its significance in life strong enough to induce him to come nearer to it. Then he finds he must challenge the mechanical way his mind is acting. N. Sri Ram wrote:

> We have identified ourselves with so many things, our bodies, our race, nationality, property, ideas, habits. We have to withdraw from identification with everything external to ourselves. Our identification with all this has taken place

in time. What came into existence in time can be seen through
and ended by us. Such disengagement. . . is not escapism.
It is the attainment of a state of freedom and universality . . .
the return of the soul or consciousness to its original state.

Be Still and Know

How is that done? Many roads and methods are described
in different sorts of yoga and meditation, but they all seem to
come to this main point: the need to still the mind, stop the
thought processes and just watch, observing things as they are.
Practices of concentration can help in this; but in them also
the important thing is to have a mind that is still, not roving
and restless. That is the portal to faculties beyond mind, to
intuitional glimpses, to an experience of unity, of all life
being one.

As the word meditation is used for thinking along a certain
line, or with certain pictures before the mind, it should be noted
that the state of mind referred to is not that of putting ideas
together, or building up something, but a state in which real
stillness makes it possible to sharpen the power of perception
so that it can cut through illusions and false ideas. To
achieve stillness of mind is something the individual has to do
himself. No one can do it for him, others can only give hints
and advice.

The same rule applies when we turn to another aspect of the
conditions necessary for the opening of the individual to unity
in himself: the way we are living, the way we meet and treat
human beings and other living creatures is of great importance.
If we are causing harm to others, if we are pursuing our own
advantage at the expense of others, if we use wrong means,
then our sight is obscured and we cannot see clearly. This,
too, we have to regulate for ourselves.

Another way of expressing this need for a right way of living is to say that what is wanted is the transforming of one's whole being into something that can better respond to the deeper notes of existence. It is a question of retuning oneself to be able to perceive notes that are purer and more beautiful expressions of the unity of Life. So also in this respect each one has to do something fundamental himself.

Rules of conduct and behaviour may come into the picture here. Many people, probably the majority of those who have been brought up in one or other of the great religions, have got an inner reaction against such rules, which come from a church or from some social class system. They know intuitively that man is born free, and so something of a revolt takes place. The way of dealing with such a situation seems to be to come to the understanding that, even if these rules have a social function, yet they stem from an insight into the conditions for man's development from the limited sphere of the strivings of worldly life to the realization of his inner unity with all. What the individual can do is to see how certain behaviour works, what are its results; and it will be clear that some modes of behaviour work more in the direction of clear sight and harmony than others. Anyone who really wants to do so can find out by experiment and observation. Often mere observing is enough.

One question is often asked: to make progress worth mentioning in the spiritual life, is it not necessary to have a teacher, a guru? The value of a competent teacher is of course very great; but some points should be noted. Even if we have a teacher, a guru, the actual work has to be done by ourselves, because of the necessary retuning of our whole life. If we think a guru indispensable, then we are probably not using our inner resources to the full: we do not rely enough on our inner potentialities, either for following guidance in a fruitful way or for going on with none.

Moreover, in order to profit by the teaching and guidance of a genuine guru, we have to be able to function on a " wavelength " that at least approximates to that of the guru and his teaching; that is, we must be clear enough of personal reactions to be open to truth and beauty, to see the needs of others, and to give help as a natural reaction. This means that we have to be open to function as a channel through which love, truth, beauty can flow. In this case we can learn from life, from the events and circumstances in our lives, to a high degree. Whether or not such experience and knowledge comes through a guru of high order is not important; the important thing is that we are open to these influences and learn from them. In any case their source is the Unity, from which all comes.

Path of Self-Realization

The whole of our path towards self-realization and unity has to be in the atmosphere of ourselves being part of the whole—mankind and all lower kingdoms. And being a part, we must not only avoid doing harm, but also act positively in the interest of the whole. The idea of spiritual development being the realization of unity, the one Life in all, is thus expressed in the *Bhagavad Gita*:

There is only *one* Self in the universe;
That Self is the self in all.

So coming to our true Self is to come to the Self of all, and our path towards the truth and self-realization must be true to this all the way.

What is the purpose in life for a person who has got a glimpse of this perspective and finds that there is a deep response in himself? First, he has to learn to be tranquil enough inwardly to be able simply to receive without colouring or distortion. Secondly, he will retune himself and his way of living to the deeper sides of life, to a note that is purer and nearer to Life at its source, to Unity. That means renunciation of many personal wishes, ceasing to respond to coarser vibrations, not because they are " evil " or to be condemned, which pertains to our intellectual set of ideas, but because we see that they counteract our retuning to the wider, the purer, the more beautiful, and we find that in the long run we prefer the latter. We make a conscious choice.

This also means that we are not screening off life around us. We take part in it. We do not omit doing what we see needs to be done if we can do it; but we hold our understanding of what needs to be done with light hands, with an open mind, ready always for deeper understanding, and ready to do our part of the work.

The keynote of all this is perhaps an open mind and reverence for life in all its expressions. There is a simile that sums up this attitude to our fellowmen and life around us. It is the simile of a well. What is a well? A well is a place where there is water, but the well has not created the water. A well is merely a place where the water, which is everywhere in the depths of the ground, can be brought to the surface for the benefit of men.

That is the way we should look at ourselves and our fellows. Eternal wisdom, truth and beauty are in each of us. Each of us has to try to become a place where that eternal truth and beauty can well up for the benefit of all. We shall find that, according to our capacity to become such wells, so will be our ability to help and to serve all those whose lives at any time or at any point touch ours.

YOGA: THE SCIENCE OF WITHOUT AND WITHIN

> Seek the way by retreating within.
> Seek the way by advancing boldly
> without—*Light on the Path*

IANTHE H. HOSKINS

Quot homines, tot sententiae. If it is true of affairs in general that the opinions of men are as many and varied as those who hold them, it is especially so in the case of attempts to circumscribe and define the Wisdom tradition presented under the name of Theosophy. To one, Theosophy is a precise body of doctrine, to another an attitude towards life, to a third all that is contained in the writings of a particular teacher, to yet others a synthesis of all these. An attempt to explore the inter-relatedness of Theosophy and any other system must therefore be prefaced by a clarification of the view of Theosophy held by the writer.

Theosophy, translated as divine Wisdom, is explained as that Wisdom that is held, or would be held, by god-like beings. As such, it is not only the totality of knowledge, but also the wisdom that must arise in an individual from the possession of that knowledge.

However remote the possibility of such possession may seem to us as we now are, an exercise of imagination playing with the words " the totality of knowledge " may be admissible as a means of picturing at least in barest outline some aspects of their infinite content. Without this exercise, the phrase is likely to remain a poetic but meaningless abstraction. All that ever has been, all that is, all that ever shall be, is there. Time and space and the laws of becoming are there. Worlds visible and invisible are there, worlds objective and subjective, the mysteries of life and consciousness, of cause and purpose, of origins and ends. All human creativity is there also, with suffering and joy and striving and seeking. Whatever gods there be must themselves be part of the totality of the knowable, and if there be none, their non-existence must just as surely be within the knowable ALL.

From the earliest records of human history, man has shown himself to be what his name implies, a thinker, an inquirer into the world in which he finds himself. When the Vedic tradition was eventually committed to writing, the great question of life beyond the grave was already old. For is not the King of Death made to say, in the *Kathopanishad*, that the gods themselves were once puzzled by the mystery of existence hereafter? And from those days down to the present time, like children in the dark who clutch the hand of an adult, men who know they do not know have put their faith in those who have professed to know.

The history of human progress is the history of individuals. Exploration and experiment by men unwilling to remain within the restricted area of the known have, now here, now there, pierced the veil of ignorance and enlarged the boundaries of experience. Little by little, and often at the sacrifice of life, these pioneers have made their discoveries and handed on to later generations an ampler heritage of knowledge and a life enriched.

A useful comparison is suggested by these facts. This globe of ours, with its seas and continents, may serve to represent the whole of existence, nature in its entirety; the navigators of the uncharted oceans and the explorers of hitherto unpenetrated lands may then represent the experimenters and explorers of nature, both without and within. The earliest maps of the Mediterranean basin, the cradle of western civilization, show how limited was the known inhabited world in the early centuries of our era. The coasts were moderately well determined, and the islands, but even in this confined area knowledge was partial and inaccurate. But adventurous mariners, sailing out into the unknown and recording their discovery of new lands, corrected and enlarged the primitive outlines, while across the continents the caravans of traders and explorers brought a rich expansion of information to the map-makers of their day. Throughout the centuries this extension of knowledge has proceeded continuously, until today only the most remote and inaccessible areas of the earth, parts of the polar regions and the great mountain ranges, remain to be mapped in detail.

Records of the Seers

As with the explorers of nature without, so has it been with the seers, the explorers of nature within, whose accumulated discoveries down the ages have been transmitted in the records and teachings of the Wisdom tradition. They saw, and recorded—so far as was possible—what they knew of the truth of things, and their records are preserved in the scriptures, myths, folklore and religious observances of all the peoples of the earth.

However, it is one thing to read an account of polar exploration or of the ascent of Everest, even to see a cinematograph record of the icy wastes or the snow-covered peaks: but it is quite another to experience for oneself the exhilaration and the agony that accompany entry into those remote and forbidding worlds. Such experience is reserved for the few, for the very few, who by personal qualifications and by training have earned the right and developed the skills without which no entry into those rarer regions of the earth is possible.

The same is true of the inner worlds discovered, explored and recorded by those whom the *Bhagavad Gita* calls " the seers of the essence of things ". Beautiful indeed are their writings, inspiring their accounts of the Reality perceived. But students of the Wisdom tradition who would experience for themselves the worlds described in the mystical literature of east and west have also to earn by personal preparation the right and the power to undertake man's ultimate quest. " It is a fact ", writes Aldous Huxley, grandly recognizing this truth in his Introduction to *The Perennial Philosophy*, " confirmed and reconfirmed during two or three thousand years of religious history, that the ultimate Reality is not clearly and immediately apprehended, except by those who have made themselves loving, pure in heart and poor in spirit."

Reverting to the earlier illustration, it may further be observed that the making of maps serves primarily to record and to convey information about a territory. The map-reader may thus learn not only what a particular territory is like but also whether it is accessible to him and what are the travelling conditions he may expect to encounter. In modern times, indeed, certain maps are designed specifically for travellers, offering them the possibility of selecting the route appropriate to their purpose.

The records of the explorers of nature within, the mystics, saints and seers of religious history, may be likened to maps of existence. To those who learn to read them—and one

13

should bear in mind that map-reading is a skill to be learned and practised—these maps offer knowledge of the accumulated discoveries made by qualified investigators from the most ancient times. The knowledge thus handed down embraces the origin and laws of the whole evolutionary scheme of which man is a part, his own origin and nature and the laws of his unfolding. But not all this only: for there on the map of existence is traced a route, marked out by the pioneers in the exploration of nature within, so that all travellers coming after them might find it and follow. These map-makers, be it understood, marked the route but did not make it, for it was there from the beginning of time, inherent in the very nature of things. What they did was to discover it, by arduous and patient toil, by trial and error and trial again until no further error was possible. And having discovered it, they marked it with signs unmistakable to those who learn to read the legend of the Wisdom cartographers.

The route so discovered and so traced runs, today as always, between two points that may be designated as point A and point B. The first of these is that point in the evolutionary process where any individual happens to be when, tired of aimless wandering, he becomes for the first time a seeker of the Way. It follows that for every man there is a distinctive point A, uniquely his, the starting-point from which he may strike away from the common levels and set foot upon the lower slopes of Mount Carmel. Point B, however, the goal of humanity's evolutionary ascent, is one only, and from whatever place the upward journey may begin, it is here that it must end for all—or seem to end, rather, for what lies beyond that point can be neither discerned nor imagined by those who are as yet beginners in the Way. In the spiritual literature of India, fountain-head of the Wisdom

tradition as given to the west, the infinite variety of routes
that converge in point B are recognized by a single
name: yoga.

The Map and the Traveller

Summarizing the facts so far presented, it may be said
that Theosophy is the total map of existence while yoga is
that area of the map that is of particular and practical concern
to purposeful travellers. Theosophy the map, yoga the
route; Theosophy the totality of knowledge, yoga the application of knowledge to individual living; Theosophy the accumulated wisdom of the ages, yoga the science by which each
student may come to know the Wisdom for himself.

Among the primary principles of the Wisdom tradition
is that Hermetic axiom which states: as above, so below;
as in the macrocosm of the universe, so in the microcosm
of man. Whether the student concerns himself first with
the broad sweep of knowledge of nature without, or with
the seemingly more circumscribed science of nature within,
he will find his attention directed to the same three areas
of information. All of these, in time, must become for
him areas of investigation and experience. As a field of
study, Theosophy could be said to begin with theory and to
end in practice, whereas yoga, beginning with practice,
must inevitably lead to an understanding of its philosophical
premises. The areas of dominant concern common to both
approaches may be thus briefly defined: the source of man's
being; his present condition; the way of enlightenment.

The Wisdom teaching on the first of these is clear and
unequivocal. There is but one origin of all things. It
is the one omnipresent and boundless Principle of *The Secret
Doctrine*, the Godhead of Meister Eckhart, the Divine Ground

of the medieval mystics, the Brahman of the Vedas, the One and Only of Thrice Greatest Hermes. The names of the One vary, inevitably, with the culture within which this seer or that has sought to give expression to his experience of Truth. No student of the Wisdom literature, however, can fail to recognize that all without exception acknowledge a single source of being, one supreme Reality that alone *is*. From this One, the many; from the blazing fire, the innumerable sparks; from the Godhead, God and all creatures. Therefore—an axiomatic, unarguable *therefore*—THOU ART THAT: the individual in his essential nature is identical with the Supreme. Theosophy begins with the affirmation of the one self-existent Reality, itself the " causeless cause " of multiplicity. Yoga, beginning with the individual consciousness, is directed towards the discovery of that Reality as one's Self. The one begins at the centre in explanation of all that emanates from there, the other starts on the periphery in order that the centre may be known in experience. " There is One only, without a second." " Realize that thou art THAT." In these two sentences lie the whole of Theosophy and the whole of yoga: the affirmation of ultimate oneness, and the call to the practical science of Self-realization.

A common feature of the mystical literature in which attempts are made to speak of the One is the insistence that—these very attempts notwithstanding—It is unknowable, unthinkable, unutterable, beyond all human conception. Turning, however, to the present condition of man, the truth is all too clearly perceived and expressed: he knows himself to be limited, ignorant, suffering, confused, beset by problems. His state is portrayed in the *Bhagavad Gita* by Arjuna appealing to Krishna the Lord for enlightenment and in the *Crest-Jewel of Wisdom* by the distraught but earnest seeker after salvation.

Yet the very consciousness of circumscription and suffering in the present self is evidence of a recognition, however dim, that a different kind of life is possible, if only one knows how to reach it. To be aware of discomfort is to be aware that comfort is possible. To recognize failure is to recognize the existence of a standard to which one has not attained and which is yet attainable.

Again now in the third area of concern the different strands of the Wisdom tradition meet in the affirmation that the human dilemma is not the final end of man. An optimism, a certainty, shines through the utterances of the mystics of both east and west. There *is* a path, a road, a way, by which a man may leave the self that he seems to be and enter into the experience of the Self that he is. There *is* a means of crossing the troubled ocean of human life. It is the way of salvation of the Christian, the way of enlightenment of the Buddhist, the way of illumination of the mystic, the way of Self-realization of the yogi. An ancient invocation appeals that the soul may be led from the unreal to the Real, from darkness to light, from death to immortality. The way of yoga, by whatever name it be known, is the route that leads from the unreality of the time-bound world to the timeless world of the Real, from the darkness of ignorance to the light of unclouded knowledge, from the death of the separated consciousness to the immortality of reabsorption in the imperishable source of being.

Erroneous Identification

Why, one may ask, if this consummation is as certain and as blissful as the ancient seers would have us believe, do we not seek the path with alacrity and eagerly embrace its disciplines? The codifier of traditional yogic instruction Patanjali, names the obstacles that prevent all but the few from following in the footsteps of the illumined ones: ignorance of one's true nature, the sense of I-ness that makes of the little self the centre of each man's universe, the seeking of pleasure in the illusory world of sense-objects, the withdrawal from those same objects when they are experienced as sources of pain, the ultimate clinging to an identifiable existence for ever and ever. All these take their rise in that primary darkness of unwisdom, the privation of knowledge of man's true being, which causes the erroneous identification of consciousness with its vestures.

Explained in terms of the meaning of the word, the purpose of yoga is commonly stated to be union with the Supreme. More correctly, yoga is shown to be the process that enables man to experience in full self-consciousness his identity with It. "The truth" affirms the sage of the Svetasvatara Upanishad, "is that you are always united with the Lord. But you must *know* this." Yoga as process is the technique of removing those above-named obstacles that have obscured the Divine Immanence. The Reality is ever present, the Timeless in the midst of time, but the consciousness in its conditioned state is unaware of it.

The disciplines of yoga are rooted in knowledge of the laws of nature without and within—knowledge, that is, of the behaviour of the material envelopes through which consciousness functions and knowledge of the causes of, and the the solution to, the human dilemma. This knowledge is Theosophy, the ageless Wisdom of life. In the pictorial language of the Vedic seers, the universe is represented as the ceaselessly turning wheel of Brahman on which all creatures are bound. When those same seers, pointing to the erroneous notion of separateness from Brahman as the cause of bondage, give instruction in the methods of release from the whirling wheel, they reveal themselves as masters of yoga.

The seers *knew*. Absorbed in contemplation they saw within themselves the ultimate Reality, the one Being that dwells hidden in the heart of all beings. Knowing this, they summon mankind all down the ages to know it also, if any will listen and obey: "Arise! Awake! Approach the feet of the Master and know THAT. Nothing further is there to know."

THREE FUNDAMENTAL PROPOSITIONS

A. An Omnipresent, Eternal, Boundless and Immutable Principle, on which all speculation is impossible, since it transcends the power of human conception and could only be dwarfed by any human expression or similitude. It is beyond the range and reach of thought . . . "unthinkable and unspeakable".

B. The Eternity of the Universe *in toto* as a boundless plane; periodically "the playground of numberless Universes incessantly manifesting and disappearing . . . The appearance and disappearance of Worlds is like a regular tidal ebb of flux and reflux".

C. The fundamental identity of all Souls with the Universal Over-soul, the latter being itself an aspect of the Unknown Root; and the obligatory pilgrimage for every Soul—a spark of the former—through the Cycle of Incarnation (or "Necessity") in accordance with Cyclic and Karmic law, during the whole term.

INTERPLAY OF INDIVIDUAL AND GROUP

We are most free when we are free
from ourselves. Our fullest freedom
lies in perfect service.—N. SRI RAM

VIRGINIA HANSON

According to the hypothesis propounded through H. P.
Blavatsky, the creation of the universe was a series of
group projects. Further, this stupendous phenomenon—
whose ultimate mysteries science has yet to unravel—continues to be maintained and operated by groups working together
at different levels and serving different functions: those
charged with the primary responsibility are the " graduates "
of past evolutionary cycles, and working under them are great
hosts of un-self-conscious beings engaged in carrying out the
multifarious and interlinking laws of Nature.

Numerous references in *The Secret Doctrine* support these
statements. Perhaps two will suffice:

> In Esoteric philosophy the Demiurge, or Logos, regarded
> as the Creator, is simply an abstract term, an idea, like " army ".
> As the latter is the all-embracing term for a body of active
> forces or working units—soldiers—so is the Demiurge the
> qualitative compound of a multitude of Creators or Builders.[1]
> The whole Kosmos is guided, controlled, and animated by
> almost endless series of Hierarchies of sentient Beings, each
> having a mission to perform. . . [and] each either was, or pre-
> pares to become, a man, if not in the present, then in a past

[1] *S. D.* I, 380, 1st. ed.; II, 95, 6-vol. ed.,   T.P.H.

or coming cycle. . . . They are *perfected*, when not *incipient*, men.[1]

Admittedly, we are inclined to place a mundane interpretation upon a concept so transcendent that it cannot be grasped by the finite mind. But we may turn to the Hermetic axiom, " As above, so below ". Or we may refer again to *The Secret Doctrine*, where we are told:

> . . . the world of Form and Substance is an immense chain, whose links are all connected. The law of Analogy is the first key to the world problem.[2] . . . Analogy is the guiding law of Nature, the only true Ariadne's thread that can lead us, through the inextricable paths of her domain, toward her primal and final mysteries.[3]

The universal law of the One and the many, referred to in these citations, is unaffected by the passage of time, and it was inevitable that later thinkers would recognize the same principle, although expressing it in different terms. For example, the Jesuit philosopher-scientist, Pierre Teilhard de Chardin, points out that if man is to become aware of the significance of himself and his world, he must develop a whole series of senses, among which are:

> A sense of number, discovering and grasping unflinchingly the bewildering multitude of material or living elements involved in the slightest change in the universe;
> A sense . . . of the organic, discovering physical links and structural unity under the superficial juxtaposition of successions and collectivities.[4]

Since the evolution of consciousness is implicit in the whole thesis of *The Secret Doctrine* (as it is in Teilhard's philosophy, although with a different emphasis), and since cyclic law

[1] *S. D.* I, 274-5; I, 318.
[2] *S. D.* I, 604; II, 328.
[3] *S. D.* II, 153; III, 161.
[4] *The Phenomenon of Man*, Harper & Brothers, New York, 1959, pp. 33-34.

operating at higher and higher levels apparently governs the process, one cannot escape the staggering speculation that perhaps our own inexpert and faulty attempts at group work are miniature rehearsals for that aeonic future when, as Dhyan Chohans—Logoi—we shall participate in creating and maintaining a universe. It will, presumably, be a " better " universe, although in saying this one risks a greatly over-simplified value judgment. It will, at any rate, surely have inconceivably greater potentials than the one in which we live, for it, too, will be the product of evolving consciousness. But we have to remember also that meshed into its whole substance and structure will be the karma of our present cosmos—what Geoffrey A. Barborka calls " the results of incompleted sequences of energies," [1] or still unresolved causes which, on a cosmic scale, have been, are being, and will be set in motion in our present scheme. The chain is unbreak-able. In the " progressive development of everything, worlds as well as atoms," each universe is a " Son of Necessity " because it is a link in the " great cosmic chain of Universes, each one standing in the relation of an effect as regards its predecessor, and of a cause as regards its successor." [2] It is a somewhat daunting thought that we are now creating the condi-tions we shall have to work with in our cosmic undertaking.

It is not beyond reason, however, to project one's imagina-tion into such a prospect, however futile this may seem from the materialistic point of view. We may, by a kind of reversal in juxtaposition, think of the future as a backdrop against which our present world drama is being enacted. That every individual has a role in that drama we must believe, or the whole chain of being falls apart.

[1] *The Divine Plan*, p. 61. T.P.H.
[2] *S.D.* I, 43; I, 115.

This is not to deny the demands of pragmatism, which form an anchor to the present and which must therefore be respected. For, regardless of the sublime prospect of a future of cosmic activity, we live in the present and are very much involved in the here-and-now of our earthly, mundane activities, which is as it should be. The " perhaps " that all of these activities may be tentative rehearsals for a future grand performance may be beside the point at the moment. No actor in any drama can afford to ignore the necessities of rehearsals, however much the ultimate performance may be the motivating factor in his efforts.

Turning our attention, then, to the rehearsals, we are immediately faced with the questions: What is a group? What is an individual? What is the relationship between individuals in the group situation? What is the relationship of the individual to the group and the group to the individual? To deal with all this interplay in depth, even if one were capable, would require endless research and a dissertation the length of an encyclopaedia. Yet some attention to it is essential.

The Jungian psychologist, Marie-Louise von Franz, defines a group as " a collection of people who are intellectually and on a feeling level related to each other and in which everybody fulfils a certain role."[1] This fits well into the concept of rehearsals, and the temptation is to accept it and go on. But the author points out that there are other collections of individuals, such as " A *crowd*, i.e., a random accumulation of people " and " A *mass*, i.e., a big crowd which is emotionally and instinctively unified and generally follows a leader."[2]

[1] *Quadrant*, Journal of the C. G. Jung Foundation for Analytical Psychology, New York, No. 13, Winter 1973, p. 4.
[2] *Ibid.*, p. 4.

That the group and the mass have sometimes tended to
" topple over " into each other she makes clear, and this
is true to the extent that instinctual behaviour replaces conscious, directed action, and vice versa. We have seen this
dramatically illustrated during the past decade when, for
example, groups organized for the promotion of peace have—
inexplicably from a logical point of view—turned to violence
and destruction as a means of promoting their ends.

Recognizing the fact that change is the only constant in the
universe and that any set of circumstances can, without
warning, become a wholly different set of circumstances
(although there will always be a thread of causation if we can
find it), and in spite of the danger of oversimplification, we
might for our theme paraphrase Dr. von Franz's definition
to apply to an ideal group at our present stage as composed
of individuals who are intellectually and on a feeling level
related to each other, who have voluntarily united for the
pursuit of a definite purpose, and in which everyone, consciously and intelligently, fulfils his own role.

Everyone Individually

This brings us to the " everyone " in the sense of individuals.
Here we come upon something quite mysterious.

The theosophical concept of man is that of a septenary
being, and the goal of evolution seems to be the development
of full consciousness at every level. As consciousness approaches the fulfilment of its potential at one level, it begins
to grope its way into the next; the previous level becomes
increasingly objective to it, while the level at which it is
working remains for a long time largely subjective. And
so on up through the septenary ladder. "Groupness" is possible
at every level, but its characteristics will reflect the level

at which the consciousness of the individuals composing the group is functioning; this will, of course, have its diverse elements. The group is a training ground for the development of individual consciousness and, conversely, the unfolding of individual consciousness brings about the evolution of group activity. Thus we find that the group has its place in the pattern for the awakening of consciousness at successively higher levels and on an ever-expanding scale.

In discussing the efforts of evolution to produce man, H. P. Blavatsky points out that the two higher principles— referred to in the Stanza under discussion as the " Indiscrete (Undifferentiated Element) and the Vahan (Buddhi) * "— "can have no individuality on Earth unless there is (a) the Mind, the Manas-Ego, to cognize itself, and (b) the terrestrial false personality, or the Body of egotistical desires and personal Will, to cement the whole." [1] More specifically, she says elsewhere that ". . . to complete the septenary man, to add to his three lower Principles and cement them with the Spiritual Monad . . . two connecting ' Principles ' are needed: Manas †. and Kama †." [2] Thus man becomes man only when this connecting link of kama-manas comes into being, and it is into kama-manas that *Ahamkara*, the I-making faculty of universal mind, reflects and functions as individual consciousness.

This is a very necessary step in the whole process; the fact that individual consciousness does stem from Universal Mind gives assurance of its legitimacy. Since there can be no consciousness without something through which to manifest,

* Direct intuitive perception.
[1] *S. D.* II, 241; III, 244.
[2] *S. D.* II, 79; III, 88.
† Manas, mind; kama, desire.

separation of the undifferentiated primordial consciousness into units was essential. It would seem logical to assume that the sense of I-ness was at first quite dim and nebulous, and that for millenia its intensification and enhancement were the unending concern of the agencies of evolution.

We know from studies of anthropology that well organized groups existed in primitive societies, but to a large extent the principal characteristic of such groups was what Lévy-Bruhl termed *participation mystique*,[1] a concept on which Carl Jung elaborated considerably from the psychological point of view. It might be thought of as groupness at the etheric, or sensation level of consciousness. *Participation mystique* comes about when there are as yet no definite boundaries to the individual psyche, and thus no clear sense of identity. The individual does not see himself as a unique element in the group; rather his consciousness is merged in that of the group. This is somewhat the condition of the infant who only gradually becomes aware that he is something separate from the objects about him. Dr. M. Esther Harding, who has contributed so richly to the understanding of Jungian ideas, comments that *participation mystique* " has to do with the projection of unconscious contents into the environment, into people or things or situations, where they are encountered as if they were properties of the object and are not recognized as having anything to do with the individual's own psyche, let alone really belonging to what should be his own contents." [2]

To some extent all of us still engage in *participation mystique*, especially when we are unaware of how much our own

---

[1] *How Natives Think*, p. 129, Washington Square Press, New York.

[2] *The I and the Not-I*, Bollingen Series LXXIX, p 42. Pantheon Books, New York, 1965.

unconscious projections affect our judgments of and our reactions to others in any group in which we are involved. There is always danger that any group, however intelligent and conscious its members, may be thrown back into this condition by some untoward circumstance or event. Constant vigilance seems essential. " . . . when a group of people get together," says Dr. Harding, "even though they may intend to form a positive organization of some sort, the negative qualities come up."[1] More forcefully she comments: "Unless the destructive energies are first transformed in individuals, a group, however optimistic its organizers, will soon be subverted for destructive purposes."[2]

But we may say that evolution uses everything, and our unconscious projections serve an important purpose, for eventually they bring us to a greater awareness of ourselves. It is only through projecting the contents of our consciousness that we become aware of them at all; until then they are, so to speak, in solution. Just as the individual cannot see his own face save as it is reflected in a mirror, so consciousness cannot see its own contents until they are in some manner reflected from outside itself; the group functions as the mirror for these reflections. And just as our own mirror-image becomes a conscious part of our being, so do the projections of the unconscious work their way into conscious attitudes and behaviour. Jung points out ". . . in the course of mental development, consciousness gradually assimilates them . . . and reshapes them into conscious ideas".[3] We might conceive of the process as one of projection, recognition,

---

[1] *The I and the Not-I*, Bollingen Series LXXIX, p. 49. Pantheon Books, New York, 1965.

[2] *Ibid.* p. 48.

[3] " Commentaries on *The Secret of the Golden Flower*, Translation by Richard Wilhelm; pp. 110-111. Harcourt, Brace & World, New York, 1967.

acceptance, assimilation, re-creation, and release, repeated over and over again at higher and higher levels—a rhythmic pulsing of " eternal motion " manifesting through points of individual awareness. Depending upon the honesty of the individuals, the process can be one of continual creation of higher potentials, so that the group becomes a culture for those genuinely human qualities of tenderness, love, and compassion which can grow only in relationship.

When we begin to " stand aside and watch ourselves go by " we begin to see ourselves in relation to our actions and our environment; we learn to separate the I from the not-I in a sane and healthy fashion. This is particularly important to a higher functioning of groupness, however far we may be from that cosmic performance toward which we are groping our way.

The Motive Power

It would seem that differentiation of consciousness really begins when kama comes into play. Kama is the dynamic aspect of the psyche—the great motive power which plunges man into all kinds of circumstances and relationships in which he learns, through conflict and suffering, that he is a *being* and therefore a problem. Recognition of the problem results in heightened awareness, which, indeed, appears to be the end in view of all experience. " . . . man is a problem intrinsically and under all circumstances," says Abraham Heschel, Professor of Ethics and Mysticism at the Jewish Theological Seminary of America. " To be human is to be a problem, and the problem expresses itself in anguish. . . . The problem of man is occasioned by our coming upon a conflict or contradiction between existence and expectation, between what man is and what is expected of him." [1]

[1] *Who Is Man?* p. 3, Stanford University Press, 1965.

Here man reaches out for support and comfort, for someone to show him how to escape from his predicament. His
efforts toward self-understanding are still nebulous and
tentative, and he wants the security that " belonging " gives
him. Therefore participation in group activity at this level
may take the form of joining with others under a strong leader,
even to the extent of unthinking acceptance of the pronounce-
ments of such a leader because they save him from the pain
of decision. We see this reflected in some totalitarian societies,
but it is not altogether absent on a smaller scale in the so-called
free cultures, where many groups have as their *raison d'etre*
a powerful leader who dominates the lives of his followers.
One is tempted to say that the former situation is forced,
while the latter comes about voluntarily, but this may not
be true; the follower may be impelled by the very nature
of his own needs to accept the security and the concomitant
lack of responsibility which membership in such a group
gives him.

As consciousness exhausts the possibilities of the group at
this level, it begins to move toward a further development.
Manas comes into play, and with it a questioning of previous
values, a faint stirring of the will to make up one's own mind
about important matters, a recognition that one need not
accept as absolute the statements and opinions of any leader.
Another danger is inherent at this stage: kama is still very
much in the picture, and one may shift his emotional allegiance
from the leader to his own opinions, which he feels called upon
to defend, often with violence. This is an intrusion of the
instinctual or etheric principle into the situation. It is understood, of course, that all levels of consciousness, save those
which man has not yet penetrated, are operative at all times;
according as he acts in one or the other fashion, the principle

14

governing one of the levels is predominating, but the others are not absent. Our rehearsals are becoming increasingly complex as we strive to assimilate new elements and transmute them into faculties and powers.

Groupness at the level of manas has some interesting characteristics, with most of which we are by now more or less familiar. There must be a leader, but he is an elected leader—on the basis of the will of the majority, but usually also on the basis of his own standing or prestige, or perhaps of the efforts he has made to achieve that status. Conflict is not absent, for competition is keen; it may take many guises, but the predominant challenges are at the level of manas. But conflict, too, has its place in the maturing of the psyche, for through it the individual discovers his own possibilities and limitations; he begins to acquire a definition of himself. This is a genuine evolutionary achievement which enormously enriches his contributions to the group and, by that measure, raises the level of the group's functioning.

Organizations for the promotion of social betterment are a prominent feature of this stage, and the proliferation of such groups is a heartening development, however imperfectly and even ineffectually some of them may function.

One startling phenomenon has been the emergence of protest groups. Great numbers of people, almost simultaneously it seems, have become aware that their status is in some way an inferior one, that they do not occupy the place in the human scheme to which they instinctively feel they are entitled, even though they may not be able in all instances to rationalize this motivation. Kama is still an insistent element, with perhaps some very faint filtering of the buddhic influence through manas to give a different flavour to the development. But here a new *mystique* comes into play.

Dr. James Hitchcock, Professor of History at St. Louis University, has commented that the inevitable law of these protest groups " has been a rapid transformation in the movement, not, as the media have so often made it appear, from moderate to extremist leadership, but from a leadership which, however angry, is essentially pragmatic and concerned with specific problems and demands to a leadership intoxicated with mystical visions of group identity, ineffable perceptions of selfhood, inchoate anger, and fathomless frustration. The final stage of social protest has in each case been the ritual assertion of a truism—that the oppressed group experiences a sense of selfhood not ultimately accessible to any outsider." [1] Nevertheless, it seems obvious that the formation of protest groups is the result of an evolutionary push—and perhaps of a pull as well, since we cannot escape the conviction that some inscrutable and irresistible power forever draws consciousness toward a denouement; the one Life works through whatever means are at hand. Greater and greater numbers of individuals must share in the increasingly complex interplay provided by group activity.

Group Function in One World

Perhaps the next evolutionary step will be a movement from the *mystique* of group destiny toward awareness of group function in a total world operation. This can come about when the manasic impulse has fulfilled itself and thus created an " opening " for the influx of buddhi.

This phase will not be represented by a merging of all groups into one amorphous mass as greater awareness of the unifying principle of buddhi comes into play. This would be

[1] " The Vital Balance," *The National Observer*, Washington, D.C., May 26, 1973, p. 22.

contrary to the laws of life.   As consciousness struggles toward
greater complexity, it seems at the same time to move in the
direction of greater individualization, or self-awareness.   What
appears to take place, over and over again, at higher and higher
levels, is that an inner pressure builds up until there is a
breakthrough to a new level and the emergence of a new
principle of organization corresponding to the next higher
evolutionary principle.

George S. Arundale, in *Mt. Everest* [1] traces this process
in a slightly different manner.   We describe a circumference about ourselves, he says, and then proceed to fill in
the space inside that circumference with the ever-expanding
contents of our consciousness.   When the periphery can no
longer withstand the pressure, it breaks at some point and
we emerge into greater freedom.   But here we describe a
larger circumference and go on to repeat the process *ad infinitum.*
It is conceivable also that the circumference will become more
and more tenuous as we proceed and that eventually it will
give way to boundlessness.

One curious and paradoxical fact emerges from all our
observations of the relationship between the individual and
the group.   The more the individual seeks to advance his
own aims, the more dependent he is upon the group as a
milieu to be exploited, and therefore the more his own freedom
is curtailed.   But the more he commits himself in clear consciousness and direction to the purposes and functions of the
group, maintaining his own freedom and encouraging the
freedom of others in voluntary cooperation, the more he
sharpens and defines his own individuality.   In the first
instance, in seeking to enhance himself, he loses that which
he seeks.   In the second instance, with no thought of his own

[1] p. 141. T.P.H.

advancement, he finds himself. This is a world apart from *participation mystique*; it is, rather, what Jung has described as " successful adaptation to the necessity of the group together with the greatest possible freedom for self-determination." [1] Without this freedom, goals become muddled and means become mangled. Group interplay in this sense does not mean the polishing of individual egos but rather the opposite; it means opening the consciousness of the group— and of all the persons comprising the group—to greater growth in mutual respect and even reverence, to clearer definition of functions, and to greater dedication and commitment to aims. This is perhaps what we are beginning to see at our present stage of group operation, which seems to foreshadow the " ideal " group as defined earlier.

In general it might be said that while, within any given stage of evolution, there must be room for almost infinite gradations and varieties of consciousness, humanity proceeds *en masse*, as it were, toward the achievement of the evolutionary goal. "The multiple rises, attracted and incorporated by the ' Already One ' " [2] says Teilhard, as he envisages the pyramid or cone whose supreme point is the all-encompassing unity. Is this supreme point what H. P. Blavatsky had in mind when she spoke of the great " Day Be With Us " [3] when every unit which initially issued from the undifferentiated consciousness will have arrived at absolute consciousness? This will be through the full unfoldment of that which is now " non-conscious, or unconscious " and will mean total consciousness at every level of being, total consciousness of essential

---

[1] *The Development of Personality*, Collected Writings of C. G. Jung, v. 17, p. 171. Bollingen Series, Pantheon Books, 1954.

[2] *Building the Earth*, Dimension Books, p. 62, Wilkes-Barre, 1965.

[3] *Transactions of the Blavatsky Lodge of The Theosophical Society*, p. 148, The Theosophy Company, Los Angeles, 1923.

oneness, ". . . yet each knowing itself, a mysterious teaching indeed."

If those who reach that goal will be the intelligent group agencies for the building and maintenance of a future cosmos —fulfilling the functions for which they are suited by virtue of their own natures and development—then we can surely grasp the importance of our present rehearsals. No one can rehearse successfully save in the company with other actors in the drama, and it is the conscious interplay of functions which defines for each the significance of his own role.

———

The nature of truth is universal; its possessors in any degree will be found to be appliers of universality in thought, speech and action. Their efforts will be for humanity regardless of sex, creed, caste or colour. To be able to afford a basis for unity to individuals or organizations in search of truth, without demanding any relinquishment of affiliation or belief, is no small thing.

If people could be brought into the position of listening to the message of Theosophy and applying it, the misery and suffering and hardship in the world would practically cease to exist. But it is beyond the reach of any power whatever to get men to listen and to apply. They must first desire and choose to listen.

—ROBERT CROSBIE

PERSONAL PROBLEMS IN A TROUBLED WORLD

Together differently.—G. S. ARUNDALE

L. H. LESLIE-SMITH

THE far-reaching scientific discoveries and developments and the many inventions of the past few decades require a wide measure of international cooperation. Time and space, which formerly kept nations and ethnic groups separate, have been so shrunk that they now bring people and peoples continually closer together. Modern communications and knowledge have contracted our earth to such an extent that organization covering the whole of it should be possible. The ever increasing economic interdependence of nations and the needs of commerce and of culture irresistibly demand an international outlook. Every sea and air route, and many an overland one too, necessitates a high degree of collaboration and team work. No group, however powerful and whatever its resources, can exist today separate from all others. Moreover, the trend is steadily towards bigger and bigger business organizations, many of them cutting across old boundaries and barriers. The tendency is in the direction of world-wide institutions, a pointer perhaps to an ultimate federation of all peoples. All the pressures would seem to be towards one world, one humanity.

Psychologically, however, the world is everywhere torn by narrow nationalism, greed, hatred, warring systems. Men are apparently determined to resist the compelling evolutionary trend and try to prevent the pattern of a unified earth from taking shape. So the global situation is tragically paradoxical. Man appears to be afflicted with an irrational madness in which mental processes and emotional attitudes become more and more restricted and parochial, instead of widening out to be universal. This regression is characterized by power complexes and cupidity. Dissension and further fragmentation follow—small groups asserting themselves, refusing to work with others, contending for a selfish and illusory independence that is an impossibility. Greater folly could scarcely be imagined. Whether political, economic, religious or ideological in flavour, the notions and practices of such groups are totally out of tune with the unity towards which mankind is being steadily impelled. The two world wars and the tremendous social and political upheavals of this century should surely have taught us that neither men nor nations can fulfil themselves unless they work together. "There is no longer any possibility of prosperity and happiness for one nation alone... It must henceforth be happiness and prosperity for all."[1] Yet the lesson is largely unheeded.

Several causes contribute to this sad and dangerous state of affairs. One big factor is the rapidity and extent of changes during the past quarter of a century. Time is needed for people to adapt to new conditions and circumstances, and the breaking up of old modes of living by one event after another has been so breathtaking as to deny reasonable time. The upsetting of customary habits within various communities has been difficult enough; but more intractable still is the result of groups of the great family of man being suddenly thrown into juxtaposition after having for centuries been distant neighbours. The altered situation is hard to cope

[1] C. Jinarājadāsa in *Theosophy in Action*, April 1940.

with. It is as if a large family brought up in a spacious mansion was suddenly forced to live huddled together in one or two rooms. Cramped and crowded conditions would cause much frustration and friction. We are becoming one world so quickly that we have had no time to adjust our ideas and our ways to the fresh outlook that is required of us. The complexities arising from the impinging of nations on one another is well illustrated by experience in the European Common Market, where sectional interests, especially in agriculture, constantly clash, and long and hard bargaining takes place before a reasonable compromise is reached.

Old Patterns Broken Up

An allied cause of the malaise of the human race is the disruption of old patterns of life by new knowledge as well as new methods. All over the world, ideas that have directed men's lives for centuries have been challenged and rejected. Not least of these are beliefs that provided a sense of psychic security and stability. Traditional habits and ways of life have been shattered and loyalties loosened. Not only have long-established religious practices and tenets been thrown over, but people have lost faith in any reality behind the forms of religion. This has left them with no guiding principles, no valid code of conduct, no spiritual anchorage, so that they drift like rudderless vessels on a stormy ocean. Money-making and status symbols have displaced the old ideals, but they can never satisfy the spirit of man. It should be no surprise that many young people rebel against the materialism of their elders and are looking, sometimes in strange places, for spiritual values.

Another reason for our human malady is constantly with us, though it has been heightened and brought more into consciousness with our changed relationship to time and space. It is commonplace that, both actually and metaphorically, we see with eyes that distort or dim what is perceived. From cradle to crematorium our environment exerts enormous pressure on us to conform. Everything conspires to mould us into a shape perhaps far other than that into which we would naturally grow. None can escape this influence of birth, family, education, social group, national mystique. The infant absorbs the atmosphere of his surroundings; and very soon his psyche is no longer his own. Its pristine purity is quickly coloured, often sullied; and usually this goes on progressively for most of his life. Again, one person has an Indian outlook; another, some variety of European; a third, an American; a fourth, a Chinese; a fifth, a Russian. Add to this that one is a Protestant Christian, another a Catholic, a Hindu, a Moslem, a Buddhist; one is a communist, another an individualist, and so on. The ramification and the magnitude and might of these forces are overwhelming.

Yet none of this would matter, but would provide picturesque variety, if it did not make us intolerant of usages and observances different from our own, if we did not always want others to adopt our views and our ways. All too often our conditioning does have precisely this effect. Differences mostly spell separateness, discord, disagreement, even unreasoning hate, instead of an enriching cooperative effort.

Nationally and ethnically the story is the same as with the individual. The dead hand of the psychological past lies heavy over all the earth. Communities everywhere are in bondage to their version of history; they cherish memories of injuries or fancied injuries stretching back sometimes for centuries. We suffer from the results of bitter differences caused by events that should long ago have been forgotten, but are instead carefully fostered. We have the capacity to understand one another, yet we go out of our way to misunderstand.

Why all the international strife and the internal contention in every country? Simply because nations, as well as groups within nations, are ruthless in seeking their own greedy advantage at the expense of others. Again, why? Because individual man is selfish and eager to exploit his fellows— to say nothing of the other kingdoms of nature. The group attitude inevitably follows from the individual attitude. A nation cannot do what the greater part of its citizens are unwilling to do. As long as we quarrel with our neighbours, so long will our country show enmity towards other lands. As J. Krishnamurti has said, "The problem of the world is the problem of the individual." Thus the trouble lies essentially not in any organized body of men, but in each man individually. It is evident, then, that outer reform and reorganization, however good and desirable, merely tinker with our problems unless they stem from a change of heart. The outer is always an expression of the inner, and is automatically modified when our thoughts and feelings take a new line.

The Only Way of Escape

Here we can discern the way by which, and by which alone, it is possible to resolve the human enigma that starts at the personal level and expands to the international sphere, to find a way of escape from the mental-emotional slavery from which we all suffer but of which most people are totally unaware.

If we would have peace on earth, we must live in harmony with our neighbours. This we cannot do unless we are at peace within ourselves. To quote Krishnamurti again,

" Where there is no inward peace, the world becomes a battle-field." Jung saw to the heart of the predicament: " If the individual is not truly regenerated in spirit, society cannot be either, for society is the sum total of individuals in need of redemption." The need, then, is spiritual regeneration, a reorientation that completely changes our lives by gradually shifting our focus of consciousness from the personal to the universal—in practical terms, from self-centredness to community-centredness. This is the royal road to redemption, and to internal peace and joy undreamt of before.

The first step towards psychological liberation is a recognition that we are in servitude to our conditioning (and also to any revolt against it, which merely reconditions us). Awareness of our thraldom enables us to allow for it, to watch the effects of our fettering, and to check our reactions. This can be done because, in spite of being impregnated with bias and prejudice, each human being has his own unique spiritual potential.   As Robert Browning put it,

> There is an inmost centre in us all
> Where truth abides in fulness.[1]

Or, to quote a modern writer, " There is a principle deep within ourselves—indeed, it is the very core of our being—which is the origin of every kind of good, equally for ourselves and for others. If we can touch it, even for a moment, withdrawing from everything else, we may be able to bring out of that moment a sense of something of imperishable value, present in everyone and everything." [2]

There is the same meaning in the ancient injunction, " Man, know thyself." For a self-seeking, and therefore separative, line of thought and action arises from ignorance of our true

---

[1] Paracelsus.

[2] N. Sri Ram, *An Approach to Reality* p. 61. T.P.H.

nature as part of and identical with universal Spirit—and consciousness of this unity comes in the experience of all mystics. The inner peace that is a prerequisite for outward peace arises from this knowledge. Even the briefest flash of this vision causes a man to begin living from his inner centre, so that by degrees he is able to act purposefully and to harmonize his thoughts, feelings and actions as an integrated being. The man is then healthy, whole. " To achieve wholeness in our-selves is to be able to live fully, and apply the whole of our being and our consciousness at any point of our contact with the external world. . . There is diversity on the surface, but the sense of unity arises from within, and that unity creates a state of harmony which is like the deep waters of the ocean that remain quiet even under the tossings on the surface." [1]

Individuals themselves have further to be integrated in groups; for, apart from relationship with one's fellows, exist-ence can have little meaning. Then the groups likewise have eventually to find their completion in larger ones, until finally the unit is mankind as a whole. In this immensely long process it will be found, as H. P. Blavatsky said, that " When people have learned to think and feel as truly human beings should think and feel, they will act humanely, and works of charity, justice and generosity will be done spon-taneously by all." [2] Thus will come a time when men and women, and consequently groups of men and women, will work together for the good of the entire community. Na-tions will similarly discard outworn notions and end their slavery to the past. They will know, for instance, that there are no economic " laws ". There are man-made

[1] N. Sri Ram, *An Approach to Reality* p. 61, T.P.H.
[2] B. C. W. IX, 241-42.

arrangements called economies, easily changed where there is the will.

Polluted World

In recent times there has been much concern about pollution, because it is threatening our well-being, possibly our lives. It seems that only when people get frightened for their own safety is anything done to remedy the defilement. It would be much wiser and simpler if we realized our obligations to our fellows and to nature without having to be spurred by fear—a positive forestalling of a harmful situation rather than a negative prohibition after the damage has been done.

Modern writers of note in many fields of human endeavour urge mankind to take charge of its own destiny, to be responsible for its future and for the further development of the earth. Humanity has tended to think of itself as a species separate from nature. But, though man may be, as has been claimed, the crown of nature, he is nonetheless an integral part of the entire natural process on the planet. He is not a being set altogether apart from it. Insensibility to this, or unwillingness to accept it, is the direct cause of many problems that the human race has made for itself. Recognition of the intimate linking of every part to every other part gives a sense of responsibility. First, responsibility of man to man; secondly, responsibility to and for the other kingdoms of nature by reason of the interrelationship of all, both living and so-called inanimate—in fact for the total environment. Only if, as stated in *The Voice of the Silence*, we help nature and work with her will she regard us as her creators.[1]

[1] By H. P. Blavatsky.   T.P.H.

Physical pollution is, however, but the result of psychic pollution. Adulteration of the psychic environment comes from crooked thinking and warped feeling, which stem from the conditioning we have already considered. Enmity and greed vitiate the psyche. Such pollution utterly inhibits any understanding that duties alone justify rights. The most vicious form of psychic defilement, however, takes the form of believing that " my religion " (whichever it may be) or perhaps just my version of my religion, is true and others false. From this has sprung the black record of the wars of religion. It can, of course, be also " my philosophy " or " my ideology ".

A further point is that modern man thinks he knows a thing when he merely knows about that thing. All the wonderful knowledge of the phenomenal world of forms is but the shadow of an inner world of life that holds the forms in being. The superb discoveries of science do but show the mechanisms through which life operates. The knowledge seems to have been mostly lost that

> . . . higher, deeper, innermost, abides
> Another life, not like the life of sense,
> Escaping sight, unchanging. This endures
> When all created things have passed away.[1]

This interior world of direct perception is common to all men, shared by all. It is where our roots are, where we truly belong. Denial of this most precious human heritage constitutes what H.P.B. called " the great dire heresy of separateness ",[2] and constantly poisons our psychic surroundings.

The awakening of the smothered spiritual nature is the basic concern of all true religion. " Religion, *per se* (wrote

[1] Edwin Arnold, *The Song Celestial*, VIII.   T.P.H.
[2] *The Voice of the Silence.*

H.P.B.), is that which binds not only *all Men*, but also *all Beings* and all *things* in the entire universe into one grand whole. This is our theosophical definition of Religion." [1]

Conditions for Survival

Genuine civilization and culture depend on the recognition of a spiritual quality in the universe. Such recognition is largely absent from most modern schemes of education. In this age of automation it is essential to train young people to use our amazing technological skills; but to bring children up to earn a living without teaching them how to live is to destroy the future. For only " how to live " concerns the spirit of man. H.P.B. urged that " children should above all be taught self-reliance, love for all men, altruism, mutual charity and, more than anything else, to think and reason for themselves. . . We should aim at creating *free* men and women, free intellectually, free morally, unprejudiced in all respects and, above all, *unselfish*." [2]

With the globe narrowed to fairly workable proportions—an epoch-making event that until now was never possible—our knowledge, our technical skill and our economic resources could soon bring in a world civilization free from want. It is only round the corner if we do not destroy ourselves first. Yet greatly lacking, except among a handful of idealists, is the will to use this knowledge and these resources for the benefit of all peoples and in the service of all mankind.

In the course of his long history man has survived because he has been able to adapt to physical environment, to changing conditions and circumstances. Otherwise our species would be extinct. What is now essential for survival is a psychic

[1] *Lucifer*, II, 177, 1888.
[2] *Key*, pp. 270-71.   T.P.H.

adjustment—a change of heart and mind.   The only remedy for the great dangers that beset our schizophrenic world is man's conversion: a conversion to a spiritual view of the universe and man, and a willingness to act in accordance with that conviction.   There is no other way to the healing, the making whole, of each man personally, and thence to the healing of the nations.

Never surely has anything been more vitally necessary than it is now for men to realize their unity: unity in depth, with the source of all life; and inevitably, therefore, unity in breadth, with all their fellows.   N. Sri Ram wrote: " The message that mankind needs is the message of its essential unity."   And there is this corollary: " Since humanity is one, in some manner our own thoughts, aspirations, efforts, must tell in the shaping of all men's thoughts and actions."   Here is responsibility; here is untold opportunity.

———

Theosophy is that ocean of knowledge which spreads from shore to shore of the evolution of sentient beings. Unfathomable in its deepest parts, it gives the greatest minds their fullest scope; yet, shallow enough at its shores, it will not overwhelm the understanding of a child.   It is wisdom about God for those who believe that he is all things and in all, and wisdom about nature for the man who accepts the statement found in the Christian *Bible* that God cannot be measured or discovered.

—W. Q. JUDGE

15

TOWARDS UNDERSTANDING OURSELVES

The proper study of mankind is man
—ALEXANDER POPE

LAURENCE BENDIT

IT will be well to make a clear distinction between the Theosophical Society and a wider cultural movement of which the Society is an organized part. Though the society bearing the name Theosophical was founded a century ago, it was really what is called technically an epiphenomenon representing the surface of a stream of thought and research already moving in the western world, at least among those with active minds. Forming itself around two highly contrasting individuals, Henry Steel Olcott and Helena Petrovna Blavatsky, with a small handful of others, it was labelled "theosophical" as the best indication of its purpose, and its concern with ultimates. It was this which made it different from a myriad other societies, and linked it with religion as defined by Paul Tillich, though it was never to be *a* religion. Moreover, in contrast with several other lines of thought, it came to stand for what is called occultism as something different from such disciplines as psychology, parapsychology and the like; though, as I shall try to show, all of these are strands in the main fabric which deserves the title of Theosophy in its wider and original sense. For all concern themselves with the nature of Man, both physical and non-physical, his place in the universe, and with how he operates in it.

One can, further, consider man's place in terms of what he does in what, for most of his earlier evolution, he sees as " outer space, " or the world he conceives as outside himself; and also in terms of what happens in " inner space ", his own field of being. For we learn that to understand the outer world, and to be effective in it, sooner or later demands also understanding of oneself as an individual, in the body corporate of mankind first, then as a denizen of Life in its entirety. The artificial division between these two sides of the matter is pragmatically useful even when, as we develop, it becomes to us a part of the *maya* or incomplete truth which eventually we discover for ourselves.

To begin with, let us look back a hundred years, a paltry period when we think that man has, as recent evidence shows us, been on earth for millions of years; yet one of very great significance because of the rapidity with which this past century has been connected with advances in self-knowledge as well as in technical affairs.

At about the time the Theosophical Society was formed, we saw the Baconian age of science floundering and almost foundering in an attempt to reduce our world picture to materialism. In contrast to this intellectual exercise, spiritualism catered for credulity and sensationalism, for what we call today " anti-science " Psychology, the science of the human mind, was virtually non-existent. It was in this mental climate that the Theosophical Society was born, bringing before the public eye esoteric doctrines hitherto kept concealed, or at least cryptic, and very largely couched in terms of factual doctrine rather than teaching the individual how to experience things for himself, to make his own discoveries.

What was given out, and what became popularly known as Theosophy because of its association with the Society was, in fact, occultism—neither science in the accepted sense, nor spiritualism, though it built a partial bridge between the two: partial because it needed the still unborn semi-science now known as depth psychology to bridge the gap entirely.

At this point it will be well if we consider the growth of this knowledge. For, on the side of science, at the time the Theosophical Movement got properly under way, there was already in existence the Society for Psychical Research, by seven years its junior; and, in spite of its prejudiced condemnation of H. P. B., it was already doing useful work. It acted in something of a judicial capacity, studying and taking evidence for certain classes of phenomena dubbed "psychical": haunts, poltergeists, the claims of mediums, and so on. It had many distinguished scientists and thinkers in its ranks; but it was condemned to dealing with material as it arose, more or less spontaneously and erratically. It was not until considerably later that a new stream of research started, using ordinary people, not mediums, in trying to prove statistically and mathematically that man was not entirely limited to perception through his five physical senses, but could, to a significant extent, perceive by some other means. It was not until the early nineteen-thirties that I myself heard Professor William MacDougal say to a group of psychiatrists: " I never believe anything absolutely, but I think that J. B. Rhine has proved paranormal cognition beyond reasonable doubt." Rhine was then virtually unknown even within the profession of psychologists and psychiatrists, but it was not long before he became famous; and, moreover, scientists, sometimes deliberately bent on proving him wrong, found to their dismay that their own findings confirmed his. Man was, henceforth, credited with powers of " paranormal cognition," later to be called extrasensory perception, or ESP. And, further, with psychokinetic (PK) power ("mind over matter") and affecting such things as the fall of dice without direct physical contact. Theorists then dubbed the newly discovered, or, as so often in science, the rediscovered function of the mind, "Psi"—initial of the Greek word for psyche, psychology etc.—in which ESP received impressions and PK was the active side.

Such an advance in our ideas about the mind clearly supported the occultist's view, and hence came into line with Theosophy. But this was not the only advance. For, by the turn of the century, what came later to be known as depth psychology was beginning to emerge. We not only had such people as Professor of Psychiatry Bucke, of the book *Cosmic Consciousness*, and William James, of *Varieties of Religious Experience*, considering irrational and transcendental subjective experience in a serious manner, but another name was coming into prominence, that of Sigmund Freud.

"Inward Space"

It may seem strange to bring Freud into a theosophical context. But we owe it to Freud, whether or not we agree with his views, that a new approach to mental problems was opened up. He deserves the credit for opening the door to what we nowadays sometimes call "inward space": the unconscious mind that underlies the thin veneer of daytime conscious life. He showed us the significance of irrational and uncontrollable things like dreams, mental habits based on emotion and then given a respectable garb of rationality only after the mind had acquired its prejudices, and so on. Freud failed, in that he believed himself to possess absolute truth, and that on a materialistic basis, which later people realized was true only in a two-dimensional manner—much as the foundations of a house are " true," but need a superstructure to make a house. He left out much that is self-evidently part of our mental working.

Then came his successor, Jung, whose greatest discovery came as a result of meeting a sinologist, Wilhelm, after which Jung provided us empirically with material which showed that Religion (with a capital) was no imposed tradition, but was in effect an outgrowth from within the human mind, an inalienable emanation from the deeper levels of himself. This led to a completely theosophical philosophy of man as both a spiritual being and a psychic and physical entity. Depth psychology, then, by its own discoveries, came into line with occultism; but it did so by teaching individuals to seek out their own experience by introspection and self-study. The result was that the student of factual occultism was able to confirm for himself, and in a living way, what was previously to him only doctrinal and theoretical information.

True, eastern disciplines of a yogic nature aimed at the same purpose. But the westerner often found these methods tedious, ineffective, even dangerous and unbalancing; which is not to find fault with them, but only with their universal application to very differently formed personalities.

To Know Ourselves

Enough has now been said to suggest that the best of depth psychology relates directly to that aspect of Theosophy which is concerned with understanding ourselves and our minds. Occultism tells us of subtle bodies, of the genesis of mind, as well as of cosmic origins and facts. Psychology can help us to know ourselves and thereby inevitably, since we live not by ourselves alone but in the context of humanity, and beyond humanity of the complete created universe, to discover this universe for ourselves. The two go hand in hand and are, in effect, the two sides of the same coin. Indeed, it might be said that while occultism can be a corrective to psychology, so is psychology a corrective to the distortion of views about ourselves that derive from the Victorian mentality in which this occultism was put before the public.

This matter needs explaining further. It shows in the bad psychological advice seen in ideas such as that desire should be killed out, that we should get rid of personality by transcending it, by refusing to let ourselves think " impure " thoughts, to feel negative emotions. H. P. B., in one of her books, constantly warns the disciple against the dangers of *Mara*, the evil one, as a result of whose spells " the path of occultism is strewn with wrecks ". But we know today that Mara, the Deceiver, is no rampant devil wandering around the psychic worlds trying to destroy us, but our own ignorant mind: virtually our own unconscious, shadow-filled because we have not brought the light of self-awareness into its depths. The remedy: to learn to know ourselves fully. But to do so does not require us to try to kill out desire, to cut ourselves off from our roots in our animal heritage, but to accept and integrate them by understanding their place in our total human nature. It may be pointed out that this is well understood in the philosophies of such people as Aurobindo today, and of ancient Tantric Buddhism, if not of its decadent modern schools.

The Growing Tip

And now it is interesting to see where Theosophy stands today. For, as I have tried to show, we have a convergence of several streams of thought about the mind of man: the " occult," represented by the Theosophical Society, that of depth psychology, and the substream of psychical research, nowadays better known as parapsychology, and becoming more and more a department of depth psychology.

No longer is occultism derided as exploded superstition: science has cleared the field of much delusion, but it has been unable to remove a residue of occult ideas well founded now in observed fact. Moreover, inner experience is being seriously considered by the modern psychologist: there is already a considerable movement, especially in America, towards what is called transpersonal psychology. This is explained and claimed to be a " fourth force ": first we have Behaviourism, then Freudianism, then Humanism; and now we have this new aspect.

It is worth noting how this is developing. First, it owes much to Abraham Maslow's perception that the future evolution in man is best studied by looking at what he called the " growing tip "—perhaps five per cent of human beings: those who excel in any field, including the record-breakers in athletics, who enable us to extrapolate and to some extent to forecast future development along a particular line. This in turn led him and others to take once more into serious consideration people who claimed to have experience of value to themselves, if not to others, which did not come within the framework of limited intellectual rationality. These people picked up where Bucke and James had started, and where " psychics " and mystics had continuously been insistent. They soon bogged down over what " transpersonal " really meant; for, it seemed, clairvoyance took a person into a realm outside the strictly personal, but it was clear (again using Maslow's term for what we might call an illuminating *spiritual* experience) that its quality and the impact it made were quite different from that of the " peak experience ".

Then, in the journal issued by the new movement, occultism came to the rescue in an article where two research Ph.D.s unashamedly put forward one of the best statements I know of the occult view of man, acknowledging H. P. Blavatsky as one of their sources. They showed the difference between a " vertical " transpersonal movement—towards the spiritual —and a " horizontal " one, where the extension is merely outward from the limits of the personal into the psychic field. This will probably bear fruit as transpersonalism moves further. And if it does, it will inevitably bring things closer to intelligent Theosophy.

All Inclusive

So, in a hundred years, things have moved. We know so much more than we did then; science and occultism and mystical religion are converging in a positive and constructive way. Modern existential thought focuses matters in the all-important present and gives us a dynamism which we did not perhaps have of old; and properly understood, it suggests that the present chaos is likely to be only a time of reorganization, similar to that which occurs in the pupation of insect life, to be followed by a new phase of human life. How big a part the Theosophical Society has played in bringing about this change cannot be assessed. It may be more than the cynic believes, it may be less than the enthusiast thinks—or feels. In any case, the Theosophical Movement, well established in the so-called " outer world, " seems likely to grow and expand until its influence spreads to include all the human race. For true Theosophy is " as wide as the great outdoors, " and has room in it for everybody. It is not an exclusive cult only for a self-styled élite.

FOR ALL TIME

THE principles of Theosophy which the articles in this volume have discussed were described by H. P. Blavatsky as " Eternal Verities ". To the extent to which this is true these principles will endure. Whatever is in fact true must inevitably be presently confirmed by seekers for truth in every field of human endeavour. If there are laws governing the universe —physically, psychically, spiritually—then those laws must constitute a body of Truth, the discovery and dissemination of which was the stated object of the Theosophical Society at its founding. In this search the test must always be " Is it true? ", remembering that truth has nothing to do with belief. No statement, no doctrine, becomes true because many people believe it, nor false because they disbelieve it. The criterion is whether it is in consonance with the laws of the universe, and our contention is that the main principles of theosophical doctrine will be found to pass that test. Students of this philosophy find that it gets to the heart both of personal and world problems as nothing else does because it presents ideas fundamental to the universe and man. This Ageless Wisdom, the core of the Ancient Mysteries, is therefore not just for a particular era but for all time because " the essence of Theosophy is the perfect harmonizing of the divine with the human in man ".[1]

[1] *B. C. W.* Vol. IX, p. 241.

In answer to the question: What do you expect for Theosophy in the future? the answer is given in *The Key to Theosophy*:

> As it has existed eternally throughout the endless cycles upon cycles of the past, so it will ever exist throughout the infinitudes of the Future, because Theosophy is synonymous with Everlasting Truth. [1]

THERE IS NO RELIGION HIGHER THAN TRUTH
            is the Motto of The Theosophical Society.

A scholarly exposition of source material of the Wisdom constitutes the following and final chapter of this volume.

[1] p. 304.

PRESIDENTS OF THE THEOSOPHICAL SOCIETY

H. S. Olcott	1875-1907
A. Besant	1907-1933
G. S. Arundale	1933-1945
C. Jinarājadāsa	1945-1953
N. Sri Ram	1953-1973
J. B. S. Coats	1973-

SOURCE OF THE IMMEMORIAL WISDOM

> Wisdom is the principal thing:
> therefore get wisdom: and with all
> thy getting get understanding.—
> *The Bible*, PROVERBS iv, 7

GEOFFREY A. BARBORKA

IN considering the source of the Wisdom from which present-day Theosophy springs, one soon discovers that many scriptures are mentioned in *The Secret Doctrine*. Each one has its own method of presenting its ideas. H. P. Blavatsky used these ancient scriptures as a means of showing that there is a golden thread which unites them all, thus indicating that they have come from a single source. This enables the student to recognize that there is a fundamental truth which each system of thought seeks to express in one way or another. In thus writing on the occult lore presented in these scriptures and about the Mystery Schools which had flourished in various parts of the world, H. P. Blavatsky was of course aware of the fact that there was a system of philosophy, often referred to as the esoteric doctrine, which had been formulated so as to convey this immemorial Wisdom to those who were entitled to receive it. Thus we find her writing on this very theme:

> There is reason to call the trans-Himalayan esoteric doctrine Chaldeo-Tibetan. And, when we remember that the *Vedas* came—agreeably to all traditions—from the Mānasa-rovar Lake in Tibet, and the Brahmins themselves from the

far North, we are justified in looking on the esoteric doctrines of every people who once had or still have it—as having proceeded from one and the same source; and to thus call it the "Aryan-Chaldeo-Tibetan" doctrine, or Universal Wisdom-Religion.[1]

Then, are the Vedas to be regarded as the source of this universal Wisdom Religion? Not as being *the* source of this Wisdom, but as the means whereby the immemorial Wisdom was presented to the early representatives of the Aryan Race, before its members came into India from the far north. For—continuing the quotation:

> The *Vedas*, Brahmanism, and along with these, Sanskrit, were importations into what we now regard as India. They were never indigenous to its soil. There was a time when the ancient nations of the West included under the generic name of India many of the countries of Asia now classified under other names.[2]

Very little is known as to how the Vedas came to be written. The Brahmans ascribe their preparation to Vyāsa, for he is regarded as a compiler, not as the author of the Vedas. There is no doubt that they are the most ancient works of the Hindus. They are mentioned in the Laws of Manu (the *Mānava-dharma-śāstra*), itself an old Sanskrit scripture. In this work only three of the Vedas are mentioned. Orientalists conclude that the fourth Veda, known as the *Atharva-Veda*, is a much later production than the first three Vedas, which are named: the *Rig-veda*, the *Yajur-veda* and the *Sāma-veda*. These three are regarded in the Laws of Manu as *sanātanaṃ trayaṃ brahma*, "the eternal triple divine knowledge." The word *veda* itself signifies knowledge, sacred knowledge.

[1] *B.C.W.* III, p. 419.
[2] *Ibid.*, p. 420.

The oldest of the three Vedas is the *Rig-veda*—literally the Hymn-veda, or the Veda of praise.   It is a collection of 1017 hymns, arranged in ten maṇḍalās—divisions or " books " —written in metre, in the most ancient form of Sanskrit, and intended to be recited aloud.   The *Yajur-veda* is the sacrificial Veda: it is a collection of mantras to be recited during the observance of sacrifices.   The *Sāma-veda* is the Veda of chants, to be used in connection with religious rites.   The later *Atharva-veda* consists principally of formulas and spells to be used in order to counteract diseases and calamities.   *Atharva* signifies a priest who uses fire and soma (the sacred juice of the soma-plant) in his religious observances.

Subba Rao, an able exponent of Brahmanical philosophy, stated:

> The *Vedas* were perhaps compiled mainly for the use of the priests assisting at public ceremonies, but the grandest conclusions of our real secret doctrine are therein mentioned.   I am informed by persons competent to judge of the matter, that the *Vedas* have a distinct dual meaning—one expressed by the literal sense of the words, the other *indicated by the metre and the svara* [intonation] which are, as it were, the life of the *Vedas*.[1]

An important consideration in connection with the Vedas is that each of the four scriptures is composed of two parts: (1) the Mantra, words of prayer and adoration; (2) the Brāhmaṇa, directions for the observance of the ceremonies during which the mantras were to be recited, as well as giving the meaning of the legends associated with the mantras. Moreover, concerning the Brāhmaṇa portion, further exposition of the legends was given in the *Āraṇyakas*, comprising the Upanishads; consequently these works are regarded as pertaining to Vedic literature.   The literal meaning of both

[1] *B.C.W.*, III, 401.

these words indicates the nature of the scriptures. *Āraṇyaka* signifies forest-born, hence writings which came into being in a forest, where the Vedas were studied. The term *Upanishad* may be rendered " what is received when seated near " thus conveying the idea that instruction was received when sitting with a teacher.

The Upanishads

At all events the *Upanishads* represent the exposition of the Vedas. In regard to the *Upanishads* H. P. Blavatsky wrote:

> Translated as " esoteric doctrine ," or interpretation of the *Vedās* by the *Vedānta* methods. The third division of the *Vedās* appended to the *Brāhmaṇas* and regarded as a portion of *śruti* or " revealed " word. They are, however, as records, far older than the *Brāhmaṇas*. . . . It is from these treatises of the *Upanishads*—themselves the echo of the primeval Wisdom-Religion—that the Vedānta system of philosophy has been developed. . . . The accepted number of these treatises is 150, though now no more than about twenty are left unadulterated. They treat of very abstruse, metaphysical questions, such as the origin of the Universe; the nature and the essence of the Unmanifested Deity and the manifested gods; the connection, primal and ultimate, of spirit and matter; the universality of mind and the nature of the human Soul and Ego. . . . There was a time, aeons before the Brahmans became a caste, or even the *Upanishads* were written, when there was on earth but one " lip," one religion and one science, namely, the speech of the gods, the Wisdom-Religion and Truth.[1]

Not only are the *Upanishads* a secret doctrine, but in dozens of other works as, for instance, in the *Aitareya Āraṇyaka*, it is plainly expressed that they contain *secret doctrines*, that are not to be imparted to anyone but a *Dvija* Brahman.[2]

---

[1] *Theosophical Glossary*, 353-4.
[2] *B.C.W.*, V, 297 fn.

Along with these Hindu scriptures, mention should be made of the *Purāṇas*, regarded as containing legendary stories of ancient India. In fact the *Purāṇas* are a collection of eighteen Brahmanical writings, allegorical and symbolical in character. They treat of the creation, passing and renovation of worlds, as well as the genealogy and activities of deities, sages and heroes. The word *purāṇa* signifies " ancient "; the writings are composed in epic couplets. In addition to the eighteen principal volumes, there are eighteen subordinate works known as *upa-purāṇas*. Although written in the form of fables there is no doubt that there is a great deal of esotericism in the ancient writings. H. P. Blavatsky comments:

> To comprehend the esoteric meaning of ancient Brahmanical literature, one has to be in possession of the key to the Brahmanical Code. To master the conventional terms used in the *Purāṇas*, the *Āraṇyakas* and *Upanishads* is a science in itself, and one far more difficult than even the study of the 3,996 aphoristical rules of *Pāṇiri*, or his algebraical symbols.[1]

> The ... teachings of the SECRET DOCTRINE, supplemented by universal traditions, must now have demonstrated that the *Brāhmaṇas* and *Purāṇas*, the Gāthās and other Mazdean Scriptures, down to the Egyptian, Greek, and Roman, and finally to the Jewish Sacred records, all have the same origin. None are meaningless and baseless stories, invented to entrap the unwary profane: all are allegories intended to convey, under a more or less fantastic veil, the great truths gathered in the same field of prehistoric tradition.... It has been shown, on the evidence of the whole ancient literary world, and the intuitional speculations of more than one philosopher and scientist of the later ages, that the tenets of our Esoteric Doctrine are corroborated by inferential as well as by direct proof in almost every case.[2]

[1] *B.C.W.*, V, 208.
[2] *S.D.*, II, 409-10, 1st ed.; III, 408, 6-vol. ed.

Ancient Scriptures

However, farther back in time than any of the scriptures which have come down to our day, there exists a " literary relic," according to H. P. Blavatsky. She first mentioned it in her initial work, *Isis Unveiled*, on the opening page:

> There exists somewhere in this wide world an old Book—so very old that our modern antiquarians might ponder over its pages an indefinite time, and still not quite agree as to the nature of the fabric upon which it is written. It is the only original copy now in existence. The most ancient Hebrew document on occult learning—the *Siphra Dzeniouta*[1]—was compiled from it, and that at a time when the former was already considered in the light of a literary relic.[2]

Later, in *The Secret Doctrine* H. P. Blavatsky wrote regarding this archaic manuscript:

> The " very old " book is the original work from which the many volumes of *Kiu-ti* were compiled. Not only this latter and the *Siphrah Dzeniouta* but even the *Sepher Jezirah*, the work attributed by the Hebrew Kabbalists to their Patriarch Abraham (!), the book of *Shu-king*, China's primitive Bible, the sacred volumes of the Egyptian Thoth-Hermes, the Purāṇas in India, and the Chaldean *Book of Numbers* and the *Pentateuch* itself, are all derived from that one small parent volume. Tradition says that it was taken down in *Senzar*, the secret sacerdotal tongue, from the words of the Divine Beings, who dictated it to the sons of Light, in Central Asia, at the very beginning of the 5th (our) race; for there was a time when its language (the *Sen-zar*) was known to the Initiates of every nation, when the forefathers of the Toltec understood it as

---

[1] H. P. Blavatsky refers to this work (also spelled *Siphra Dtzeniuthah*) as " the oldest book of the Kabbalists." It has been rendered into Latin by C. K. von Rosenroth under the name of *Liber Mysterii* in his *Kabbala denudata*. An English translation is available in M. Mathers's *Kabbalah Unveiled* under the section entitled " The Book of the Concealed Mystery "—which again is one of the divisions of the *Zohar* (the " Book of Splendour ").

[2] *Isis*, I, 1.

16

easily as the inhabitants of the lost Atlantis, who inherited it, in their turn, from the sages of the 3rd Race, the *Manushis*, who learnt it direct from the *Devas* of the 2nd and 1st Races.[1]

An elucidation of the ancient works quoted in this extract from *The Secret Doctrine* produces some interesting side-lights. (The *Kiu-ti* will be considered later.)

The *Sepher Jezirah* (also spelled *Yetzirah*) signifies the Book of Creation. It is another Kabbalistic work, attributed to Rabbi Aqībah (who died A.D. 135). H. P. Blavatsky described it as:

> The most occult of all the Kabbalistic works now in the possession of modern mystics.[2] Its alleged origin, of having been written by Abraham, is of course nonsense; but its intrinsic value is great. It is composed of six *Perakim* (chapters), sub-divided into thirty-three short *Mishnas* or Sections; and treats of the evolution of the Universe on a system of correspondences and numbers. Deity is said therein to have formed (" created ") the Universe by means of numbers " by thirty-two paths (or ways) of secret wisdom," these ways being made to correspond with the twenty-two letters of the Hebrew alphabet and the ten fundamental numbers. These ten are the primordial numbers whence proceeded the whole Universe, and these are followed by the twenty-two letters divided into *Three Mothers*, the seven double consonants and the twelve single consonants.[3]

The three mother letters are A, M, S; the seven double consonants signify the seven sacred planets; the twelve simple consonants stand for the twelve signs of the zodiac.

---

[1] *S.D.* I, xliii; I, 64, 6-vol. ed.

[2] " The *Sepher Yetzirah* now known is but a portion of the original one incorporated in the Chaldean *Book of Numbers*." *S.D.* III, 199 fn.; V, 205.

[3] *Glossary*, 165. The three mother letters stand for the three Elements: Air, Water, Fire.

The *Shu-King* is described as the Book of Historical Documents, a collection of records which were regarded as antique in the time of Confucius (550-478 B.C.). In its preface 100 books are mentioned, of which only 59 are extant, the oldest going back to the 23rd century B.C., the latest to the 8th. It also has an astronomical interest, for among other items there is a reference to a partial eclipse of the sun.

With regard to the sacred volumes of Thoth-Hermes, H. P. Blavatsky, first giving the meaning of Hermetic, wrote:

> Any doctrine or writing connected with the esoteric teachings of Hermes, who, whether as the Egyptian Thoth or the Greek Hermes, was the God of Wisdom with the Ancients, and, according to Plato, " discovered numbers, geometry, astronomy and letters.[1] "

> The forty-two Sacred Books of the Egyptians, mentioned by Clement of Alexandria as having existed in his time, were but a portion of the Books of Hermes (*Stromata*, II, 324). Iamblichus, on the authority of the Egyptian priest Abammon, attributes 1,200 of such Books to Hermes, and Manetho, 36,000.[2]

> There is also the additional evidence of Clemens Alexandrinus, that ought to be credited to some extent. Clemens testified to the existence of an additional 30,000 volumes of the Books of Thoth, placed in the library of the Tomb of Osymandias, over the entrance of which were inscribed the words, " A Cure for the Soul."[3]

Reference is made to the Hermetic books in *The Mahatma Letters to A. P. Sinnett* under Hermetic Philosophy in this manner:

> Hermetic Philosophy suits every creed and philosophy and clashes with none. It is the boundless ocean of Truth, the

[1] *Glossary*, 140.
[2] *S.D.*, III, 37 fn.; V, 58 fn.
[3] *S.D.*, III, 37; V, 58.

central point whither flows and wherein meet every river, as every stream—whether its source be in the East, West, North, or South.   As the course of the river depends upon the nature of its basin, so the channel for communication of Knowledge must conform itself to surrounding circumstances. The Egyptian Hierophant, the Chaldean Mage, the Arhat, and the Rishi, were bound in days of yore on the same voyage of discovery and ultimately arrived at the same goal though by different tracks, . . . TRUTH has no ear-mark and does not suffer from the name under which it is promulgated—if the said object is attained.[1]

The Book of Numbers

Turning now to another book of wisdom, given the name of the *Book of Numbers*, which originated in Chaldea.   This book should not be confused with the fourth book of Moses called " Numbers " in the Pentateuch (the first five books of the Old Testament).   The Chaldean *Book of Numbers* is

A work which contains all that is found in the *Zohar* of Simeon Ben-Jochai, and much more.   It must be the older by many centuries, and in one sense its [the Zohar's] original, as it contains all the fundamental principles taught in the Jewish Kabbalistic works, but none of their blinds.   It is very rare indeed, there being perhaps only two or three copies extant, and these in private hands.[2]

We are not aware that a copy of this ancient work is embraced in the catalogue of any European library; but it is one of the " Books of Hermes," and it is referred to and quotations are made from it in the works of a number of ancient and medieval philosophical authors.[3]

The *Books of Hermes* are the oldest repositories of numerical Symbology in Western Occultism.[4]

[1] *M.L.*, Letter 85, p. 399 1st ed.; p. 393, 3rd ed.
[2] *Glossary*, p. 75.
[3] *S.D.*, III, 99 fn.; V, 114 fn.
[4] *S.D.*, III, 100; V, 115.

In a word, ther eal, genuine Kabbalah, the only original copy of which is contained in the Chaldean *Book of Numbers*, pertains to, and teaches about, the realm of spirit, not that of matter.[1]

The use of all the seven keys to unlock the mysteries of Being in this life, and the lives to come, as in those which have gone by, show that the Chaldean *Book of Numbers*, and the *Upanishads*, undeniably conceal the most divine philosophy —as it is that of the Universal Wisdom Religion.[2]

The Book of Dzyan

Even though the passage quoted from *The Secret Doctrine* mentioned some of the works which had been derived from the archaic manuscript, it did not include the specific work which was pre-eminently used and which formed the basis for the writing of H. P. Blavatsky's work, namely the *Book of Dzyan*. This book originated from the *Kiu-ti*. From this same source came the *Stanzas of Dzyan*. The word *Dzyan* is thus explained:

> *Dan*, now become in modern Chinese and Tibetan phonetics *ch'an*, is the general term for the esoteric schools, and their literature. In the old books, the word *Janna* is defined as "to reform one's self by meditation and knowledge," a second *inner* birth. Hence Dzan, *Djan* phonetically, the "Book of *Dzyan*."[3]

The book of Dzyan—from the Sanskrit word "Dhyan"[4] (mystic meditation)—is the first volume of the Commentaries upon the seven secret folios of Kiu-te,[5] and a Glossary of the

---

[1] *B.C.W.*, VII, 267.

[2] *B.C.W.*, VII, 260.

[3] *S.D.*, I, p. xx fn.; I, 44 6-vol. ed.

[4] *Dhyāna*, derived from the verb-root *dhyai*, to meditate. Cf. the symbolical words in *The Voice of the Silence*: "Dhyāna whose golden gate once opened leads the Naljor [a saint, an adept] toward the realm of Sat eternal and its ceaseless contemplation." p. 48 or. ed.

[5] Also spelled Kiu-ti. In the next sentence "Gelugpa Lamas" signify "Yellow Cap Lamas," indicating those Tibetan Lamas who adhere to the reforms in Buddhism instituted under the administration of Tsong-Kha-pa in 1417

public works of the same name. Thirty-five volumes of Kiu-te for exoteric purposes and the use of the laymen may be found in the possession of the Tibetan Gelugpa Lamas, in the library of any monastery; and also fourteen books of Commentaries and Annotations on the same by the initiated Teachers.

Strictly speaking, those thirty-five books ought to be termed "The popularised Version" of the Secret Doctrine, full of myths, blinds, and errors; the fourteen volumes of *Commentaries* on the other hand—with their translations, annotations, and an ample glossary of Occult terms, worked out from one small archaic folio, the *Book of the Secret Wisdom of the World*[1] —contain a digest of all the Occult Sciences. These, it appears, are kept secret and apart, in the charge of the Teshu Lama of Tji-gad-je.[2] The Books of Kiu-te are comparatively modern, having been edited within the last millennium, whereas the earliest volumes of the *Commentaries* are of untold antiquity, some fragments of the original cylinders having been preserved. With the exception that they explain and correct some of the too fabulous, and to every appearance, grossly exaggerated accounts in the Books of Kiu-te—properly so-called—the *Commentaries* have little to do with these. They stand in relation to them as the Chaldaeo-Jewish *Kabbalah* stands to the Mosaic Books.[3]

No student, unless very advanced, would be benefited by the perusal of those exoteric volumes. They must be read with a key to their meaning, and that key can only be found in the *Commentaries*.[4]

---

[1] Here H. P. Blavatsky added the following footnote: " It is from the texts of all these works that *The Secret Doctrine* has been given. The original matter would not make a small pamphlet, but the explanations and notes from the Commentaries and Glossaries might be worked into ten volumes as large as *Isis Unveiled*." (*S.D.*, III, 405 fn; V, 389 fn.)

[2] Tji-gad-je (modernized spelling Shigatse) was the seat of the Tashi-Lama of Tibet; situated near the joining of the Nyang-Chu with the Tsang-po river. Southwest of Shigatse is the celebrated monastery Tashi-Lhünpo, founded by Ganden Truppa in 1445.

[3] *S.D.*, III, 405-6; V, 389.

[4] *S.D.*, III, 406; V, 390.

There is a passage in *The Mahatma Letters to A. P. Sinnett* regarding the *Kiu-ti* which should be included at this point. The Mahatma was describing that:

> The monad performs not only "world rings" or seven major inmetalliations, inherbations, zoonisations and in-carnations—but an infinitude of sub-rings or subordinate whirls all in series of sevens. As the geologist divides the crust of the earth into great divisions, sub-divisions, minor compartments and zones; and the botanist his plants into orders, classes and species, and the zoologist his subjects into classes, orders and families, so we have our arbitrary classi-fications and our nomenclatures. But besides all this being incomprehensible to you, volumes upon volumes out of the Books of Kiu-te and others would have to be written. Their commentaries are worse still. They are filled with the most abstruse mathematical calculations the key to most of which are in the hands of our highest adepts only, since showing as they do the infinitude of the phenomenal manifestations in the side projections of the *one* Force they are again secret.[1]

This truly indicates that there is a vast treasure house of occult lore which is available only to one who is qualified to contact it. It should be borne in mind that H. P. Blavatsky was selected to give certain portions of this occult lore in *The Secret Doctrine*. Yet regarding the immemorial Wisdom she wrote:

> The now *Secret* Wisdom was once the one fountainhead, the ever-flowing perennial source, at which were fed all its stream-lets—the later religions of all nations—from the first down to the last.[2]

---

[1] Letter 14, p. 81; p. 80, 3rd ed.
[2] *S.D.*, I, xliv-xlv; I, 66.

EXCERPTS FROM INAUGURAL ADDRESSES OF THE SIX PRESIDENTS

H. S. Olcott, November 17, 1875

We are of our age, and yet some strides ahead of it . . . We seek, inquire, reject nothing without cause, accept nothing without proof: we are students, not teachers.

What is it that makes me not only content but proud to stand for the brief moment as the mouthpiece and figure-head of this movement, risking abuse, misrepresentation, and every vile assault? It is the fact that in my soul I feel that behind us, behind our little band, behind our feeble new-born organization, there gathers a Mighty Power that nothing can withstand—the power of Truth. Because I feel that we are only the advance-guard, holding the pass until the main body shall come up. Because I feel that we are enlisted in a holy cause, and that truth, now as always, is mighty and will prevail.

Annie Besant, June 26, 1907

The Society asserts itself as a nucleus of Universal Brother-hood, and its speciality as such a nucleus is indicated by its name—theosophical. It is its function to proclaim and spread abroad Theosophy, the divine Wisdom, the Brahma Vidya, the Gnosis, the Light of all lights, that man may know God, may attain the knowledge which is eternal Life, because he is himself of that nature which he seeks to know.

On this fact, this all-pervading identity of nature, this Unity, is based the Universal Brotherhood; and, to bring the outer proofs of it, it searches through all religions and philosophies, and dives into the hidden secrets of nature and of man.

G. S. Arundale, June 21, 1934

Theosophy asks you to examine, to study. It does not ask you to believe or to accept on authority. But it does ask you not to make up your mind in a hurry, not to assume that that which your mind does not conceive nor understand cannot be true. And it also asks you to make up your mind for yourself, not to allow it to be made up for you by somebody else, still less by public opinion.

First . . . Theosophy is a body of truths for study, investigation and experiment, and every member has the right, and indeed the duty, to pursue such study, investigation and experiment in the utmost freedom, no matter whither these may lead him, just as he has the duty to accord the same right to his fellow members in a spirit of sincere goodwill and understanding; second . . . there is no effective search for truth save as truth becomes the actual possession of its seeker through his own personal experience.

C. Jinarājadāsa, February 17, 1946

It was said by Solomon about the Wisdom: " Sweetly doth she *order* all things." Wisdom is a power . . . Each theosophical lodge should become a power plant generating ideas, especially the ideas which the world needs today to lessen the struggle for existence. Take, for instance, the most powerful and dynamic idea which we have as our " marching orders," the Universal Brotherhood of Humanity. Only imagine a world peopled in the majority with men and women who not only believe but have discovered the joys inherent in that principle; would a man or woman then care to ask to what race another belongs, to what God he or she bends the knee? How could wars ever arise in such a civilization? How could poverty exist as contrasted with callous luxury?

All our theosophical studies, then, are a mere accompaniment, an elaboration in harmonies, of the glorious chant of Unity which rings throughout the universe, linking angel and man, beast and plant, in one joyous embrace.

N. Sri Ram, February 24, 1953

The Society is an organization which is as broad-based as it is noble in structure, with a breadth of Brotherhood that excludes none, but includes all men and women, nay all lives, and an aim that reaches up to the summit of human perceptions and aspirations . . . Besides this Brotherhood, all that is asked of a Theosophist, by the three objects to which he subscribes, is the desirability of the comparative study of science, religion and philosophy—all science, all religion, and all philosophy—and the investigation of those powers which are latent in man, and of the laws of Nature which are still unknown and unexplained.

If our Society is to be a truly theosophical society, and to progress and fulfil its mission, it must embody a mode of living on the part of its members, in which there is an ever-deepening realization of brotherhood and, as an open sky stretching over the earth, an ever-widening horizon of thought, bringing ever-new intimations to the human spirit.

Our duty is to work for a new order in which all things will be different from what they are, will have a different purpose and a different beauty, because each man will in some degree have realized his kinship and duty towards all other men, nay towards all life, including our younger brethren, the animals.

J. B. S. Coats, November 17, 1973

A balanced Theosophist is one who goes out to the circumference as he goes in towards the centre—inwards to experience more of the reality of the One, and outwards to share this understanding in a useful service to others . . . Hence the need for us to interest ourselves in the world in which we live and in all that is going on, in the findings of science and in the efforts being made by the United Nations and other international groups to bring about a widespread understanding of man's essential unity with the universe around and with his fellows nearer at hand . . . The world of tomorrow—the *One* world of which we often speak—will demand of each one of us, whether he lives in a quiet village in India or a bustling city of the United States, a far greater awareness of the needs, interests, customs and hopes of all the rest of us, not only within our Society but in relation to the larger world, which is also after all *our* world, with its countless problems and pains.

THE THEOSOPHICAL SOCIETY

The Theosophical Society was formed in New York on November 17, 1875, and incorporated in Madras on April 3, 1905. Its three declared Objects are:

1. To form a nucleus of the Universal Brotherhood of Humanity, without distinction of race, creed, sex, caste or colour.
2. To encourage the study of Comparative Religion, Philosophy and Science.
3. To investigate unexplained laws of Nature and the powers latent in man.

The Theosophical Society is composed of students, belonging to any religion in the world or to none, who are united by their approval of the Society's Objects, by their wish to remove religious antagonisms and to draw together men of goodwill whatsoever their religious opinions, and by their desire to study religious truths and to share the results of their studies with others. Their bond of union is not the profession of a common belief, but a common search and aspiration for Truth. They hold that truth should be sought by study, by reflection, by purity of life, by devotion to high ideals, and they regard truth as a prize to be striven for, not as a dogma to be imposed by authority. They consider that belief should be the result of individual study or intuition, and not its antecedent, and should rest on knowledge, not on assertion. They extend tolerance to all, even to the intolerant, not as a privilege they bestow but as a duty they perform, and they seek to remove ignorance, not to punish it.   They see every religion as an expression of the divine Wisdom and prefer its study to its condemnation, and its practice to proselytism.   Peace is their watchword, as truth is their aim.

THEOSOPHY is the body of truths which forms the basis of all religions, and which cannot be claimed as the exclusive possession of any.   It offers a philosophy which renders life intelligible, and which demonstrates the justice and the love which guide its evolution.   It puts death in its rightful place, as a recurring incident in an endless life, opening the gateway to a fuller and more radiant existence.   It restores to the world the science of the spirit, teaching man to know the spirit as himself and the mind and body as his servants.   It illuminates the scriptures and doctrines of religions by unveiling their hidden meanings, and thus justifying them at the bar of intelligence, as they are ever justified in the eyes of intuition.

Members of the Theosophical Society study these truths, and Theosophists endeavour to live them.   Everyone willing to study, to be tolerant, to aim high, and to work perseveringly, is welcomed as a member, and it rests with the member to become a true Theosophist.

FREEDOM OF THOUGHT

Resolution passed by the General Council of the Theosophical Society

As the Theosophical Society has spread far and wide over the civilized world, and as members of all religions have become members of it without surrendering the special dogmas, teachings and beliefs of their respective faiths, it is thought desirable to emphasize the fact that there is no doctrine, no opinion, by whomsoever taught or held, that is in any way binding on any member of the Society, none which any member is not free to accept or reject. Approval of its three Objects is the sole condition of membership. No teacher or writer, from H. P. Blavatsky downwards, has any authority to impose his teachings or opinions on members. Every member has an equal right to attach himself to any teacher or to any school of thought which he may choose, but has no right to force his choice on any other. Neither a candidate for any office, nor any voter, can be rendered ineligible to stand or to vote, because of any opinion he may hold, or because of membership in any school of thought to which he may belong. Opinions or beliefs neither bestow privileges nor inflict penalties. The members of the General Council earnestly request every member of the Theosophical Society to maintain, defend and act upon these fundamental principles of the Society, and also fearlessly to exercise his own right of liberty of thought and of expression thereof, within the limits of courtesy and consideration for others.

OUR CONTRIBUTORS

GEOFFREY A. BARBORKA was educated at the Theosophical School, Point Loma, California, and at the Theosophical University there. He is a deep student and has conducted many courses on the works of H. P. Blavatsky. Among his major writings are *The Divine Plan; H. P. Blavatsky, Tibet and Tulku; The Mahatmas and Their Letters;* and *Peopling the Earth.*

LAURENCE J. BENDIT, psychiatrist, lecturer and author, held the degrees of M.A., M.D., and B.Chir. from Cambridge University and also various British medical diplomas. He has made a substantial contribution to the literature of psychology and Theosophy. Among his best known works are *Self-Knowledge, a Yoga for the West; The Mirror of Life and Death; The Mysteries Today;* and, with his late wife, Phoebe D. Bendit, *The Psychic Sense* and *This World and That.* He was a former General Secretary of the English Section of the Theosophical Society. He continued writing valuable articles up to the time of his recent death.

CURT BERG took the degree of M.S. of Civil Engineering in Stockholm, of which he is a native, and he joined the Theosophical Society about the same time. His professional work has been in the field of town planning; he is the head of the Land Development Section of the Real Estate Department of the City of Stockholm. After some years as editor of the national magazine of the Theosophical Society in Sweden, he was its General Secretary from 1949 to 1953 and has held the same office since 1968. He has lectured on Theosophy in the Scandinavian countries as well as at international gatherings throughout Europe and in India.

17

E. JAMES BURTON is a first-class honours graduate and Quain Research Essay Prizeman of University College, London. He has been a university and college lecturer, and is an examiner and consultant to various colleges and universities in speech, drama and communication, including film and audio-visual media. His many books include *Student's Guide to World Theatre* and *Communication of Religious Experience* and his special field is inter-cultural developmental studies. He is Chairman of the British Section of the World Spiritual Council (UNESCO) and a worker in other inter-religious organizations, the Churches Fellowship for Psychical Research and Sufi movements. From 1967 to 1974 he was Executive Secretary, Society of Teachers of Speech and Drama. He has done considerable lecturing for the Theosophical Society, of which he has been a member for many years, and has contributed to theosophical journals. He is Regionary Bishop, Province of Great Britain and Ireland, of the Liberal Catholic Church.

BORIS DE ZIRKOFF is a native of Russia. After the revolution he studied in various European universities, specializing in languages and the classics. Emigrating to the United States, he went to the Headquarters of the Point Loma Theosophical Society where he worked for eighteen years in literary, scholastic and secretarial capacities. Since 1925 he has been compiling and editing a uniform edition of H. P. Blavatsky's *Collected Writings*. He is editor of *Theosophia*, an independent quarterly published for the past twenty-five years in Los Angeles, where he maintains a Theosophical Information Centre. Mr. de Zirkoff is believed to be the only living direct relative of H. P. Blavatsky.

GEOFFREY A. FARTHING, T. D., is a chartered electrical engineer who retired from the Yorkshire Electricity Board (England) in 1967 to take up full-time theosophical work. He has served on various British Standards Institution and European and world committees concerned with the safety of domestic electrical appliances; and was Chairman of the British Committee for ten years. Major Farthing served throughout the 1939-45 war in the Royal Signals. He joined the Theosophical Society in 1946 and from 1969 to 1972 was General Secretary of the English Section. He has lectured throughout Europe and also in India, the United States, Canada and in East, West and South Africa. His publications include *Theosophy, What's it all about?* and *When we Die.*

VIRGINIA HANSON has been on the H.Q. staff of the Theosophical Society in America since 1962. She is editor of *The American Theosophist* and senior editor for the Theosophical Publishing House in America. Before her retirement from U.S. government service Mrs. Hanson was for some years Publications Editor in the Department of Justice. She has written various works of fiction and many articles for literary and theosophical journals.

GEOFFREY HODSON has served the Theosophical Society for many years as lecturer, writer and teacher in many countries. Notable among his books are *The Kingdom of the Gods* and *The Hidden Wisdom in the Holy Bible.* Born in England, Mr. Hodson served in the British Army in the first world war, later making his home in New Zealand. He has been active in animal welfare work and penal reform. He has several times been Director of the School of the Wisdom at the International H.Q. of the Theosophical Society at Adyar, Madras, and also guest teacher at the Krotona Institute School of Theosophy, Ojai, California.

IANTHE H. HOSKINS graduated in French at the University of London. After a career in teaching and teacher-training, she became a full-time worker for the Theosophical Society in England which she had joined in 1936. She served for three years as Director of the School of the Wisdom at Adyar, the International H.Q. of the Society. She has lectured in several European countries and in Pakistan and East and West Africa. Miss Hoskins is now General Secretary of the English Section.

LESLIE H. LESLIE-SMITH, M.C., M.A., is an Oxford graduate who served in the Machine Gun Corps of the British army in the first world war and for thirty eight years was on the editorial staff of *The Times*, London. He joined the Theosophical Society in 1936 and for many years has been on the Executive Committee of the English Section, being General Secretary from 1965 to 1969. He has done considerable lecturing and writing on theosophical subjects, and he is Chairman of the Theosophical Publishing House, London. He is a member of the General Council of the International Society.

MADELEINE LESLIE-SMITH has been a member of the Theosophical Society since 1936. She was for some years Publicity Secretary of the Society in England and has for a number of years served on its Executive Committee. Mrs. Leslie-Smith is Chairman of the European Federation of National Sections of the Theosophical Society, and has lectured in many European countries.

JEANINE MILLER was born in China and was attracted to the eastern philosophies early in life. She made a special study of Sanskrit, the Vedas, Indian philosophy, Taoism and the Persian and Sufi poets. Miss Miller is a keen student of comparative religion, in particular Hinduism, Islam and Christianity, and has been a member of the Theosophical Society since 1956.

JOY MILLS, International Vice-President of the Theosophical Society, was for some years National President of the Society in the United States. She is a graduate of the University of Wisconsin-Milwaukee and she did post-graduate work at the universities of Chicago and Washington. A teacher by profession, Miss Mills has in recent years devoted her full time to the work of the Theosophical Society, lecturing in various countries throughout the world. She is the author of *Theosophy and Psychology* as well as of many articles on theosophical subjects.

WILLIAM J. ROSS is a retired naval architect now living in Australia. Born and educated in England, he joined the Theosophical

Society in Birkenhead while serving his apprenticeship there. In 1923 he went to the United States and after holding various engineering posts was appointed to the U.S. Navy Department. In 1943 Mr. Ross was transferred to Long Beach, California, to help organize the new naval shipyard and to take charge of the Hull Design Section. He retired in 1962. During this entire period he worked for the Theosophical Society, and he became a member of the Board of Directors of the American Section. He has travelled widely and lectured for the Society in Britain, India, Australia and New Zealand as well as throughout the United States.

PETER SEDGWICK was educated at Winchester College and Grenoble University, where he graduated in History and Philosophy. He worked in the British Foreign Service from 1931 to 1953 in London, Cairo, Milan, New York, Baltimore and in various countries in Central and South America. He joined the teaching staff of the Institute for English Philology at Graz University in 1958 and retired in 1974. He is a long-standing member of the Theosophical Society, first in the English Section and later in the Austrian, and has lectured for the Society in a number of European countries.

HUGH SHEARMAN graduated in History from Queen's University, Belfast, and got his Ph.D. from Dublin University for work on economic history. He is the author of various books on public affairs and history, as well as novels, and is well known as a contributor to works of reference, periodicals and newspapers, and as a broadcaster. Dr. Shearman joined the Theosophical Society in 1940 and served first as Presidential Agent and then as Organising Secretary in Northern Ireland from 1949 to 1973. He has been a member of the General Council of the International Society since 1950. His talent has found valuable expression in a number of books on Theosophy, including *Modern Theosophy*, and in numerous articles and lectures.

V. WALLACE SLATER, a science graduate of London University, is by profession a research chemist and became director of research of a world-wide chemical company. He joined the Theosophical Society in 1920 and was General Secretary of the English Section from 1961 to 1965. He is a well-known lecturer and the author of books and articles on science and on Theosophy, among the latter being *A Simplified Course of Hatha Yoga* and *Raja Yoga, a Simplified and Practical Course.* Mr. Slater is a member of the General Council of the International Society and is Chairman of the Theosophical World Trust for Education and Research.

N. SRI RAM graduated from Madras University in 1909, when he was already a member of the Theosophical Society, and he devoted his entire life to theosophical work. He taught in a number of theosophical schools, and was assistant editor of *New India* and *Commonweal*, edited by Annie Besant, then International President of the Society, whose private secretary he was from 1929 to 1933. He filled many offices in the Society, including Treasurer, Recording Secretary and Vice-President, and he lectured in countries all over the world. He was elected International President of the Theosophical Society in 1953 and re-elected in 1960 and 1967, having served for 20 years in that office when he died in 1973. Mr. Sri Ram wrote a number books, including *Man, his Origins and Evolution*, *An Approach to Reality*, *Life's Deeper Aspects* and *Seeking Wisdom*, and a large number of articles for *The Theosophist* and other magazines.

CORONA TREW, a graduate and Doctor of Science of the University of London, was a Senior Lecturer in Chemistry at that university. She has been a member of the Theosophical Society for fifty years and has served on the Executive Committee of the English Section for a considerable time. She is widely known as a lecturer and writer on theosophical subjects in relation to philosophy, science and mysticism. Dr. Trew is Vice-Chairman of the Theosophical World Trust for Education and Research.

CHARLES S. J. WHITE, Associate Professor of Philosophy and
Religion and Co-Director of the Centre for Asian Studies,
The American University, Washington, D.C., took his Ph.D,
in Hinduism at the University of Chicago. He has taught at
various major universities and has done extensive field work
research in India, and has published numerous essays.

HELEN V. ZAHARA, a New Zealander by birth, lived for a number
of years in Australia, where she was for some time General
Secretary of the Theosophical Society there. Miss Zahara was
an accountant by profession, but devoted her full time to the
Theosophical Society from 1946 until her death in 1973. She
went to work at the H.Q. of the United States Section in 1965
and was Chairman of the Department of Education and co-
ordinator of special programmes sponsored by the Kern Foundation, including the production of Quest books. She had lectured
in over thirty countries for the Society, and was for a considerable period Recording Secretary of the International Society
at Adyar.